CREATING EXCELLENCE

CREATING EXCELLENCE

Managing Corporate Culture,
Strategy, and Change
in the New Age

by

Craig R. Hickman
and Michael A. Silva

NAL BOOKS

NEW AMERICAN LIBRARY

NEW YORK AND SCARBOROUGH, ONTARIO

NAL BOOKS TRADEMARK REG. U.S. PAT. OFF. AND FOREIGN COUNTRIES
REGISTERED TRADEMARK—MARCA REGISTRADA
HECHO EN HARRISONBURG, VA., U.S.A.

SIGNET, SIGNET CLASSIC, MENTOR, PLUME,
MERIDIAN and NAL BOOKS
are published *in the United States* by New American Library,
1633 Broadway, New York, New York 10019,
in Canada by The New American Library of Canada Limited,
81 Mack Avenue, Scarborough, Ontario M1L 1M8

Designed by Julian Hamer

LIBRARY OF CONGRESS CATALOGING IN PUBLICATION DATA

Hickman, Craig R.
  Creating excellence.

  Bibliography
  Includes index.
  1. Management. I. Silva, Michael A. II. Title.
HD31.H48   1984   658.4   84-20612
ISBN 0-453-00482-2

First Printing, December, 1984

5   6   7   8   9

PRINTED IN THE UNITED STATES OF AMERICA

TO

Winston,
Al,
Verla,
Agnes,
Pamela,
and Karen

For all they've done

Contents

Part II: Six Skills for New Age Executives

Part III: Creating Excellence

Acknowledgments

A number of people contributed their time and talent to *Creating Excellence*. They deserve to share the credit for the book's strengths, although we alone accept the blame for any of its flaws. First we have deeply appreciated the efforts of Michael Snell, our agent, editor, and partner, who skillfully guided us through all phases of this project. His patience and good humor made the writing enjoyable throughout. Many people at New American Library offered valuable assistance: Robert Diforio, Chairman of the Board, and Arnold Dolin, Vice President and Editor-in-Chief, caught our vision of *Creating Excellence* and marshaled their organization's finest efforts behind the book. Jill Grossman deserves special thanks for quick and insightful editing of the final manuscript.

We owe special thanks to Dixie J. Clark and Mary H. Kowalczyk for their endless hours at the word processor and for skillful handling of all the administrative tasks related to the manuscript. Our schedule demanded rapid turnaround of material, and Federal Express demonstrated its excellence almost daily for several months without a single delay.

Special thanks goes to the team of Lee and Nan Conant, Executive Vice President of Bennett Enterprises and President of Conant Associates, respectively, who have helped us shape Bennett Enterprises and who provided creative stimulus throughout the writing of our book. The other senior executives of the Bennett Enterprises have always helped and supported us in our quest for excellence: Senator Wallace F. Bennett, Chairman of the Board and source of encouragement and trust as we have applied the principles of *Creating Excellence* to the Bennett Enterprises; DeVon Johnson, President of the Paint and Glass Company; Peter van der Heyde, President of National Car Rental; Lynn Stauffer and Alan Bradshaw, President and Executive Vice-President of Personal Business Computers; John Bennett and Leon

Nason, President and Executive Vice President of the Leasing Company; Craig and Jim Bradley, President and Executive Vice President of the New Zealand Trading Company; Porter Sutton, President of SCI; Floyd Mori, President of Pacific Basin Resources; Paul Barron, President of Mountain West; and Jack Stevens, Chief Financial Officer.

We are also grateful to a group of professors at Harvard and Brigham Young University who have helped develop our ideas. Their devotion to excellence in teaching and training business leaders should not go unrecognized: Michael Yoshino, Harry Hansen, Paul Lawrence, and Anthony Athos of the Harvard Business School; Bonner Ritchie, Stephen Covey, Alan Wilkins, and Wayne Clark of Brigham Young's organizational behavior and economics schools.

We owe a special debt of gratitude to the individuals who helped us grow throughout our business career. Their lasting influence has served us well: Phil Matthews, former Chief Financial Officer at Dart & Kraft; Bill Ewing, Management Consultant; Marlon Berrett and Joe Ahlin, Partners of Arthur Young & Company; Sam Okinaga, Former Chairman of State Savings and Loan; the Warren Pugh Family, owners of Cummins Intermountain; and the Lowell Christensen family.

Finally, we thank Arthur Young & Company for the example of excellence it offers in delivering results-oriented consulting services to its clients. This emphasis on implementation beyond the realms of formulation and planning has allowed Arthur Young to help its clients achieve excellence. Our relationship with Arthur Young & Company represents our shared long-term commitment to welding strategy and culture to create excellence.

Preface

If we had to choose one essential characteristic of what we call the New Age, that characteristic would be change. Until fairly recently executives operated with the assumption that they enjoyed limitless resources and plenty of time to build profitable enterprises, but today finite resources, new technology, and accelerating change are placing unprecedented pressure on every organization. Only those leaders who learn to anticipate and even invent the future will profit from, rather than be surprised by, change. We know about the great effort and even pain involved in inventing a successful future because we've done it ourselves. The principles outlined in this book have grown out of, and eventually guided, our management of the Bennett Enterprises, a hundred-year-old private corporation originally formed with a single purpose: to meet the business challenges of a new century with bold and innovative ideas. For many decades that vision created excellence, but as times changed, Bennett also needed changing. When in 1981 the owners began looking for someone to position the company for its second century, they picked one of us (Michael Silva) to assume the presidency and become the CEO. Shortly thereafter Michael brought co-author Craig Hickman aboard as a member of the executive committee to help redirect Bennett Enterprises' future.

Within one year, our strategy to diversify Bennett from a base of paint and glass and leasing businesses that had been highly vulnerable to economic downturns began to pay off as we moved into expanded financial services, computer sales and service, advertising, specialty retailing, interior design, and management consulting. Conant Associates, which was recently profiled in *Interior Design* magazine as one of the nation's fastest growing and most successful interior design firms, offers a good example of the strong culture that now permeates the organization. Making the necessary strategic and cultural changes at Bennett Enterprises has not been an easy task. Throughout the undertaking we have had to draw on each of the six executive skills outlined in this book in order to retain useful parts of the old strategy and culture while simultaneously introducing new directions and values. Many of the changes occurred rapidly, and in the midst of it all we learned a great deal about maintaining the harmony between strategy and culture that is so crucial in creating long-term excellence.

Since Bennett remains a privately held corporation, we do not disclose specific financial information, but we can tell you that the company currently ranks in size with companies in the Fortune 1000 and, based on current growth rates, will soon rank with companies in the Fortune 500. But more important than size is Bennett's commitment to superior performance in each of its businesses. This commitment has already brought substantial increase in profitability and return on equity, and we are confident it will continue.

We came to Bennett's with firm academic backgrounds and strong beliefs, which have continued to evolve through the hands-on running of the business. Craig has an MBA from Harvard and Michael completed graduate work in Brigham Young University's nationally acclaimed organizational behavior program. We have held a variety of executive positions and have both worked as management consultants for Arthur Young & Company. We feel that our experience, both in management theory and in the real world, gives us a special vantage point. Too many business books are either studies written by academics without practical experience or simplified quick-fix guides by businessmen with no theoretical background. While some academics may think they know how to run a business, we have actually done it, dealing firsthand with the frustrations line managers feel in the face of labor demands, foreign competition, federal intervention, vendor and client bankruptcies, employee theft, quality control, community involvement, and even a secretary's twenty-four-hour flu.

It seems obvious to us that the best advice should encompass both a thorough theoretical foundation and useful applications. Therefore, in each chapter of this book we try to provide a clear definition of a concept, such as strategy or culture, and we also illustrate each concept with actual case studies. At the end of each chapter you will have a chance to evaluate your growing knowledge with self-tests and exercises designed to relate the concepts to your own situation.

Our examples fall into three categories: factual accounts of real companies, hypothetical situations, and role-playing cases. In the first group you will find examples of successes and failures from a variety of industries. Bear in mind that we use a negative example not to place blame on an individual or organization, but to help you learn from the lapses or mistakes of others. Taken together, these case histories paint a broad picture of the past. To make our ideas as current as possible, and to give you a chance to test your learning, we have incorporated a number of hypothetical present-day situations throughout early chapters. These examples grapple with the sorts of problems that now confront many companies and their leaders. We conclude the book with four role-playing cases set in the future that will help you contemplate the kinds of problems you are likely to face in the years to come.

We have written *Creating Excellence* to teach people the practical skills they must acquire before they can become the sort of leaders we call New Age Executives. Today's executives must learn more than their predecessors ever needed to know in order to establish and maintain excellence. Our book gives you the tools you need to set about this important task. It will take a huge investment in time and effort, and the road will be hard, but down that long road lie not only financial and lifestyle rewards, but the pure joy of a job well done. Like all journeys, it begins with a single step—*commitment*. And it starts not in the halls of a top business school or on the carpet of a prestigious consulting firm. It starts, and ends, in the very heart of the executive suite.

PART I

THE FOUNDATION OF EXCELLENCE

• CHAPTER I •

Creating Excellence:
Toward A New Age
Renaissance

> We must welcome the future, remembering that soon it will
> be the past; and we must respect the past, remembering
> that it was once all that was humanly possible.
> —GEORGE SANTAYANA

> Those things that hurt, instruct.
> —BENJAMIN FRANKLIN

What Is Excellence?

A Baccarat crystal vase displaying a dozen long-stemmed American Beauty roses. New Hampshire's technicolor hardwood forests in October. The cry of a newborn baby. Whatever your definition of excellence, you would probably agree that such experiences deserve the label. In fact, we seem to easily recognize excellence. Beethoven, Mozart, Shakespeare, Hemingway, and Leonardo da Vinci created it. Gandhi, Socrates, Franklin, Confucius, and Einstein had it. John Wooden, the legendary UCLA coach, brought it to the basketball floor, Vince Lombardi inspired it on the football field, and Jesse Owens showed it at the 1936 Summer Olympics. Everyone recognizes that an Olympic gold medal and a Nobel prize reward it.

Such recognizable excellence extends to the business world. Rolls-Royce, Mercedes-Benz, and Porsche have crafted world-respected automobiles. Products such as Kleenex, Xerox machines, and Scotch tape have come to refer generically to all similar products, regardless of manufacturer. When we think of American companies that embody excellence, IBM, Hewlett-Packard, Citicorp, Delta Air Lines, McDonald's, General Electric, and American Express leap to mind. How did such companies create models of excellence? Did they provide outstanding products and services to their customers? Did they bestow unparalleled benefits on their employees? Did they dominate their competitors? Did their annual reports consistently display record growth and earnings? Yes, they accomplished all these goals, but they did more. They exploited ideas, inventions, and innovations; they never rested on their laurels but always sought to pioneer products and services; and they promoted and rewarded individual leaders within their ranks.

As in most fields of endeavor where you wish to gauge excellence, you can measure organizational excellence with both objective and subjective yardsticks. Neither one, however, provides a complete test. Peters and Waterman set forth six objective criteria for gauging excellence in their book *In Search of Excellence*: compound asset growth; compound equity growth; average ratio of market to book value; average return on total capital; average return on equity; and average return on sales. At the other end of the scale, *Fortune* magazine has adopted rather more subjective criteria for ranking corporations: quality of management; quality of products or services; innovation; value as a long-term investment; financial soundness; ability to attract, develop, and keep talented people; community and environmental responsibility; and use of corporate assets. Although both objective and subjective criteria help identify truly excellent organizations, they do not do justice to every type of organization at any given stage of development. For example, Peters and Waterman concluded that Dana Corp., Boeing, and Texas Instruments provide excellent models, yet in the last four years each of these companies has suffered setbacks that might, at least according to the Peters and Waterman yardstick, knock them off the list. And what about the breathtaking turnarounds of Chrysler, Baldwin-United and Firestone? Shouldn't their progress count for something?

Fortune's ranking of corporate reputations can also fail to capture a perfect picture. Johnson & Johnson, previously number five on the "ten most admired" list, had a serious earnings problem in 1983. J & J 1983 versus 1982 margins (net income before extraordinary items as a percent of sales) dropped a full 23 percent in the fourth quarter. The market value of their stock plummeted 17 percent. The worst nose dive, however, was taken by Eastman Kodak, number four on *Fortune*'s 1983 list, but gone completely from the 1984 list. Kodak 1983 versus 1982 profits plunged 51 percent. Are such companies no longer excellent? Or, do the measures of excellence listed above provide insufficient yardsticks? Instead of adopting a rigid set of criteria for judging excellence, we recommend that you measure your organization against your own unique standards. Your tailor-made criteria may measure customer satisfaction with your products and services, the rewards and benefits your employees receive, dominance in a defined market, progress toward growth and profit goals, or innovation. If you're a banker, you may weigh these categories differently than a computer manufacturer would, and you might rank the categories in a different order. But you must never overlook one crucial factor: developing individual executives into leaders.

No matter what all the surveys, studies, and comparative statistics indicate, the real race for excellence is the one you run against yourself. Can you lead your organization toward your own definition of excellence?

Individual Leaders, Not Organizations, Create Excellence

Individual executives who have developed specific skills create superior organizational performance. Excellence doesn't happen miraculously but springs from pacesetting levels of personal effectiveness and efficiency. Great business, government, and nonprofit organizations owe their greatness to a few individuals who mastered leadership skills and passed those skills on to succeeding generations of executives and managers.

James C. Fargo, the third president of the American Express Company, returned from a trip overseas in 1890 fed up with the inconvenience of the "letter of credit" system for obtaining cash in foreign countries. He immediately commissioned one of his executives, Marcellus Fleming Berry, to solve the problem. We imagine the following conversation. Fargo said, "Berry, the moment you get off the beaten track, letters of credit are of no more use than so much wet wrapping paper. If the president of American Express [then a respected shipper of goods, specializing in money and valuables] has that kind of trouble, think about the trouble the ordinary traveler has. Something must be done. Do it." Eventually Berry developed the original "traveler's cheque" to replace the inconvenient letter of credit, an innovation that made world travel much more convenient. Fargo's insight and vision combined with Berry's versatility and focus set the tone for future generations of American Express executives who strengthened American Express's status as one of the most admired diversified financial corporations in the world, with over $10 billion in revenues.

A handful of visionary pioneers created the U.S. airline industry. C. R. Smith at American, Eddie Rickenbacker at Eastern, Juan Trippe at Pan American, William Patterson at United, and C. E. Woolman at Delta each established highly profitable airlines, but only one of them successfully passed his skills on to his successors. Though each of these pioneers had mastered the skills required to build strong corporations, only Woolman assembled a management group capable of carrying on the skills that had won Delta its early success. His rival pioneers held on to their power too long, neglecting the development of those who would inherit their leadership, and set the stage for eventual reorganizations, shifts in direction, and alarming earnings fluctuations. Delta, however, sustained its excellence because Woolman slowly but surely shifted the burdens of management to a group of executives committed to his own basic tenets and philosophies. Although the transition didn't occur overnight, when Woolman died suddenly in 1966 his corporate heirs smoothly grasped their mentor's reins. Woolman's management skills, characterized by his three famous tenets (treat employees like members of a family, maintain strict consistency, and thoroughly plan facilities and equipment) guided the new leaders. The financial result of Woolman's transfer of skills? Delta is the most profitable airline in the world. In the past ten years the company's cumulative net earnings have been double those of any other carrier.

Individuals, not organizations, create excellence. With their unique skills they lead others along the pathway to excellence, carefully cultivating those who will later assume the controls. To groom future leaders successfully, the mentor makes sure he passes on both his gift for strategy and his flair for building a strong corporate culture.

The Foundation of Excellence: Strategy and Culture

Before you can apply the six important leadership skills we will be discussing in much greater detail in Part II, you must understand that you cannot succeed without laying a strong foundation of strategic thinking and culture building. In Chapters 2 and 3 we will explore these two concepts thoroughly, but for now we can simply define *strategy* as the hard-nosed American approach to business that traditionally stresses the impact of competitive advantage on the bottom line, and *culture* as careful attention to organizational and people needs (an approach for which many Americans greatly admire the Japanese). To unite strategy with culture (Chapter 4) you first need to develop a vision of the firm's future and then in order to implement strategy for making that vision a reality, you need to nurture a corporate culture that is motivated by and dedicated to the vision.

The marriage of strategic thinking and corporate culture building requires that leaders not only cultivate broad vision but master the skills to implement that vision. Such leaders see crisis as opportunity, not danger, and create a future equally responsive to the bottom line and to an organization's people. We all know Detroit lost its preeminence in auto making by believing that "customers will drive whatever we build for them," while Japanese car manufacturers rethought the automobile's role in a changing world and designed a car better suited to that world. Now Toyota, not GM, dominates world markets with excellence.

Transforming mediocre organizations into excellent ones, converting crisis into opportunity, and shaping vision into reality demand more than theoretical formulas or quick fixes. Although it takes a tremendous investment of time and effort, anyone can learn to do it. Unfortunately, most top executives can either think strategically or build cultures creatively but cannot do both simultaneously. The challenge is to become both visionary and realistic, sensitive and demanding, innovative and practical. The leaders who achieve this are the ones who do things first, sometimes before others even dream of them. They thrive on always being on the leading edge of new trends and ideas. They are people like Peter Schutz.

When Schutz, an American, became president of Porsche in 1980, German newspapers blared the headline "GASTARBEITER [foreign worker] IN THE PRESIDENT'S CHAIR!" An old family-run company, building one of the world's supreme motorcars, Porsche had languished under a previous president, not a family member, who so antagonized employees that Ferry Porsche, the founder's son and chairman of the board, had felt it necessary to move his offices out of headquarters so as not to be associated with the management regime. Pride sank to an all-time low. In came Schutz, whose first act was to ask Herr Porsche to return to the fold. Then for ninety-five days, nothing happened. The workers, at first hostile and suspicious, turned speculative: what's was going on? One day the racing engineers decided to brief Schutz on their plans for Le Mans, where Porsche cars had won five times. This year, they explained, they would not race to win, because it was a marketing year for showing off the new Porsche 944. Schutz replied, "I don't care what you have to do but Porsche is going to win at Le Mans."

A scant two months before the race the team worked furiously to get cars ready for the twenty-four-hour endurance trial. Schutz, accompanying the team to the race, spent the entire time in the pits. Looking back on the experience, he said, "Never in my life have I witnessed such professionalism, team spirit, and dedication. I kept telling myself, we can't lose, we can't lose." Not only did Porsche win the race and renewed pride, but Schutz won Porsche, establishing himself as a leader capable of strategically positioning the company and revitalizing its culture. Afterwards an engineer summed up the employees' respect when he said, "Peter Schutz has proved he is the right man for Porsche."

Strategic thinking and culture building work in tandem. Actions based on strategic thinking must effectively satisfy customer needs, gain a sustainable advantage over competitors, and capitalize on company strengths. Actions aimed at corporate culture building instill a collective commitment to a common purpose, foster distinctive competence among employees to deliver superior performance, and establish a consistency that helps attract, keep, and develop leaders at all levels.

All firms follow some kind of strategy and function with some form of culture, but most do this only halfheartedly. Sometimes a company develops a strategy it can't implement. When Exxon tried to run its new office systems business like an oil company, it lost millions of dollars to more agile high-tech rivals who knew their business. When Quaker Oats moved into toys and restaurants, it almost destroyed a once invincible food marketing culture. Some senior executives attempt to correct problems in the culture with confusing and alienating policy memos and dictums. Jim Edwards reorganized Bausch & Lomb's instruments group overnight into new reporting relationships, governed by IBM-like operating policies, such as a matrix-style structure that had people reporting to more than one boss. However, the Bausch & Lomb crew didn't respond the way Edwards's IBM experience had taught him they should. Confusion skyrocketed, earnings crashed, and Edwards resigned. Roy Ash of AM International lost his job the same way when his seemingly brilliant strategy failed to launch the company into the high-tech future. Too much change too fast.

By sharp contrast, Hewlett-Packard has instilled a sense of shared purpose and a striving for technological innovation in its organization by encouraging rather than stifling an entre-preneurial spirit. The company has successfully kept entrepre-neurs within its ranks, while many rival companies lose theirs to start-ups. The consistency of this purpose has outlasted its founders. H-P's strategy depends on innovation to satisfy cus-tomer needs, better products to gain advantage over competi-tors, and individual entrepreneurial spirit. This strategy differs dramatically from that of U-Haul, which cancelled agreements with its independent dealer network and tried to open com-pany-owned moving centers, a thoughtless strategy that demol-ished U-Haul's culture, obliterating the good dealer relationships the company had so carefully cultivated. Within a year U-Haul lost half its business to Jartran and Ryder.

Most firms are either strategy-deficient or culture-deficient. Deficiencies in either sphere usually lead to failure. Who can overcome such deficiencies? Strong leaders. Fortunately, lead-ers are made, not born. Any executive willing to make the commitment and investment of time and energy can learn six essential skills for constructing excellence on the foundation of strategy and culture. But before embarking on the arduous path toward excellence, the executive must develop what we call the New Age attitude.

The New Age Attitude

Just as most people recognize excellence when they encoun-ter it, most of us accept the fact that the world has changed dramatically in the past thirty years. We might characterize the Old Age of Management as one in which opportunities seemed to abound. Andrew Carnegie, Henry Ford, John D. Rockefeller, and others embodied the early American "we can do anything" spirit that took advantage of vast natural resources and the fact that hard work alone could make dreams come true. During the 1950s our country enjoyed an explosion of growth after which the Aquarian Age of the 1960s and early 1970s brought a deep questioning of Old Age values and assumptions. Many young people in the sixties found business distasteful and flocked to the social sciences; then in the 1970s the emerging "me" generation flooded back to schools of management, law, and medicine. However, we woke up one day to find that we had correctly questioned the assumptions of the Old Age but had not replaced them with acceptable new ideas. The world had changed: could *we* change with it?

The 1980s have spawned new management approaches and techniques. But quality circles, team building, Japanese-style management, and other measures recommended by books, consultants, and academics continue to fail because the executives who try to follow their advice have not made fundamental changes in their attitudes and approaches. In the words of Michael Maccoby, author of *The Leader,* "A new model of leadership that expresses an ethic of self-development is needed, not just at the top, but at all levels of large business, government, union and non-profit organizations." He goes on to suggest that we don't have time to educate the next generation. We need the benefit of this new model of leadership right now. That means executives and managers throughout corporate America must immediately develop new skills and abilities, not through simple formulas, mechanistic techniques, or imitation but through a deep dedication to fundamental new skills, skills that characterize the New Age executive.

Can American executives surmount their crisis of confidence? The business world recognizes the need for powerful, influential leaders like Bank of America's A. P. Giannini, IBM's Thomas J. Watson, Sr. and Jr., and Henry Ford. Unfortunately, such leaders do not abound. These days companies often import their presidents and CEOs: PepsiCo's John Sculley went to Apple Computer, James Morgan of Philip Morris took over Atari, and Archie McGill left IBM for A T & T. But can such transplanted talent transfer management approaches and techniques? Not easily. Confronted with an indifferent and sometimes hostile environment, they find their tried and true techniques don't work as well as before. RCA's musical chairs in the executive suite, which has seen four CEOs since 1966, has created nothing but confusion and lagging profits. Xerox's Archie McCardell, president and chief operating officer, jumped to ailing International Harvester and staved off the hungry bankers with cost-cutting magic for two years. But by the end of the fourth year, it became apparent that McCardell had neglected the company's long-term strategic position by remaining in markets the company should have departed from long ago. With Harvester on the verge of bankruptcy, the bankers closed in. McCardell was forced to resign.

When morale sags and excellence declines, many managers begin to feel frustrated and powerless. They grow defensive, a posture that makes it impossible to adapt skills to a new environment. You cannot impose iron-clad techniques and procedures on organizations. Rather, you must master a whole group of new skills that help you flow with different or changing conditions.

Six Skills for New Age Executives

Most business schools teach six fundamental managerial skills that supposedly insure success in today's business world:

- set goals and establish policies and procedures
- organize, motivate, and control people
- analyze situations and formulate strategic and operating plans
- respond to change through new strategies and reorganizations
- implement change by issuing new policies and procedures
- get results and produce respectable growth, profitability, and return on investment

While these may have worked in the past, declining American productivity and competitiveness prove they no longer suffice. To achieve corporate excellence in the dynamic future, managers must learn to transcend the past with what we call the New Age skills:

- Creative Insight
- Sensitivity
- Vision
- Versatility
- Focus
- Patience

The first two skills help forge a strong *foundation* for excellence because insight informs successful strategies and sensitivity helps build strong cultures. Vision and patience help you *integrate* your skills. While vision helps you invent an excellent future, patience allows you to take the necessary time to implement it successfully. And since any organization must be able to evolve, versatility and focus provide for *adaptation*, the former stimulating anticipation of future needs, the latter directing implementation of change efforts. Vision logically comes after insight and sensitivity because it yokes the two, while patience naturally follows versatility and focus because it links all the other skills by providing exquisite timing.

These foundational, integrative, and adaptive skills help New Age executives to harmoniously orchestrate strategy and culture. You do not need to be born with these skills, but you do need to work at acquiring and developing them. In Chapters 5 through 10 we will explore these skills in depth, but let's take a brief look at them here.

Creative Insight: Asking the Right Questions. Insight, which involves adapting a variety of critical perspectives, forces executives to strike at the heart of a problem, not just at its visible symptoms. Executives lacking insight see either the forest or the trees, but never both. Without insight, executives waste valuable resources because they don't get at the roots of problems and are therefore unable to design successful solutions. By asking the right questions, you obtain the key to the increased insight that informs superior strategies. Chapter 5 includes instruction in basic meditation and six exercises designed to improve insight and overcome the most common obstacles to maintaining it.

Sensitivity: Doing Unto Others. If, in the final analysis, people are an organization's greatest asset, then New Age managers must understand how to bind them together in a culture wherein they feel truly motivated to achieve high goals. Face-to-face communication, ongoing training and development, creative incentive programs, and job security all display the sort of sensitivity that nurtures strong cultures. Every strong culture derives from management's sensitivity. Without it, employees feel unmotivated, underutilized, and even exploited. Most executives are sensitive in some ways but not in others. To heighten your sensitivity, Chapter 6 helps you address key areas with a Sensitivity Chart.

Vision: Creating the Future. Leaders who develop clear vision can mentally journey from the known to the unknown, creating the future from a montage of facts, figures, hopes, dreams, dangers, and opportunities. By applying the art of meditation to organizational introspection, you gain a deep understanding of a business and its environment. In Chapter 7 you'll learn the step-by-step process that clarifies your vision. You'll master scenario building and then see how to test your unique scenarios with a proven ten-part examination.

Versatility: Anticipating Change. A difficult skill to master, versatility presumes that some goals other than immediately pressing business problems should concern you. Unless you aggressively pursue interests outside your field, you will never be able to comfortably adapt to change. To improve your versatility, Chapter 8 presents six steps for previewing change, walking you through a realistic situation in an effort to teach ways of mentally anticipating and adapting to it.

Focus: Implementing Change. Everything that happens in your organization either contributes to or erodes its efforts to implement change and keep strategy and culture in harmony. Focus enables leaders to invest available resources toward implementing successful and lasting change. How do you acquire focus? By eliminating unfocused activities and understanding the steps to successful implementation. Through a series of exercises, Chapter 9 explains how to identify contributive, partially contributive, or noncontributive activities. Once you categorize your activities, you can select one of three alternatives for action: eliminating, modifying, or adding to your work.

Patience: Living in the Long Term. Executives must rise above the thoughts and actions of others and commit themselves to the long-term perspectives of their enterprises. If you believe in your firm's long-term purpose, you must be patient enough to see it through. In Chapter 10 you'll find nine guidelines for controlling impatience, reducing your stress level, achieving greater peace of mind, and creating the ideal environment for carrying out your vision.

Since New Age executives find themselves in so many different types of organizations, and since any given organization evolves through fairly predictable stages, you'll employ these skills in different combinations and with varying levels of emphasis, depending on the situation. Therefore, you must bear in mind while learning these skills that no single one ever works alone but that each depends on mastery of all the others.

Can you master and apply these skills overnight? No. As we cautioned earlier, New Age executives can't rely on quick fixes, magic formulas, and cure-all theories. It takes just the same kind of dedication, hard work, and pure grit to create excellence as it does to win a twenty-six-mile marathon.

No Pain, No Gain

In the early 1930s, James O. McKinsey began what has become one of the most respected international management consulting firms, and McKinsey's original vision continues to place his firm in a dominant position. With offices throughout the world, McKinsey & Company serves clients who rank among the biggest and the best. How did it all begin? Three goals preoccupied the founder: technical competence, reputation for superior management advice, and constant contact with businessmen. His commitment to superior management advice won the company a reputation for always making valuable contributions during the first meeting with a prospective client. McKinsey wrote thousands of follow-up letters to businessmen after luncheons, presentations, and meetings, immediately offering advice that would benefit them. He peppered every meeting with questions about the nature of an executive's enterprise and the problems it faced. By maintaining constant contact and visibility with businessmen, meeting with a different executive every day for lunch or dinner, he managed to affect more than three hundred new businessmen each year. On one occasion he rented an apartment in the center of town for the sole purpose of developing a relationship with a businessman who lived next door. As a result of such perseverance and hard work, James O. McKinsey helped father modern management.

Little of lasting value comes easily. Although at times ostensibly miraculous events seem to happen effortlessly, don't be misled by superficial appearances. The achievement of excellence requires effort and, at times, pain. The very process of confronting and addressing problems head-on calls forth our greatest effort, but only by expending our greatest effort can we win exceptional and durable skills. New Age executives might think of themselves as marathoners who must toil to prepare themselves to go the distance, surmounting all the obstacles that block their paths. Such marathon-distance managers recognize obstacles and problems as the very impetus of their own growth. Winston Churchill summed it up when he said, "To every man there comes in his lifetime that special moment when he is figuratively tapped on the shoulder and offered the chance to do a very special thing, unique to him and fitted to his talent; what a tragedy if that moment finds him unprepared or unqualified for the work which would be his finest hour."

But it's getting tougher, not easier, to create excellence. In a business environment that is increasingly characterized by turbulence, fundamental changes in consumer behavior, intensified domestic and global competition, the radically fluctuating cost of borrowed funds, accelerated technological breakthroughs, economic uncertainty, and constantly shifting markets, today's executives must bear unprecedented burdens. If we have suffered at the hands of ruthless competition and our own complacency, we must suffer even more to win back dominance and aggressive leadership.

Three Deadly Attitudes

Deeply ingrained attitudes often prevent you from developing a New Age outlook. From our own experience with hundreds of firms we have identified three basic attitude problems that most American executives suffer from today: short-term orientation, shallow thinking, and quick-fix expectations.

Short-term orientation. Over the past few years the business press has diligently focused on the short-term orientation of most American corporations. Much of the criticism has addressed such problems as preoccupation with quarterly earnings and annual earnings-per-share increases, pinpointing this short-term orientation as one of the primary reasons for America's decline in world competitiveness. Even when management recognizes this problem, it often remains trapped by traditional approaches. In a recent meeting with a group of eighteen chief executive officers largely from Fortune 500 companies, we heard most of them accept short-term orientation as a major problem. Unfortunately, these same executives had to confess their own inability to solve the problem. The elaborate system that has developed in the United States for tracking corporate performance can unwittingly strangle executive action. Stockholders, financial analysts, and business journalists scrutinize every quarter's earnings, looking for information, trends, and news. How could Coleco Industries take decisive and sometimes painful steps to overcome its shaky start with the Adam computer when the company's leaders found every move subject to the microscope, with the press pronouncing the company's planned layoff of over a thousand manufacturing workers as a sign of doom rather than smart streamlining? Fortunately Coleco's long-term results should generate more headlines than their immediate crisis caused.

Since the drive to maximize short-term profits robs long-term developement needs and prevents a company from creating or exploiting opportunities, companies can only create excellence when they replace short-term needs with long-term development and well-being. Obviously, New Age executives must find a way to balance short-term with long-term expectations.

Shallow thinking. Too much concentration on dousing the flames of daily crisis can drain the executive's reservoir of creative energy and result in superficial or shallow thinking. Such thinking has triggered "low-risk" strategies vulnerable to more aggressive Japanese and European ones. It has spawned "market-driven" behavior that satisfies customer needs in the short run, but doesn't produce new, superior products over time. Good business requires deep thinking; and deep thinking only comes from a deep and abiding commitment to success.

Quick-fix expectations. An overreliance on shallow thinking leads many American executives to look for cheap and easy, rather than costly and difficult, solutions. Ignoring serious problems by providing temporary relief for symptoms can eventually aggravate rather than eradicate pain. According to Yale sociologist Charles Perrow, "Managers want the quick and easy fix. It pays to go heavy on schlock. That's the way of the market, to beef up the image of the executive as being all-powerful." But the way to create excellence is to confront problems (suffering the inevitable pain of doing so) and develop effective solutions (which takes good old-fashioned hard work). As we tell our consulting clients, "If you don't want to sweat, don't hire us."

Using Strategic Thinking, Culture Building, and the Six Skills

A piano student who does no more than memorize the notes of a concerto will never become an accomplished virtuoso. The same holds true for mastering the skills of the New Age executive. You must apply them judiciously, sparingly, and in just the right combination, at just the right time, depending on the situation. In Part III we demonstrate how you can apply strategy, culture, and the six skills to a wide assortment of settings that represent the common stages of any organization's life cycle. The applications vary from the most stunning achievements to the most miserable failures, from Horatio Alger stories to dramas of agony and defeat. The four common stages are:

Start-up: Originating Strategy and Culture. To help readers solve the problems associated with organizations starting from scratch, we spotlight companies living in the fast lane, whose emerging corporate cultures can be hard to find. But managers in such enterprises must realize from the outset that they are either building a forceful culture or creating a Frankenstein. During the early-growth phase, strategy and culture tend to separate unless a leader guides and coordinates them. Uncontrolled strategy and culture can undermine the best product or service. In Chapter 11 Part III readers will see how to deal with the start-up stage of a business, discovering how to avoid such pitfalls as bureaucratic red tape and knee-jerk behavior as we take apart a booming high-tech firm and ask the reader to make strategy and culture decisions. Here the foundation skills (creative insight and sensitivity) plus one of the integrating skills (vision) come dramatically into play.

Growth: Holding Strategy and Culture Together. Growth often brings innovative strategies that may demand a new culture. In Chapter 12 readers watch a professional service firm struggling to gain market share. Any growth-oriented organization bent on launching a brilliant new strategy needs to carefully weigh the consequences for its culture. If management cannot commit the time (it could take years) and money (it could take millions) to develop the new culture or adapt the old one, it should reconsider its goals. We will present a difficult situation facing the professional service firm, and you will decide the best course of action and then evaluate your decisions. Here you will see the integrative skills (vision and patience) in action.

Crisis: Radically Altering Strategy and Culture. Many organizations face serious crises as they move along their development paths. When crisis threatens the organization's very survival, drastic action is needed. The only option at this point is to radically alter strategy and culture, but too much or too little change will destroy the organization. The ability to make effective decisions about what to change and how to change during a crisis is the quality that separates the New Age executive from the rest. In Chapter 13 you will face the crisis experienced by a manufacturing company. You will have to decide how much you can change the company's strategy and culture, then match your decision against the New Age executive's. The skills of insight, versatility, and focus are extremely important here.

Evolution: Fine-Tuning Strategy and Culture. When you examine formerly excellent organizations in changing environments, you see living, throbbing, changing, growing creatures constantly evolving to insure their survival. As a firm's vision and strategies evolve, culture must adapt as well, but only within certain bounds. Can you reasonably expect a benevolent service firm to transform itself into a manufacturing giant? Can engineers become marketers? Perennially excellent organizations feed off common purpose, satisfied customers, distinctive competence at delivering products and services, dominance over competitors, and consistency in hiring and keeping good people—but they must constantly withstand the threats of a changing environment. Strategy must assume a reinforcing role to bolster the culture and adapt it to the changing environment. In Chapter 14 we dissect a large consumer products company that has developed a strong culture over years of operation but now faces a changing environment which requires a new strategy that may threaten its culture. Can it respond to change and still protect its culture? You will take the helm, choosing from among several possible courses of action, and then observe how a chosen path measures up against the choices of New Age executives. Here you'll exercise the adaptive skills (versatility and focus) and one of the integrative skills (patience).

Marathon runners begin to get their minds and bodies in shape by visualizing the goals they wish to attain, then sharpening the skills to get there. Before we delve into the six New Age skills, let's learn how to visualize our goals for excellence by becoming strategic thinkers.

CHAPTER 2

On Becoming a Strategic Thinker

Without competitors there would be no need for strategy.
—KENICHI OHMAE

There are techniques of being intelligent. It is not easy to acquire the proper use of the mental tools which we have thoughtlessly inherited or which are implicit in the construction of our brains. Severe effort and long practice are required.
—PERCY W. BRIDGMAN

What Is Strategy?

In any game that pits competitors against one another—tennis, chess, Space Invaders, business—victory usually belongs to the competitor who can outthink, outplan, and outplay adversaries. Such thinking, planning, and implementation can serve as a working definition of strategy. A top tennis pro visualizes the game, plans a series of shots, and tries to control the game according to a predetermined plan. The same holds true for the chess master, the video-arcade addict, and the corporate executive. Throughout history strategy has helped determine success. Ancient tribes, villages, nations, armies, and merchant groups attempted to achieve their goals by finding new ways to conquer enemies, improve living standards, extend political influence, or increase wealth. The biblical Joseph, foreseeing seven years of famine, developed a grain storage system that created great wealth for Egypt and reunited his family. Alexander the Great conquered nations and then wisely drew

41

their cultures into the dominating Greek empire. And Great Britain's colonization won it global economic advantage and political influence.

In the early days of American enterprises executives wise enough to recognize and use strategy also achieved success. In the 1870s Gustavus F. Swift began a livestock-meat business in Massachusetts. Then, as the cattle market moved westward, he moved the company's headquarters to Chicago. When demand for meat in populous eastern cities outstripped that region's ability to supply it, Swift began formulating a plan to take advantage of what he saw as a great opportunity. Could he find a way to distribute fresh meat over a wide area? Though the railroad companies had only just begun building refrigerated cars, Swift thought they held promise, so he had several such cars built and soon began shipping fresh meat on the only railroad smart enough to cooperate. Despite strong opposition from the railroads, which charged exorbitant rates because they preferred the greater tonnage of shipping live cattle, and despite the fact that the primitive refrigerating system couldn't guarantee results in unusually cold or hot weather, Swift's strategy eventually paid off. By the 1880s his company had developed a reliable refrigerator car, and the railroads slowly capitulated to the inevitable future. Shipping fresh beef in refrigerated cars to markets around the country, Swift and Company won a significant advantage over competitors by rapidly opening branches in all major cities. The strategically adept Swift singlehandedly restructured an entire industry. He had devised a better future, he had planned a series of moves to position his company not only to exploit but to create that future, and he had executed his plan masterfully. The result? Swift and Company planted the seed from which sprang billion-dollar Esmark, Inc., now a part of Beatrice Foods.

In 1853 the Otis elevator company opened its first plant, ironically in a one-story building that still houses corporate headquarters in Chicago. Elisha Graves Otis, after developing an automatic safety device to keep hoists from falling, visualized a strategy that could position Otis as the premier elevator company in the country. Even though numerous hoist manufacturers competed for dominance in the 1850s, customers only used their hoists for freight. Assuming people could also take advantage of the technology, Otis developed the "safety hoister," which he rode high above the startled crowd at America's first World's Fair in New York City. People watched aghast as Otis's assistant cut the supporting rope and the brilliant entrepreneur did not fall. This stunt demonstrated to the world that people could ride elevators without fear. In the years that followed, Otis's elevators changed the skyline of America. Outthinking, outplanning, and outplaying his competitors from the beginning, Otis laid the foundation for a lasting leadership position. Today Otis operates as a highly successful subsidiary of $14-billion-a-year United Technologies.

Before New York Life pioneered the branch-office concept in 1887, insurance companies operated out of centralized offices, working regionally through agents who routinely represented several insurance companies instead of one. New York Life's new concept included a branch-office manager who hired and trained individual agents who, in turn, worked directly for the company. This plan resulted in increased operational and organizational efficiency and improved service to policyowners. New York Life eventually opened branch offices throughout the United States, catapulting the company beyond its competitors. Like Swift and Otis, New York Life implemented a visionary game plan long before the word "strategy" became a business school buzz word.

Sophisticated Techniques: Enlightenment and Confusion

In 1969, Fred Borch, then CEO of General Electric Company, commissioned McKinsey & Company to study the effectiveness of GE's planning activities. The results of McKinsey's study eventually led to the reorganization of the company's 190 departments into forty-three strategic business units (SBUs) and to the development of a nine-block matrix the company used to summarize business and investment strategies. The nine-block matrix compressed complex strategic planning data into one efficient display, thus enabling Borch to evaluate the business strategies of each SBU on an annual basis. Finally, GE executives could evaluate the performance of each SBU without having to examine reams of documents. GE's experience marked the beginning of a trend that would make strategic planning the hottest topic in boardrooms and business schools throughout the 1970s.

Soon thereafter, eagerness for formal strategic planning increased as the Boston Consulting Group concocted the "experience-curve" and the famous "growth-share matrix" for its clients. The experience-curve concept suggested that a large increase in the cumulative production of a standardized product would bring a predictable decrease in cost per unit. The growth-share matrix offered a four-block grid for evaluating businesses on the basis of two criteria, market growth and market share, allowing an enterprise to categorize individual endeavors as cash cows (low growth, high share), stars (high growth, high share), problem children (high growth, low share) or dogs (low growth, low share).

Throughout the 1970s sophisticated strategic-planning techniques proliferated, spawning an army of corporate strategists, specialists tutored in all the complexities of strategic management. Unfortunately, these masters of scientific techniques took planning out of the hands of line managers, a development that undoubtedly contributed to the decline in American productivity. Corporate America's romance with strategy fathered a lot of confusion and misdirection. Borden, Inc.'s snack food group created huge corporate staffs to do all the strategic thinking, thus immobilizing line managers who retained bottom-line responsibility but insufficient strategic decision-making authority. Frenzied analysis and activity at the corporate and division staff levels didn't have much impact on the marketplace. Borden has experienced twenty years of ineffective diversification and lackluster performance despite its proliferation of planning staff. But Borden's CEO, Eugene Sullivan, is changing all that through an aggressive restructuring and repositioning effort that began in 1980. Through 1983, Borden's return on equity increased from 12 percent to 14 percent, and net income increased 14 percent in 1983 alone.

When Dart Industries fell in love with sophisticated strategy techniques, the company adopted high-growth businesses, such as real estate development, which the parent knew nothing about. Strategy theory persuaded Dart it should balance its slower-growth, cash-generating businesses with high-growth, cash-consuming businesses to achieve success, so Dart plunged into real estate. But the company wound up courting disaster and ultimately sold its real estate acquisitions after losing millions of dollars.

Procter & Gamble, smitten by the theory that more planning is better planning, overgathered and overanalyzed mountains of strategic data and felt cocksure that the new Pringle's potato chips would succeed. The public would delight in the uniform shape, in a package that prevented breakage, and in all the product's healthful ingredients. But the public didn't accept Pringle's and went on happily munching the competitors' brands.

What soured American executives' obsession with formal, complex planning? Jolted by the Japanese threat, then enlightened by a revolution in thought prompted by William Ouchi's influential book *Theory Z*, American executives soon saw that strategic *thinking*, not a complex planning process, creates excellence, so they gradually returned responsibility for strategy to the line managers who should have been handling it all along. Today the Borden snack food group, composed of nine separate companies, employs only a small corporate staff (six people), properly allocating authority to line managers. In 1984 Borden's introduction of Cottage Fries, a premium-priced and extra-thick potato chip, really accomplished something by beating Frito-Lay's brand, O'Gradys, to the punch. Cottage Fries outsold O'Gradys across the country. Borden expects snack food sales to jump from $315 million to $450 million by the end of 1984. What accounts for such results? Borden put its strategic muscle where it packed the biggest wallop, in the hands of its line managers.

An article in *Fortune*'s December 27, 1982, issue rang the death knell for the era of fascination with utopian strategy techniques and concepts: "We're going to miss corporate strategy, that sweet collection of surefire concepts—matrices, experience curves—that promised an easy win. Oh, it'll still be around here and there, showing its by now slightly grimy face in this corner or that, but things won't be as they were." New Age executives can feel thankful that strategy has resumed its proper uninflated role.

The flirtation with scientific strategy did produce some useful results. From it executives learned how to break down a business system (the system that gets a product to market) into component parts to better isolate value to customers and relative costs. Isolation of such factors helped executives compare their achievements to those of their competitors, thus enabling them to figure out why some products succeed better than others, and supporting decisions about adding value or reducing costs. Adding value that your competitors can't easily duplicate can make a product more attractive and win you a competitive advantage, while reducing costs at key points can provide a price advantage over rivals and put more dollars on the bottom line.

Also, certain strategy concepts, displays, and formulas, while no longer viewed as sure-fire solutions, do continue to provide valuable insight and understanding. A number of these appear in Chapter 5 on insight. Since we believe that strategic *thinking* should replace detailed planning in the New Age executive's repertoire, we'd like to explain what we mean by that term before we discuss how you can use it in your quest for excellence.

The Essence of Strategic Thinking

Locating, attracting, and holding customers is the purpose of strategic thinking. Without such a concrete goal, strategic thinking degenerates into an ivory tower experience. To the chagrin of American manufacturers, the Japanese brought their thinking about forklifts down from the ivory tower. As recently as 1973, low-priced forklifts didn't exist. Hyster, Eaton, Towmotor, and Clark Equipment dominated the market with deluxe, high-quality forklifts selling for as much as $250,000 each. The companies basked in their success, assuming they could never lose such strong positions in a stable, mature industry. Enter Toyota, Nissan, Komatsu, and Mitsubishi. Led by Toyota, the Japanese companies recognized that at least 20 percent of the market didn't need the luxury and frills of the high-priced American models, so they concentrated on the low end of the market, customers in retailing and construction industries who would appreciate less sophisticated and less expensive lifts. Before long, Toyota established a dominant position among such customers, and the Japanese group now owns more than 20 percent of a worldwide forklift market in which they had *no* position ten years ago. A fluke? Hardly. Savin Corp. photocopy machines stung Xerox the same way a few years ago. As photocopying won the hearts of Americans, Xerox gravitated to where they thought they'd make the most money, large organizations. While Xerox offered high-speed, fancy copiers at premium prices to all customers, Savin saw an opportunity for attack. Knowing no company can be all things to all customers forever, Savin (with the help of Ricoh of Japan) perfected an inexpensive but reliable copying machine for small users. Fat and happy Xerox treated the upstarts as mere pests and just waited for them to go away. But they didn't. Savin took such a big bite out of Xerox's market share that Xerox has never fully recovered.

Volkswagen, with its "Think small" advertising slogan, offered an attractive alternative to Detroit's cries that "bigger is better." Perched at the other end of the automobile industry, Mercedes, whose prices ran little higher than American products fifteen years ago, has steadily increased prices because it knows wealthy customers value quality, technical sophistication, and exclusivity. IBM's unparalleled strategy of stressing customer service, Frito-Lay's strategically impressive store-door delivery system, Cullinet's software strategy, Dow Jones's emphasis on disseminating quality information, Merck's commitment to research and development in pharmaceuticals, and Hewlett-Packard's innovation and product performance all attracted and kept customers, an achievement that is the best test of any strategy's effectiveness.

How to Think Strategically

Unfortunately, finding, getting, and holding customers is not as easy as the success stories make it seem. To create excellence with strategic thinking, you must master three aspects of the game: your customers, your competitors, and your own company.

REQUIREMENTS FOR SUCCESSFUL STRATEGIES

Strategy Components	Action You Must Take
Customers	Satisfy customer needs, recognizing that different customers have different needs.
Competitors	Gain a sustainable competitive advantage, keeping product "differentiation" in mind.
Company	Capitalize on company strengths, remembering that it takes time to develop them.

How did Swift, Otis, and New York Life satisfy customer needs? Swift fulfilled its customers' demands for readily available fresh meat at reasonable prices by lowering distribution costs with the refrigerator car. By shipping fresh, chilled meat rather than live cattle, they cut distribution costs and slashed the retail price of meat. Otis met two important customer needs, the need to feel safe riding elevators and the need for buildings higher than five stories in major cities. New York Life's offices in home towns provided security and accessibility, thereby gaining its customers' trust and confidence.

How did these companies gain sustainable competitive advantages? Swift's technologically superior refrigerator car and its outlets in every major city propelled the company years ahead of its rivals. In Otis's case, while opponents were feverishly developing competitive safety hoists, Elisha's two sons refined an electric elevator to keep their technological edge. By parlaying its original technological breakthrough into additional significant innovations, Otis remained the most prominent elevator manufacturer in the United States. And it took New York Life's competitors many years to imitate the branch-office system that eventually became the industry standard. By then New York Life had won the public's confidence.

Finally, how did these companies capitalize on company strengths? Swift exploited its founder's ability to spot trends, Otis relied on Elisha's engineering savvy and his flare for publicity, and New York Life continued to build a bond of trust.

But consider what befalls a company that does not pay attention to all three requirements of a successful strategy. When deregulation hit the airline industry, Braniff Airways immediately extended its long-haul routes to many cities it had not served in the past. Why? Since profitable long-haul routes had always opened the door to success, Braniff decided to become the number one long-haul carrier. Sadly, Braniff failed to realize that deregulation would make long-haul routes strikingly less profitable as airlines waged price-cutting wars. Braniff found itself struggling with routes far from its home base, and it soon dove behind the shelter of bankruptcy. How did Braniff go wrong? First, the company failed to envision a future any different from the past, thereby crushing its hopes for a sustainable competitive advantage. Second, Braniff didn't capitalize on its own strengths when it ignored its Dallas "hub" of operations. Third, though the company did fill customer needs for additional flights to major cities, it failed to take into account the effect on profitability of overall airline expansion spurred by deregulation. In summary, weak strategic thinking guaranteed failure.

Replacing Planning with Strategic Thinking

Ironically, the planning processes established in most corporations often stifle strategic thinking because dependency on formalized strategic planning builds a false sense of confidence. To revitalize itself, American business needs less, not more, complicated approaches.

General Electric Company, always a trendsetter in the area of strategic management, has recently pruned its corporate planning staff in favor of decentralized planning wherein responsibility for strategy sits squarely on the shoulders of line managers. Says William Rothschild, staff executive for business development and strategy at GE, "Over half of our managers are strategic thinkers. Another 20 percent to 25 percent lean that way. The rest don't understand it, and if they're fortunate enough to be in the right business where there is a stable environment, it doesn't matter too much." GE has also streamlined its requirements for planning by no longer demanding that each SBU submit plans to the highest corporate level. Instead, it has structured a sector level (the next management level down) review, and it has eliminated burdensome annual strategic planning. With these steps General Electric has delivered an unmistakable message: successful strategies do not result from plans, formulas, or systems but from managers who think and act in ways that meet customers' needs, create competitive advantage, and capitalize on existing strengths.

Can everyone do it? Yes. To develop your strategic thinking, you can practice using twelve viewpoints, each of which provides a different perspective on the issues that perennially confront any organization. If done regularly, this exercise can turn anyone into a strategic thinker.

STRATEGIC-THINKING VIEWPOINTS

Satisfying Customer Needs

1. Customer Segments — Creatively segment your customers into as many distinct groups as you can imagine. Force yourself to find new ways to segment your customers.

2. Customer Perceptions — Consider all the different ways your customers perceive your organization. Push yourself to uncover previously unconsidered customer perceptions.

3. Unmet Customer Needs — Mentally explore all your customers' unmet needs. Don't be satisfied until you visualize at least one such need.

4. Future Customer Needs — Identify all potential future customer needs. Consider needs you can create rather than merely satisfy.

Sustaining Competitive Advantage

5. Competitive Interaction — Detail how each of your competitors attacks the market. What are their stated or implied assumptions? Analyze every direct and indirect competitor.

6. Competitor Gaps — Locate any gaps that competitors in your industry haven't filled. Can your organization fill them? Pretend you are entering the market for the first time.

7. Value and Cost — Identify the value you provide your customers. At what stage in the business system does it occur? What value do competitors offer and where does it occur? Spot obvious and hidden costs, tangible and intangible value.

8. Competitor Reaction — Predict your competitors' reactions to your organization's potential actions.

Capitalizing on Company Strengths

9. Strengths and Weaknesses	Carefully list each of your organization's strengths and weaknesses. Be ruthless and objective. Look for strengths and weaknesses you've never considered before.
10. New Applications	Think of all the new ways you could apply your organization's strengths to new products, markets, or approaches. How can you strengthen weaknesses? As in brainstorming, you should consider outlandish, futuristic, and even weird possiblities.
11. Business Portfolios	Evaluate the products, services, or businesses in your organization as if they were a portfolio of investments. Which would you bet your own money on? Don't overlook even the most routine aspect of your organization.
12. Opportunities and Threats	Think of all the opportunities your organization's strengths can seize, and the threats that could take advantage of your weaknesses. Search for unsuspected opportunities and threats.

Let's look at a hypothetical situation in which you can see how these viewpoints assist you in becoming a better strategic thinker capable of developing superior strategies for your organization. Imagine the president of a $45-million bank struggling to find a way to distinguish his bank from the many large, medium, and small competitors in his geographical market area. Committed to improving his strategic thinking, he considered all possible viewpoints. Scheduling a week each for contemplation of one of the twelve viewpoints, he invested ten hours per viewpoint for a total of 120 hours. He shared the schedule with his marketing director and assistant, who were instructed to gather relevant customer, competitor, and company data for each week's viewpoint every Monday morning. The twelve-week schedule dictated their data-gathering priorities. At the start, the bank president set a goal of gaining at least one new insight each week. He didn't just sit behind his desk poring over reports and gazing out the window, he practiced the art of meditation that we will teach you in Chapter 5.

Over the twelve-week period the president followed his schedule religiously. In the first three weeks he assumed viewpoints related to customer segments, perceptions, and needs. He then spent one week trying to anticipate future customer needs and identify what new needs his organization might create. Next, he embarked on viewpoints related to competitors, examining competitor positions, strategies (especially strategies taking advantage of deregulation), and strengths. Remembering Dizzy Dean's baseball strategy, "Hit 'em where they ain't," he spent one arduous week looking for holes in the market, places where competitors "ain't." Finally, he zeroed in on the bank itself, evaluating strengths and weaknesses, opportunities and threats, and ranking the profitability of various bank services and products. He also looked hard at new applications of the bank's expertise, particularly in light of new avenues deregulation had opened up.

In the middle of his twelve-week marathon a surprise bank examiner's review interrupted his schedule, so it actually took fourteen weeks to complete the task. However, he had achieved his goal of one new insight for each viewpoint. Finally he could tackle the task of charting his bank's strategic direction. It had taken more effort than he had imagined, but the results were more than worth it because three major insights could form the foundation of a new strategy.

Contemplation of customer-related viewpoints brought the insight that the medical customer segment was very profitable, extremely loyal, and currently underserved. Despite that segment's relative smallness, it offered an opportunity because the doctors enjoyed high income levels and needed sophisticated financial services for their practices. The banker had discovered that while every bank offered so-called special services to doctors, such services were basically traditional ones, so he immediately commissioned a market research survey which confirmed his suspicion that doctors, while loyal to their banks, expressed general dissatisfaction with the services they received and would be willing to switch banks given a truly better alternative.

Second, his contemplation of competitors uncovered the interesting fact that not one of them was focusing on a specific customer segment. Most bankers are generalists who pay attention more to the nature of the customers' transactions than to the nature of the customers themselves. Intensified competition after deregulation had not caused competitors to alter traditional practices. Advertising campaigns and brochures may have abounded, touting this or that "special" service for "special" customers, but when the president hacked away the rhetoric, he saw the same old bankers doing business as usual. None of them had yet targeted the medical profession as a segment. Had the president found an opportunity to beat his competition to the punch? Deregulation and increased possibilities for competition made specialization inevitable. If smaller banks didn't specialize, they'd be squeezed out by the large ones.

Finally, introspection concerning his own bank substantiated the fact that the bank's most profitable and loyal customer group consisted of doctors. In fact, doctors represented a much larger percentage of the bank's customers than anyone realized. Not until the president had scoured the records did he appreciate the extent of the bank's dependency on the medical segment. Further examination showed that two of his bank's branches operated in locations ideally suited for serving most of the medical community. One branch sat just east of the city center with five major hospitals within three miles of it, while the other perched across the street from a major medical center ten miles outside the city. Remarkably, the services doctors most demanded from banks besides checking accounts, credit cards, and loans were services the president's bank could probably provide without too much difficulty: financial planning and counseling, credit/collections assistance (a service the bank already provided in excellent fashion), tax assistance, brokerage and trust services, leasing, prequalified lines of credit and ATMs.

Within one year, the bank president's strategic-thinking marathon paid off. The initial ad campaign communicating the new focus and specialization brought an unprecedented response. Over fifty doctors called the bank to arrange appointments to discuss their financial needs. Most of them quickly became loyal customers. Quite a success story. Did the president then sit back and congratulate himself on his successful strategy? Not for a minute. Every six months he conducts a rigorous meditation marathon to keep ahead of the scrambling pack. And before he ever launched the bank's new strategy, he carefully assessed the organization's culture, which you will observe in the next chapter.

New Age Strategy

Running a successful business has always required smart strategy. Yet the business world has undergone radical changes since World War II. Before the war, W. T. Grant was the largest variety-store retailer in the country; today, it's out of business. Before the war, Xerox did not exist; today it has revenues in the billions of dollars. Up until 1956, IBM took little interest in computers, choosing instead to make electro-mechanical calculators; today, everything it makes is secondary to computers.

Since managers in the 1970s went astray with complex, multifaceted strategic planning, we feel they should concentrate on evolving their strategic planning into more of a way of thinking. In the words of Walter M. Miller, head of planning at Becton, Dickinson & Co., "What we're moving toward is an integrated theory of management, one that assigns strategy its proper place and identifies the other factors you have to manage to make strategy work." With strategy in its proper place, let's explore the realms of corporate culture, the work environment that can make or break a strategy.

• CHAPTER 3 •

On Becoming
a Culture Builder

You can take my factories, burn up my buildings, but give
me my people and I'll build the businesses right back again.
—HENRY FORD

What Is Culture?

Webster's offers several interesting definitions of "culture"
(our emphasis added): "...the *act* of developing...the intellectual and moral faculties," especially by *education*; "*expert care and
training*"; "*enlightenment and excellence* of taste acquired by intellectual and aesthetic training"; "acquaintance with and taste
in *fine arts, humanities, and broad aspects of science as distinguished
from vocational or technical skills*"; "the *total pattern of human behavior*...embodied in thought, speech, action, and artifacts and
dependent upon man's capacity for *learning and transmitting
knowledge to succeeding generations....*"

Families, organizations, and entire nations possess cultures.
In a family, parents and even older siblings perform the act of
developing children by caring for and educating them, setting
certain standards for excellent behavior. A family may show
taste in art, food, entertainment, and even work, and each family distinguishes itself from others by unique patterns of behavior, which it passes along from generation to generation.

One might think of corporations as big families. Management
acts to develop its people by caring for and training them,

setting goals and standards for excellent performance. Every member of the organization, from the CEO to the lowliest clerk, shares some responsibility for the organization's products and services, and the unique patterns with which they carry out their responsibilities distinguish their "family" from those of their competitors. To perpetuate the culture, each employee passes valued traits along to succeeding generations.

The Japanese have always fostered culture as a nation and, amazingly, have inculcated their unique culture in their business organizations. Cradle-to-grave employment, worker participation in setting standards, quality circles, and tremendous familylike loyalty have created the strong Japanese corporate cultures that have, in part, thrust their corporations into dominant positions worldwide. Can we Americans do likewise?

Of course, some American companies have developed widely admired corporate cultures. IBM, McDonald's, and Hewlett-Packard frequently receive praise for their internal cultures. However, even smaller, less well known American enterprises provide instructive models.

Nordstrom, a public company still run by the Nordstrom family, is a $1-billion retailer with twenty-six department stores in the western United States. Sales increased from $12 million in 1963 to $1 billion in 1984. Nordstrom's culture wins high marks over that of many other department store chains for three reasons: employees share an unrelenting commitment to superior customer service, management strives to hire and keep good people, and employees themselves enforce a high standard of performance. Nordstrom's culture has been passed along so consistently to so many succeeding generations that no one who works for the family can escape it. If a new employee doesn't suit Nordstrom's culture, fellow employees, not managers, blow the whistle. Universally accepted standards and expectations throughout the firm force any nonperformer to the company's notice quickly, and Nordstrom management doesn't waste time getting rid of people who won't or can't adapt.

When the firm moved into southern California for the first time in 1978, many observers doubted its ability to succeed in that fiercely competitive market, but from the day it opened its 127,000-square-foot South Coast Plaza store it attracted more than its share of customers. "Beyond our wildest dreams," beamed Jim Nordstrom, president. After several years of successful operations in California, Nordstrom is opening another fifteen stores in the state. Earnings? In 1983, on increased sales of 25 percent, earnings leaped 50 percent. The Nordstrom culture has certainly made an impact on the bottom line.

Another less famous firm is one with which we interact daily as part of the Bennett Enterprises. According to the business press, Conant Associates has taken the interior design industry by storm. Ranked in *Interior Design* magazine's "giants list," Conant operates offices in Denver, Houston, San Diego, and Salt Lake City. Conant designs interior space for major corporations, marshalling architectural, marketing, and graphics skills into total design solutions that fully satisfy client needs. Other design firms provide similar services, but they lack Conant's unique culture, which has been erected on four pillars: problem-solving orientation, intensity of effort, mutual trust and respect among all levels of employees, and an unusual commitment to helping solve an employee's personal problems.

Pillar number one prompts the firm to go to extraordinary lengths to satisfy a customer. On one occasion, when a supplier had delivered the wrong carpet, Conant's promised installation date seemed doomed. When a frantic call to the supplier got an unsatisfactory response to the crisis, Conant spent $10,000 to air-freight the right carpet to its destination overnight.

The second pillar supports intense effort toward superior performance. As one proud employee exclaims, "If we weren't a great design firm, we'd be a great bakery, or any other business you want to name."

The third pillar fosters great trust and respect among all levels of employees. Encouraged to speak their minds and respect the views of others, people within the organization strive for strong, ongoing communication. The source of this philosophy? Both the chairman and the president, Lee and Nan Conant, always support their people. When mistakes happen, the firm, not the employee, takes the heat, although Lee and Nan expect the employee to learn from the mistake.

Last, but by no means least, the company avoids getting itself into the middle of sticky situations but still helps its people solve personal problems. Conant runs its own day care center for the children of designers and maintains an unusually flexible work schedule, allowing employees to attend to personal business whenever necessary. The result? Conant has grown from $500,000 in 1980 to over $20 million in 1984. By 1989, Nan and Lee project $100 million in revenues, a milestone that will surely establish Conant Associates as one of the largest design firms in the world.

What Culture Is Not

Like excellence, culture seems easy to recognize, but sometimes it helps to consider what a concept is *not* rather than what it is. Not long ago, Bausch & Lomb's instruments group consisted of some thirty different product lines that competed against such successful giants as Hewlett-Packard. This loosely bound group of businesses had languished for almost a decade before Jim Edwards, an IBM whiz kid, rode to the rescue. The first phase of Edwards's rehabilitation program was a wrenching overnight reorganization, creating four new divisions—three oriented to manufacturing and one dedicated to sales and service support for all product lines. In addition to the new divisions, Edwards brought aboard the matrix form of organization he had learned at IBM. The reorganization seemed brilliant, just what the doctor ordered, because it united all the fragmented product lines under the direction of one business unit, thus taking advantage of economies of scale, shared resources, and the group's combined position as one of the largest analytical-instrument producers in the world. But the loose-knit family at Bausch & Lomb didn't fall into step like the disciplined professionals at IBM, and Edwards found himself valiantly struggling to bind the family together with brochures and videotapes selling the new organization and mode of operation. Despite all his efforts confusion blossomed, and the group grew demoralized. Before long the company announced a quarterly earnings drop of 32 percent, soon followed by Edwards's resignation. One former executive summed up the experience by saying, "Edwards didn't take the measure of the company before he started." Apparently Edwards forgot for the moment that culture does not grow out of overnight reorganizations, policy directives, or matrix-style management.

Allyn and Bacon suffered a similar setback. One of Boston's oldest educational publishers, the company had been started in 1865 by two men deeply dedicated to education. Over the years, teachers and school administrators throughout the United States developed respect for A & B as a reliable supplier of textbooks. Yet in 1980, the $30-million firm found itself in financial trouble. While top management tried to lay blame on the economy, competition, and high production costs, it ignored a serious culture problem. The old culture, which had commanded respect and admiration, had withered away, replaced by one dominated by people who lacked the founders' love of books. Top management snared line managers from competing firms and created a massive bureaucracy wherein new recruits emulated their bosses' behavior, working halfheartedly and always ready to jump ship for better positions elsewhere. Lower-level employees received shallow attention and had to account for pencils and paper clips. As a result, disgruntled employees unionized, a turn of events that tore the organization apart. Despite a recent takeover by Esquire, Allyn and Bacon has its work cut out for it in overcoming what one former employee calls "culture shock."

In stark contrast to Bausch & Lomb and Allyn and Bacon, consider Piggly Wiggly, a southeastern grocery chain and distribution business. A few years ago, Piggly Wiggly was enticed by a buy-out offer, but eventually decided to turn it down. Gratified employees (Piggly Wiggly offers its people excellent benefits and doesn't lay employees off even during rough economic times) bought their company a $40,000 refrigerated semitractor trailer to say "thanks." Clearly, the employees appreciated the loyalty of their superiors. Says a ten-year mechanic, "When you can work for a company as good to you as this one, you just feel like doing good for them."

New Age Awareness

A recent *Fortune* article reported, "For all the hype, corporate culture is real and powerful." For all the hype, the concept of culture has been around for a long time. Seventy-five years ago, John Patterson created a bond of commitment among National Cash Register's sales staff with slogans and the One Hundred Percent Club, the models on which Tom Watson, Sr., built IBM with its famous "THINK" signs on every wall and its blue-suit-and-white-shirt sales and service uniforms. Harley Procter, cousin to one of the founders of Procter & Gamble, took weeks to hit on the name for a new white-soap formula he was assigned to sell. With the simple and elegant "Ivory" he initiated the first tenet of a culture that would make P & G famous: consumer-product marketing thoroughness. Strong cultures have always thrived in the best organizations, but we're just beginning to be able to articulate, describe, and use them to create excellence. One positive side effect of the decade-long passion for strategic planning was the realization that no brilliant strategy can succeed if you can't *implement* it. Notice how Webster's definition of "culture" stresses the *act* of developing desired traits with *expert care and training*. With its emphasis on implementation, culture building offers New Age executives a tool for turning well-formulated strategies into results.

In a recent survey of 305 chief executive officers, a New York compensation consulting firm found that most of the respondents consider corporate culture critical to their companies' success, and almost half of them claimed to be emphasizing corporate culture a great deal. Unfortunately, the same business leaders who once supported armies of strategic planners have now hired legions of culture consultants. Such outsiders, no matter how technically well-trained or hardworking, have as much chance of building strong corporate cultures as an anthropologist would have turning a Stone Age tribe into urban gentry overnight. Strong corporate cultures, like strong family cultures, come from within, and they are built by individual leaders, not consultants. Fortunately, as with strategic thinking, any executive willing to invest the time and trouble can shape an outstanding culture.

Gaining Increased Culture Awareness

Culture building requires renewed application of some "soft" management skills, but that doesn't mean it's a simple or easy matter. Just as any living organism thrives in a delicately balanced environment, so does a corporate culture exist within a finely tuned system. If you tinker with the system thoughtlessly, you can cause the culture to shrivel and die. Bitter experience has taught many organizations that blithely trying to change culture through reorganization or shifts in policy, rules, or strategy can easily poison it. Every collection of human beings displays a culture, but the degree of commitment to a common purpose, the distinctive competence, and the methods for consistently passing on these traits to future generations vary widely. In the words of Marvin Bower, former managing director of McKinsey & Company, corporate culture is "the way we do things around here." But a strong, successful culture is even more than the way things get done, it's also the unique ways people unify behind a common purpose, deliver superior performance, and pass skills along to others. An excellent culture is a resource, an asset that helps implement corporate strategy. Delta Air Lines could not have survived industry hardships without knowing beforehand that its employees would stand behind the company, no matter what. Braniff, Continental, and Eastern, lacking Delta's strong corporate culture, asked their employees for the same sacrifices Delta obtained but got bankruptcy, strikes, and internal strife instead.

Douglas Richardson, senior vice-president of W. K. Gray & Associates, urges a reapplication of the "soft skills": "I am not suggesting that we throw away the considerable technical managing skills we have picked up in recent years. But I am suggesting that unless due recognition is given to the other factors—the ones that turn out to control commitment, dedication, and loyalty—we run the risk of ignoring powerful forces that will exist anyway."

We recently encountered a typical culture awareness problem while consulting with a multidivision company. After we asked top management to outline its plans for implementing a new strategy, the answer was, "We'll have to get the right person for the job. The current division manager hasn't made it happen, so we'll hire someone who will." Why had they sought our services? Only to hear suggestions about hiring this "right" person? They obviously lacked culture awareness. Patricia O'Toole, in her book *Corporate Messiah*, nicely summarized our client's problem: "A company in need of a messiah is also a company in a hurry. Eager to find a hero, the search committee often puts more energy into persuading the candidate to take the job than into considering how well he will mesh with the company."

Many American executives share our client's lack of corporate culture awareness, and three common attitudes that get in the way of creating excellence (short-term orientation, shallow thinking and quick-fix expectations) are among the most common causes. Whatever the reasons, New Age executives should heighten their culture awareness and grow even more sensitive to their cultures or they'll risk catastrophe. Consider Caterpillar, which shaped its corporate culture on the sort of quality and service that make its competitors look like Tonka toys by comparison. Then contrast Caterpillar's achievement with International Harvester's failure. The latter's name was once synonymous with farming. The first IH tractor stands on display in the Smithsonian, but its last is being plowed under by Caterpillar, Deere, and Komatsu. What made the difference between Caterpillar and IH? Corporate culture, an organization of many hands but one mind devoted to building the best product possible, fully satisfying customers, and taking care of one's own people. At Caterpillar, quality and service are second nature to every employee.

The following checklist should force an executive to heightened cultural awareness, an awareness that must always precede understanding, developing, changing, and perfecting a culture. Like other aspects of excellence, a good culture takes time to build, and it must be able to evolve with changing conditions. If you answer "never" to a question, try to find a way to improve your answer to "often" or "always," and even if you answer "always" today, keep the question in mind because "always" can easily slip overnight to "often" or "seldom" or even "never." Your total score on this checklist should never fall below 116. Chapter 6 will show you how to ask and answer these and similar questions at the deepest, most sensitive level.

CULTURE AWARENESS CHECKLIST

Commitment to a Common Purpose

		ALWAYS	OFTEN	SELDOM	NEVER
1.	Can you state your organization's purpose, philosophy, or central theme in one clear sentence?	4	3	2	1
2.	Do all employees in the organization fully grasp your purpose?	4	3	2	1
3.	Do 90 percent or more of your people display commitment to the common purpose?	4	3	2	1
4.	Do individual employees perceive personal benefits from committing themselves to the common purpose?	4	3	2	1

5. Do you know which
    employees fail to grasp or
    display commitment and
    why?   4   3   2   1

6. Can you measure the level
    of individual and collective
    commitment to the common
    purpose?   4   3   2   1

7. Do you recognize the
    warning signals associated
    with an employee's decline
    in commitment?   4   3   2   1

8. Do you take action on
    employees who are not yet
    committed?   4   3   2   1

9. Are you genuinely
    committed to the common
    purpose yourself?   4   3   2   1

10. Do you consider the impact
    on the organization's
    common purpose when you
    evaluate strategic and
    operational alternatives?   4   3   2   1

Competence to Deliver Superior Performance

ALWAYS OFTEN SELDOM NEVER

11. Does your organization
    develop a distinctive
    competence with one or
    more business skills, such as
    marketing, R and D, or
    distribution?   4   3   2   1

12. Can every employee
    recognize the organization's
    areas of distinctive
    competence?   4   3   2   1

13. Are people committed to maintaining distinctive competences at any cost?   4   3   2   1

14. Does the organization pay attention to its areas of distinctive competence?   4   3   2   1

15. Are new employees sufficiently trained and developed to have the competence to deliver superior performance?   4   3   2   1

16. Do you act to enhance and improve areas of distinctive competence?   4   3   2   1

17. Do the organization's distinctive competences operate consistently over time, despite environmental changes?   4   3   2   1

18. Do your organization's areas of distinctive competence produce superior performance?   4   3   2   1

19. Do your employees recognize the superior performance delivered by the organization?   4   3   2   1

20. Do customers, competitors, and observers value your organization's superior performance?   4   3   2   1

21. Do *you* recognize competence?   4   3   2   1

22. Do *you* recognize superior performance?   4   3   2   1

Consistency in Perpetuating Commitment and Competence

ALWAYS OFTEN SELDOM NEVER

23. Is the organization's
commitment to a common
purpose and its competence
to deliver superior
performance emphasized
and discussed throughout
the organization?   4   3   2   1

24. Will the current degree of
commitment and
competence remain at a
high level?   4   3   2   1

25. Do employees consistently
communicate their
commitment and
demonstrate their
competence to their peers
and new employees?   4   3   2   1

26. Do you thoroughly screen
candidates for employment
to ensure a match with the
organization's commitment
and competence?   4   3   2   1

27. Are new employees
sufficiently motivated and
stimulated to commit
themselves to the
organization's common
purpose?   4   3   2   1

28. Do you deal swiftly with a
new employee's lack of
commitment by providing
additional development or
terminating that employee?   4   3   2   1

29. Are veteran employees who lose their commitment to the common purpose quickly retrieved or terminated?	4	3	2	1
30. Is your organization able to attract and keep the right kind of people?	4	3	2	1
31. Do you carefully consider the impact of new strategic or operating directions on your people?	4	3	2	1
32. Do employees in your organization readily recognize the difference between committed and uncommitted employees?	4	3	2	1
33. Do you perpetuate your own commitment and competence daily?	4	3	2	1

Now that you've become more aware of culture, you can learn to take the three steps required to shape the one in your organization.

How to Build Culture

By culture building we mean selecting, motivating, rewarding, retaining, and unifying good employees. Unfortunately, American management does too little of this. For too long, our business schools have accentuated hard, quantitative management techniques over supposedly "soft" people skills. Returning to Webster, we see that culture derives from "acquaintance with and taste in *fine arts, humanities, and broad aspects of science as distinguised from vocational or technical skills.*" Culture building requires a sharpening of the "soft" people skills, and it involves three steps: instilling commitment, rewarding competence, and maintaining consistency.

THREE STEPS TO A STRONG, SUCCESSFUL CULTURE

Culture Components	*Action You Must Take*
Commitment	Instill commitment to a common philosophy and purpose, recognizing that employee commitment to a corporate philosophy must coincide with both individual and collective interests.
Competence	Develop and reward competence in key areas, keeping in mind that you will foster greater competence by focusing on one or two key skills at a time rather than by addressing a host of skills all at once.
Consistency	Consistently perpetuate commitment and competence by attracting, developing, and keeping the right people.

Did Nordstrom and Conant Associates use these components to fashion their cultures? Let's consider commitment to a common purpose. Nordstrom employees feel so committed to superior customer service and high standards of performance that a new recruit who doesn't fit the mold quickly becomes obvious. Nordstrom people vigilantly police their standards in such major matters as personal selling initiative and even in such seemingly minor ones as dress, grooming, attitude, and attentiveness. In the case of Conant Associates, commitment to a common purpose manifests itself in the way employees routinely work around the clock to meet deadlines and take extreme pains to solve customers' problems. Designers never grumble when they have to redo renderings and drawings to satisfy a customer's new concern, and whenever someone makes a mistake, the company accepts the blame and pays for it. An employee error is viewed as an opportunity for learning, not punishment.

What about competence? Nordstrom's successful penetration of the California market testifies to its ability to deliver superior performance. When customers walk into a Nordstrom store, they enjoy a pleasurable experience at the hands of competent, responsive sales people. By the same token, Conant Associates has developed a strong competence in solving client problems and meeting employee needs, which go hand in hand at Conant. Employees show clients the same respect their company shows them. The essence of Conant's competence lies in its ability to see, analyze, and resolve problems. When clients meet with Conant people, they see thorough attention given to the minutest details. Conant people are trained to anticipate problems and devise creative solutions well in advance of any emergency. Like Nordstrom, Conant pays as much attention to its employees' personal problems as it does to its most prestigious clients' needs.

Do these companies consistently perpetuate commitment and competence by attracting, developing, and keeping the right people? Nordstrom conducts an extensive screening and interviewing process to eliminate the wrong people, but if it makes a mistake, the company admits and corrects it swiftly. Indecisive personnel action benefits neither the culture, other employees, nor the needs of the mismatched employee. Conant Associates also uses an extensive interviewing process during which current employees tell prospective ones about their Conant experience. After a strenuous round of these interviews, unlikely prospects may well conclude that they don't fit the mold. Whether a person can fit into the Conant culture usually becomes apparent during interviewing, but if applicants occasionally fool themselves (and Conant in the process), they seldom last long. President Nan Conant insists, "They either fit or they don't, and it only takes about a week to find out when we've made a mistake."

What happens when a company even momentarily forgets to pay attention to commitment, competence, and consistency in its culture? In the mid-1970s, Texas Instruments impressed the world with its ability to forge new technologies, cut costs to the minimum, and deliver millions of calculators to customers. During the late 1970s and early 1980s, TI tried to apply its winning formula to watches and home computers, but it did not enjoy the same success. Why? Wasn't Texas Instruments one of America's best-run companies? In the beginning, the company had unified its employees in a quest for new technology and a drive to make that technology accessible to millions of customers by keeping prices low. Their twin competencies were technological innovation and cost-cutting. With an incredible success in calculators under its belt, TI assumed it could transport its culture into other fields. But when you've been a long-jumper all your life, it's hard to become a pole-vaulter overnight. TI did not yet have the marketing expertise to compete successfully in the watch or home computer markets. By not sufficiently weighing the abilities of its strong culture, management embarked down what in retrospect seems to have been an ill-advised road.

Assessing an Organization's Culture

Assessing an organization's culture is the first step any executive must take before considering if and how a culture needs to be built, adapted, or changed. Any culture grows up over many years of operation, and you must first analyze it at a molecular level before using the culture to achieve an organization's purposes. Eighty to ninety percent of all executives find themselves inheriting some kind of culture, whether a carefully nurtured one or one that developed almost haphazardly. Regardless, managing cultures in the New Age requires extreme care. Because cultures, like the personalities of individuals, take a long time to develop and a long time to change, in most cases you can achieve better results by using an existing culture, good or bad, than by destroying an old culture and building a brand-new one. Unlike strategies, cultures cannot survive dramatic change every time a new CEO takes over. Organizations, especially those with more than a hundred employees, can't adapt quickly. Attempts to force them to do so inevitably cost a lot of money and take a lot of time. However, some executives find themselves in start-up or turnaround situations that require building a brand-new culture. Chapters 11 and 13 address these two special situations in detail, but at this point we'll focus on existing cultures.

Effectively assessing an existing culture not only allows executives to put culture to use but also allows them to adapt and modify culture over time as the environment and organization evolve. Let's see how our hypothetical bank president from Chapter 2 assessed his bank's existing culture. Prior to launching the successful initial advertising campaign targeted at the medical community, our banker spent another three months of grueling assessment to find out whether the bank's culture could implement the strategy he had formulated earlier. He knew he could adjust the bank's culture to some degree, but he also knew that major adjustments would be expensive and take a long time, severely hampering a successful attack on the medical market niche. If the culture did not support the campaign, changing the bank's proposed strategy might make more sense than trying to dramatically alter the culture.

Since his marathon of meditation had enhanced his strategic thinking, the bank president decided once again to allocate a full month to each of the three culture components: commitment to a common purpose, competence to deliver superior performance, and consistency in perpetuating commitment and competence by getting and keeping the right people. For one month he would spend at least sixteen hours a week pondering and evaluating. Before he began, he tapped five basic sources of information:

- The bank's history—events, decisions, and people that had shaped the bank's ten-year history.
- The dreams, ambitions, and values of the bank's key managers and employees, the opinion leaders who strongly influenced other employees.

- The performance, motivation, and relationships of the bank's two hundred employees.

- Organizational stories containing important messages about the bank's priorities, values, commitment, concerns, star employees, do's and don'ts, and general way of getting things done.

- All the bank's idiosyncrasies including unique ways of doing jobs, relating to people, approaching problems, and responding to success or failure.

To gather the necessary information the banker decided to adopt an informal rather than a formal approach, so he enlisted the help of his vice-president of personnel, an extremely competent woman who had risen through the ranks during eight years at the bank. This woman had seen it all, from the luckless romance between a teller and a vice-president to the stormy implementation of a new company-wide performance evaluation program two years before. She was the bank's unofficial historian. The banker took care to tell her he would hold everything she said in the strictest confidence, and she expressed her delight in helping her boss in such an important matter. They agreed on a series of both verbal and written reports. She would submit a formal written report at the beginning of each month, addressing one of the culture components (commitment, competence, or consistency) and she would spend a full day each week verbally relating all she knew about the bank's people. A major goal at each discussion session would be to identify those employees whose opinions strongly affected other employees so the president could schedule meetings and lunches with them, too. The bank president looked forward to immersing himself in his organization's culture and meditating on all that he learned.

The first month's marathon uncovered a clear and almost unanimous commitment on the part of bank employees to offering customer service superior to that provided by larger competitors. This commitment to superior service revealed itself in all aspects of banking, from taking loan applications to dealing with overdrafts to handling transactions at the teller window. The personnel vice-president reported that several employees liked to tell about a bigger bank's poor treatment of customers and about their own positive effect on these same customers. She also offered a number of anecdotes about how the previous president himself had been driven to provide superior service. "Mr. Bond once worked for the largest bank in town and hated the fact that rules and regulations came before service. He lost a key account when his superiors refused to bend a rule in an emergency, so he quit and came here nine years ago with a burning desire to provide a level of service beyond anything the big banks could offer. I remember one payday when even the Grady cement plant was closed because of a terrible blizzard. Not only did Mr. Bond take his snowmobile to work and open the bank himself, he inspired six employees to help him hand-deliver almost all the cement plant paychecks to people's doors. No one forgot that gesture."

The president's lunches with opinion leaders disclosed their firm commitment to the example Mr. Bond had created. "I like being the underdog," said one teller. "Old Mrs. Grady said the other day that she comes to our bank just to see me smile. I always have a box of dog biscuits at my window, and I give her a biscuit for each of her three poodles. She's a pretty big customer, you know. She inherited the Grady cement fortune." Many others expressed their pride at being part of a caring organization that treated its customers well. The bank guard, who had been with the company longer than anyone, said, "No other bank telephones its customers once a year on the anniversary of their opening an account to thank them for their business and to ask if they need better service. My Aunt Sally thinks of us as part of her family. That makes me feel great!"

When, during the second month, the banker tackled competence, he developed additional insights. Both he and the vice-president had known all along about their firm's commitment to superior service, but neither of them had ever thought of customer relations as the bank's most distinctive competence.

Didn't the bank's greatest areas of competence lie in delivering superior service, matching services to customers needs, and solving customer's problems? Yes, but the bank accomplished such goals with superb customer relations. Realizing that commitment to superior service had motivated employees to take a personal interest in customer needs, now a crucial competence at the bank, the president quickly saw how the trait was present in most of his organization's stories: "We want people to know we care about *them* more than their money." Such an attitude pleased customers even more than superior banking services, technical knowledge, problem-solving, financial systems, or innovative approaches. "You know what I like best about working here?" said the teller. "That we get to call our top three hundred customers by their first names. When Mr. Bond first handed out the list, we all groaned. It seemed like homework. But, you know, it turned out to be pretty easy. I've made a hundred friends who greet me on the street. They wouldn't bank anywhere else."

Stimulated by the insight gained during the second month, the president and vice-president eagerly entered the third and final month of their culture assessment. They were delighted to confirm that the bank had consistently hired, motivated, trained, and unified employees to maintain the bank's commitment and competence over the years. In fact, the "underdog" spirit appeared to grow stronger every day. "I'll tell you something interesting," said the vice-president. "Anyone can have a bad day, but when someone treats a customer curtly, she finds a happy-face button on her desk. It's a company joke, but it's a subtle way of saying, 'It never hurts to smile and be polite.' Whenever someone turns out to be grumpy all the time, peer pressure usually forces that person out quickly." A review of personnel files revealed that the bank had hired almost eight hundred employees over the previous ten years and 95 percent of the six hundred who left the bank for one reason or another did so within a year of joining. The average tenure of the bank's two hundred employees was over five years. Talks with opinion leaders uncovered accounts of employees who just couldn't hack the "pamper every customer" style and subsequently left, seldom for another bank. The records also confirmed that new hires as a percent of total employees had fallen sharply over the past five years. The bank was getting better at recognizing who fit and who didn't before offering a job. "I don't tell many people this," confessed the veteran bank guard, "but I had a drinking problem before I came here. Mr. Bond got me into a counseling program, and all the employees here helped me stay dry. Working here has changed a *lot* of people's lives for the better."

After three months, the bank president concluded his assessment and summarized three distinct characteristics of the bank's culture: a commitment to the common purpose of providing superior service to customers, a strong competence in developing exceptional customer relations, and consistency in perpetuating the bank's commitment and competence by finding and keeping service-and-relationship-oriented employees. As a result, he could articulate in detail the bank's culture, but more important, he now understood how that culture could support his strategy.

Before uniting his strategy with his company's culture, he had to undertake yet more evaluation of the match between them (see Chapter 4). However, at this point, he felt confident that his six-month investment would eventually help him carve out a profitable and secure niche in medical banking services.

Strategy plus Culture Equals Excellence

Strategy and culture each contribute to the success of any organization. In the past, we have seen brilliant strategies bring great business success, and we have seen strong cultures survive great upheavals in the marketplace. In a few exceptional cases, a strong culture has overcome a stupid strategy, or a smart strategy has prevailed despite a weak culture, but don't count on such exceptions in our increasingly competitive and sophisticated business world. Long-term success and perennial corporate excellence require alloys of superior strategies and strong cultures. In the next chapter we'll learn how to develop those alloys.

CHAPTER 4

Matching Strategy
and Culture

The fusion of knowledge is the most creative act of the
human mind.

—Elwood Murray

Any approach to strategy quickly encounters a conflict
between corporate objectives and corporate capabilities.
Attempting the impossible is not good strategy; it is just a
waste of resources.

—Bruce Henderson

One plus One Equals Three

One plus one doesn't always equal two. Sometimes the combination of two independent substances results in an alloy with
qualities far superior to the sum of the original ingredients.
Look around at all the "one plus one equals three" alloys in
your world. What would happen to your city's skyline if builders
could not use steel and glass alloys? Where would your home,
your car, or your streets be without the alloys that make up
bricks, tins, safety glass, and concrete? Likewise, if you separate
strategic thinking from culture building or don't combine them
properly in the management of an enterprise, you weaken both
the foundation and the structure of excellence. The quality of
products and services declines, morale sags, sales and profits
plummet, and the enterprise plunges into a sort of corporate
Stone Age. Without this unification of strategy and culture,
executives cannot create New Age excellence for their organizations.

To appreciate the strength of the strategy-culture alloy, consider Nolan Bushnell, the founder of Atari. In 1969, Bushnell worked on the video game that eventually spawned an entire industry. Though his first product, Computer Space, failed because it was too sophisticated for typical consumers, Bushnell did not give up. Guided by a strategy bent on technological innovation and revolution, Atari chalked up two shattering successes—arcade and then home versions of an electronic Ping-pong game called Pong. By 1975, sales blasted to $39 million, net income to $3.5 million. In three short years Bushnell had built a forceful culture at Atari committed to innovation and fun. Creative, game-loving engineers set the pace, management allowed people to come to work in T-shirts at any hour they chose (as long as the ideas and innovations kept flowing), and workers at all levels engaged in marathon brainstorming sessions. Atari's "one plus one equals three" equation created such excellence that its success lured scores of competitors into the business.

To retain its competitive edge, Atari developed a cartridge-based computer system that would tremendously expand the number of game options for its users, but Atari needed more capital to beat well-financed competitors. Bushnell raised the capital by selling Atari to Warner Communications in 1976 and quickly went from CEO to chairman to director. With the subsequent infusion of capital, Atari seemed poised to surpass its earlier success, but a new chief executive, Raymond Kasser, began making changes. Kasser, a recent Warner recruit, had learned efficiency and order during twenty-five years at Burlington Industries. As a marketing specialist, he figured that once customers bought Atari home consoles, they would continue to purchase a neverending stream of new cartridges, so he shifted Atari's strategy from innovation to exploitation, from engineering to marketing and finance. For his new strategy to succeed, Kasser would have to turn the once loosely governed Atari organization into an efficient machine. Among other things, this meant no longer "pampering" prima donna engineers, but in ceasing to do so Kasser tinkered with Atari's innovative and spirited culture, replacing it with one guided by opportunism. When the engineers lost their forceful culture, many of them left the company (former Atari employees include the founders of Apple and Activision).

Could Kasser's new strategy survive the shock to Atari's culture? When sales soared to $2 billion, with profits at $320 million in 1982, it seemed possible, but in the fourth quarter of 1982, disaster struck. Retailers began cancelling orders, and Atari's strategy got tangled in a web of "efficient" policies, procedures, and structure. Teamwork vanished, factions within the company waged internal warfare, and product development suffered. In-house software developers, accustomed to receiving credit for their games, languished in anonymity and soon followed on the heels of the engineers. Customers who expected computer hardware and software prices to steadily drop grew disillusioned with Atari's mark-ups and handsome quarterly profits and flocked to competitors' systems. The bottom line for Warner was a $418 million loss in 1983. Mismatching strategy and culture resulted in zero rather than three.

Before Jack Tramiel bought Atari from Warner in 1984, Atari continued to suffer major problems. In 1983, Kasser left Atari in disgrace and James Morgan, former vice-president of marketing at Philip Morris, swept in to take his place. Morgan's first goal was to restore the old innovative and spirited teamwork culture. However, Morgan and Warner faced the twin problems of rebuilding a culture and formulating a new strategy to deal with the declining game and rising home computer markets.

Brilliant strategies that capitalize on exciting new products or exploit unserved market niches can bring short-term success, but even with such advantages, a company cannot create lasting excellence in a dynamic world without developing a strong strategy-culture alloy.

The Strategy-Culture Alloy

Only when you pay active and simultaneous attention to both strategy and culture, always striving to harmonize them, can you create an organization capable of achieving and sustaining excellence. In the early 1980s, such writers as Ouchi, Pascale and Athos, Peters and Waterman, and Deal and Kennedy helped us recognize the importance of culture, but they did not show us how to blend it with strategic thinking.

In order to compete effectively in the world market of the future, we must put it all together. Though you can't expect to do it the same way IBM, Hewlett-Packard, Johnson & Johnson or Delta did it, you can create striking success in your own way by taking into account your organization's unique circumstances. Before you begin to learn the six skills that combine strategic thinking and culture building, you must understand the strength of the alloy.

Companies fail and go out of business for numerous reasons, including lack of product and service innovation, marketing incompetence, operational ignorance, and financial irresponsibility. Although no executive plans to go out of business, too few take the crucial first step toward establishing the strong foundation and structure that can guarantee successful battle with the New Age Forces of global marketing, economic uncertainty, and intense competition. The first step is to weld the two basic raw materials, strategy and culture, into a tough new alloy. But, as with forging Space Age metals, selecting the wrong materials or combining too much of one with too little of the other invariably produces unsatisfactory results. Consider how your own mind and body function as an interdependent unit. Zen masters, psychologists, and philosophers suggest that you can attain greatness only when your mind and body operate harmoniously. As the mind conceives bold new ventures, it depends on a healthy body to carry them out. When the body reaches beyond its physical limits, however, not even the best mind can push it further.

Similarly, if a brilliant strategy cannot rely on a healthy culture to carry it out, little hope exists for achieving greatness. On the other hand, not even the strongest culture can implement an impossible strategy. Yet why do executives continue to conceive strategies their companies cannot implement without making major changes in their corporate cultures? Our experience has uncovered three major reasons: 1) some exec-utives don't consider the time and energy it takes to match strategy and culture; 2) others lack the New Age skills necessary for successfully managing strategy and culture in tandem; 3) still others change either strategy or culture, but not both.

Before we consider examples of imperfect blends of strategy and culture, let's take a look at the near-perfect blend achieved by the St. Paul Companies. Unlike many firms in a mature insurance industry struggling with profit declines of more than 50 percent, the St. Paul Companies, a Minnesota property ca-sualty insurer, reported 1983 revenues up 9 percent to over $2 billion and profits up 11 percent to $196 million. What accounts for St. Paul's success? While its rivals have been diversifying, St. Paul has pursued strategies that take advantage of a powerful culture based on a commitment to specialization and the com-pany's ability to offer superior products through a carefully developed wholesale distribution network. St. Paul chairman Carl Drake knows that diversification would require a major change in St. Paul's culture, a change that would invite great risk, considering the firm's happy customers, strong products, and effective distribution system. Therefore, while Drake has watched an increasing number of financial service companies get into insurance, he has guided St. Paul to increasingly em-phasize the sort of specialized, sophisticated insurance products that even St. Paul's competitors, who have ignored them in favor of "easier to write" insurance packages, must use. As rivals adopt many of St. Paul's products to fill out their own lines, they become increasingly dependent on St. Paul, making it even more unlikely that they will develop their own competitive pack-ages. To cement its position, St. Paul uses its specialization to continually develop increasingly superior products. Such per-formance allows St. Paul to further expand and strengthen its wholesale distribution network. What an effective welding of strategy and culture! The strategy enhances the culture which, in turn, enhances strategic opportunities. Insurance industry analysts believe St. Paul will forge a long-range dominant po-sition. But for every success story like St. Paul's, there are several horror stories.

Deadly Mismatches

After painstaking study and analysis, strong and healthy U-Haul dramatically shifted its strategy by replacing its nation-wide dealer network of independent service stations with company-owned moving centers. An excited U-Haul management team anticipated many benefits from the new strategy, ranging from greater control to increased market share, and it felt confident the shift would only strengthen the company's dominant position in the self-moving industry. Just two years later, however, management scrapped the moving center approach in favor of the original dealer network. Couldn't the executives have foreseen that setting aside U-Haul's ability to attract and keep dealers would demand new capabilities? In a way, they did, but new capabilities such as construction and store management did not lie within easy grasp of the existing culture. Everything took much longer and cost much more than planned. By formulating the new strategy without building a culture to implement it, U-Haul lost half of its business as former U-Haul dealers turned to rivals Jartran and Ryder. Today U-Haul is finding that hard-won loyalty, once betrayed, cannot easily be won back.

Quaker Oats also made a mistake when it tried to transfer the strategy and culture it had developed in food products to the toy and restaurant businesses. In the early 1970s Quaker management grew tired of its mundane, mature position in such staple food businesses as oatmeal and pancake mixes. When it decided to diversify by turning its stable food marketing culture, capable of winning and maintaining prized supermarket shelf space, into a trendy toy and theme-restaurant marketing culture, it ran into trouble. Serious problems developed in the company's food marketing operations, store service deteriorated, shelf space declined, and sales calls became unproductive. One product, Quaker's 100% Natural Cereal, found itself with the same shelf space as its nearest competitor, though that competitor enjoyed only half as much market share. Quaker offered too few new items, introducing only one major product from 1970 to 1978, and thus failed to use the best means for maintaining shelf space in supermarkets. While the company applied its old marketing strategy to new businesses, it ignored a strategy-culture mismatch. Shifting the advertising and promotion-oriented strategy from foods to toys and restaurants wasn't the problem; it was ignoring and tampering with the existing culture that brought Quaker difficulty. The company's strong food marketing culture had grown through strict attention and commitment to grocery store sales calls, in-store product servicing, and product innovations. With the entry into toys and restaurants, attention to these key elements of the culture slackened in favor of attention to the needs of the new businesses. The result? Near destruction of Quaker's successful culture. Quaker has since taken steps to reunite strategy and culture in its food marketing business, dumping an acquired toy company and trimming its restaurant operations in favor of renewed emphasis on its core businesses. To do so the company has increased its food marketing sales force by more than 25% and has refocused its efforts on innovative food products. By taking such decisive action, Quaker may regain its former harmony between strategy and culture.

Weak alloys make weak tools. While at one time we may have gotten away with treating our organizations as machines we could easily retool to meet change, we can no longer do so. Strategy alone can't create excellence. Neither can culture. Like a sound mind in a sound body, only by working in harmony can strategy and culture bring excellence to an organization.

How to Match Strategy and Culture

When executives set about the arduous task of forging an ideal alloy from a brilliant strategy and a strong culture, they begin by carefully analyzing two important groups: customers and employees. While strategic thinking aims at getting and keeping customers, culture building attracts, develops, motivates, and unifies the right kind of employees. When the organization's strategy to get and keep customers requires employees to act and think in unaccustomed ways, employees may respond poorly or even feel resentful. On the other hand, no matter how strongly an organization's culture motivates and develops employees, if customers do not perceive better products and services as a result, the culture has been wasted. The intertwined relationship between customers and employees requires watchful management by well-trained executives with New Age skills. Like parts of a complicated jigsaw puzzle, each piece of an internally consistent strategy must fit snugly with each piece of an internally consistent culture. A single mismatched piece can destroy the overall picture. In earlier chapters we discussed three fundamental elements of strategy (satisfying customer needs, gaining advantage over competitors, and capitalizing on company strengths) and culture (commitment to a common purpose, competence to deliver superior performance, and consistency in perpetuating culture by attracting and keeping the right people). You can arrange these six elements in a strategy-culture matching grid that forces you to compare nine different combinations of strategy and culture elements.

STRATEGY-CULTURE MATCHING GRID

| | *Culture* | | |
	COMMITMENT	COMPETENCE	CONSISTENCY
Strategy			
CUSTOMERS	Match?	Match?	Match?
COMPETITORS	Match?	Match?	Match?
COMPANY	Match?	Match?	Match?

Let's explore each of the nine combinations:

- *Customers/Commitment.* An organization's collective commitment to a common purpose must coincide with the organization's way of satisfying customer needs. Although F. W. Woolworth developed a strategy to meet customers' needs with the Woolco discount store chain, the company lacked a common commitment to the idea. Consequently, the chain's image wavered over a twenty-year period until the parent firm closed all Woolco stores in late 1982.

- *Competitors/Commitment.* Commitment to a common purpose must augment the organization's method for gaining a sustainable advantage over competitors. IBM's employees share a common commitment to superior customer service, the company's primary method of sustaining advantage over competitors.

- *Company/Commitment.* Commitment to a common purpose must support the company's attempt to capitalize on its strengths. The St. Paul Companies' strength in specialized products has rallied employees to a common purpose, which in turn rules the company's strategy.

- *Customers/Competence.* An organization's competence to deliver superior performance must satisfy the customers' needs. Emerson Electric has developed a distinctive competence in cost-cutting and product improvement over the years, but today Emerson finds itself incapable of satisfying its customers' demand for new technologies. To succeed in a changing market, Emerson must solve this potential mismatch.

- *Competitors/Competence.* Competence to deliver superior performance must match the organization's method of gaining a sustainable advantage over competitors. Procter & Gamble has long enjoyed a distinctive competence in product marketing thoroughness, but recently, small and faster-moving competitors have beaten P & G to the punch. P & G must solve this potentially serious mismatch.

- *Company/Competence.* Competence to deliver superior performance must agree with the organization's efforts to capitalize on its strengths. U-Haul's competence in attracting and managing independent dealers came into conflict with the company's attempt to build on important company strengths—reputation and image. By undervaluing its real strength, dealer loyalty, U-Haul suffered a serious mismatch.

- *Customers/Consistency.* An organization's consistency in perpetuating commitment and competence by attracting and keeping the right people must parallel efforts to get and keep customers. Delta Air Lines satisfies its customers' needs for superior airline service by consistently treating employees the way it would like customers treated.

- *Competitors/Consistency.* Consistency in perpetuating the culture must agree with the organization's methods of gaining advantage over competitors. Hewlett-Packard perpetuates its culture by hiring entrepreneurially oriented managers who will fit into the company's culture. These same entrepreneurs fuel H-P's advantage over competitors by maintaining technological innovation.

- *Company/Consistency.* Consistently perpetuating the culture must enhance the organization's efforts to capitalize on its strengths. Apple Computer attempted to build on its strength in personal computers by developing the more sophisticated Lisa and MacIntosh machines, but the company kept the people who worked on the MacIntosh project isolated from the rest of the organization. Which employees will perpetuate the Apple culture, those in the mainstream organization or those isolated with MacIntosh? Apple, too, must solve a potential mismatch.

While the negative effects of a mismatch in one area may appear more deadly than those of a mismatch in others, *any* mismatch can thwart an organization's attempts to create and maintain excellence. Whenever a mismatch occurs, either the strategy or the culture must be modified accordingly. A mismatch flashes a red light to management, warning it to take action before irreparable damage occurs.

Matchmaking In Action

Executives must remain constantly alert to discover matches and possible mismatches among the six elements of strategy and culture. When they spot danger signals, they must be prepared to act decisively. Let's observe how our bank president develops his strategy-culture alloy, constantly refining and adjusting it.

The president set the strategic direction of the bank by targeting the medical community (doctors, nurses, and other medical staff) as a major market segment. The bank could win a sustainable competitive advantage by focusing on these customers before rivals did so, and it could sustain that advantage through constant attention to detail. The new strategy allowed the bank to capitalize on three major company strengths: branch location, existing customer base, and current service offerings. The executive easily summarized his bank's internally consistent strategy as follows: satisfying the medical community's banking needs, gaining competitive advantage by dominating the medical segment, and capitalizing on the bank's location, customer, and service strengths.

During his thorough review of the bank's culture, the president identified its three basic characteristics: employee commitment to superior service instilled by the bank's previous president; the bank's distinctive competence in customer relations, particularly with high-income customers; and the bank's history of hiring and developing employees capable of delivering superior service. Despite an expectable level of turnover involving the comings and goings of a restless work force, the bank had consistently hired, motivated, developed, and unified the right kind of people to build a strong culture.

Once the bank president finished his review of the bank's

culture, he tested his strategy-culture alloy with the matching grid. What follows is a summary of his evaluation.

BANK PRESIDENT'S STRATEGY/CULTURE MATCHING GRID

Strategy	Culture		
	COMMITMENT (TO SUPERIOR SERVICE)	COMPETENCE (IN CUSTOMER RELATIONS)	CONSISTENCY (IN NURTURING SERVICE-ORIENTED EMPLOYEES)
CUSTOMERS (SATISFY MEDICAL CUSTOMERS' NEEDS)	Strong Match	Strong Match	Match
COMPETITORS (DOMINATE MEDICAL COMMUNITY NICHE)	Weak Match	Weak Match	Weak Match
COMPANY (CAPITALIZE ON LOCATION CUSTOMER, & SERVICE STRENGTHS)	Strong Match/ Weak Position	Strong Match/ Weak Position	Match

To understand how the bank president arrived at his strategy-culture matching conclusions, let's review his evaluation step by step.

- *Customers/Commitment.* Comparing the strategy's focus on satisfying the medical community's banking needs to the culture's commitment to superior service, he found a strong match because the medical community, particularly doctors, has long complained about the poor service at other banks.

- *Competitors/Commitment.* Looking at the strategy's method of gaining competitive advantage by a commitment to superior service, he identified a somewhat weaker match. Although doctors expressed deep concern about the banking service they received elsewhere, the president's bank would have to tailor its services to the specific personal and technical banking needs of the medical community.

- *Company/Commitment.* Reviewing the strategy's effort to capitalize on its strengths—location, customer base, and services offered—in light of the culture's commitment to superior service, he saw another strong match. However, while building on the bank's strengths would reinforce attention to superior service, this alone would not guarantee success. Only carefully tailored products could accomplish it. He found a strong match, but a weak overall position, meaning this area would require continuous effort and monitoring along the way.

- *Customers/Competence.* Asking himself whether the culture's distinctive competence in customer relations could help meet the medical community's banking needs, he found another strong match. Doctors needed and wanted more attentive service, and the bank had the competence to provide it.

- *Competitors/Competence.* Weighing the strategy's method of gaining competitive advantage (dominating the medical community niche) against the culture's competence in customer relations, he felt he had found a weaker match. Although customer relations would always be important, dominating the niche would take more than superior customer relations in the long run. The bank would have to make its services readily apparent to prospective medical customers. Such services would have to include financial planning, tax consulting, trust and brokerage services, and equipment leasing.

- *Company/Competence*. Considering the strategy's effort to capitalize on strengths of location, customer base, and existing services in relationship to the culture's strength in customer relations, he found a strong match. Customer relations depend on convenient banking locations, a loyal customer base, and good services, although, as with commitment to superior service, merely relying on present strengths would not suffice. Along with a strong match, he also found a weak overall position.

- *Customers/Consistency*. Comparing the strategy's focus on satisfying the medical community's banking needs with the culture's consistency in nurturing the right kind of employees, he concluded that the bank generally had the right employees for the strategy. Hiring or training employees to provide certain sophisticated financial services needed by doctors could strengthen the match.

- *Competitors/Consistency*. Comparing the strategy's method of gaining competitive advantage by dominating the medical niche with the culture's consistency in nurturing the right kind of employees, he again saw a somewhat weaker match. Dominating the niche in the future would require more than consistently nurturing employees skilled in customer relations and in providing superior service. It would also require employees with more sophisticated skills.

- *Company/Consistency*. Testing the strategy's effort to capitalize on the bank's strengths against the culture's consistency in nurturing the right kind of employees, he confirmed a match. Because the bank's employees had created its strengths, any effort to enhance or capitalize on those strengths supported the bank's efforts to nurture certain kinds of employees.

Once the banker had explored the matches among the six strategy and culture elements, he felt confident that the bank's culture could successfully implement the new strategy. To his delight, he had also identified areas where he could enhance the match between strategy and culture, as well as improve the bank's overall position, by developing increased competence and hiring additional people to deliver sophisticated financial services. Without further deregulation, the bank would not be able to directly offer all possible services, but it could negotiate arrangements with affiliate firms to enhance the quality and quantity of services aimed at the medical community.

Putting New Age Tools to Work

With strategic thinking, culture assessing, and strategy-culture matching behind him, the bank president launched the new strategy and inaugurated a careful plan for improving the bank's culture. It worked. Two years after introducing the new strategy, the bank had captured 38 percent of the local physicians. Revenues had increased by 24 percent and profits by 28 percent. While two other small banks had aggressively launched similar strategies, they had not succeeded because potential customers perceived them as "second-best." The big banks in town merely paid lip service to meeting doctors' needs and had not convinced the medical community they could deliver on their promises.

As expected, the bank's culture responded with great commitment and competence. A concentrated three-day retreat for the bank's management and a one-day "company party" for all employees at a local ski resort, where three prominent doctors talked about the pressures of contemporary medicine, helped everyone rally behind the strategy. Employees relished this challenge to their competence. The president was careful to communicate that, despite his own commitment, he knew that only the employees could guarantee the bank's future success.

At the management retreat, the banker reviewed his conclusions on the strategy-culture match and invited criticism and other ideas. As the managers discussed the new strategy and its relationship to their culture, they not only accepted the new strategy, they began to think of it as their own. "I wish Old Man

Bond were alive to see this," said a senior vice-president. "It's just his style." After three days of intensive discussion and planning, management had specified the details of implementing the strategy with advertising programs, research into new services, and a training program for all personnel.

To introduce employees to the strategy, the senior vice-president invited a surgeon, a cancer specialist, and a family physician to the company's annual ski holiday. The bank had always scheduled an educational discussion during the gathering, and this year it focused on the new strategy. "Banking on Health" became the employees' motto after the doctors heightened their awareness of the special pressures and needs of the medical community. In the weeks that followed, management held a series of company-wide training sessions to continue defining and illustrating the initial slogan. Once a week, a hospital administrator, nurse, or doctor would speak on the subject of health care, diet and exercise, or preventive medicine. Soon the bank's staff developed a greater appreciation of the entire field and its value to the community.

To create stronger strategy-culture matches in competitive advantage, management outlined five new services it could introduce over the next twelve months: financial planning, tax consulting, trust services, equipment leasing, and prequalified lines of credit. Each service would be carefully introduced with an emphasis on the bank's dominant skill, customer relations. As a result, employees would feel good about helping to create not only a healthier bank but a healthier environment in which to raise their children. And doctors, nurses, and medical technicians would become part of the bank's "family."

To manage each of these new services, five existing employees were promoted to "service managers," each responsible for managing a different service, much the way a product manager manages a product at Proctor & Gamble or General Foods. These five service managers had sufficient budgets to hire one new employee each if they found it necessary to bring additional technical expertise into the bank. Each new employee would have to display skill in public relations, especially with professional clients such as doctors.

Six months after launching his new strategy, the president hosted a company-wide picnic to bring everyone abreast of developments. Just as the employees were finishing their dinners, the bank president spoke. In the style of a true culture builder, he paid ten minutes of tribute to the bank's former president, Mr. Bond, not only extolling his personal virtues but attributing the bank's strong organization to his vision and commitment. He then praised the critical roles certain key employees were playing in the bank's development, mentioning at least a dozen people by name. Their influence had affected everyone present, and they had all pitched in to accept the new challenge. No other bank, he concluded, could have taken such advantage of the opportunity to serve the medical community. And he ended by putting the new strategy in a broader context: "A financially healthy medical community means a healthy community and an excellent banking future."

After he finished his prepared speech, he invited questions and comments and was gratified by the excited buzz that filled the room. By the end of the hour, dozens of people had offered suggestions on how to accomplish the bank's goals even more effectively. The bank president's efforts had paid off. His alloy of strategy and culture had set the stage for excellence.

Of course this executive, like all others on similar quests, does not just relax and let the organization operate on its own. Continued excellence depends on fine-tuning old strategies and cultures, initiating new ones, and constantly responding to and creating change. In the chapters that follow you will learn the six basic skills that we think every New Age executive should master.

PART II

SIX SKILLS FOR NEW AGE EXECUTIVES

CHAPTER 5

Creative Insight: Asking the Right Questions

Experience is not what happens to you but what you make of what happens to you.

—ALDOUS HUXLEY

As is your sort of mind,
So is your sort of search; you'll find
What you desire.

—ROBERT BROWNING

Insight Creates Successful Strategies

On your desk sits a twelve-inch cube of solid ice. Define it. Simple, pure, clear, and cold? Now consider it from different points of view. If you were trekking across Death Valley, that cube could quench your thirst. A doctor could use it to reduce the body temperature of a fevered woman and rescue her from death; a madman could use it to crack a victim's skull; an engineer could boil it to produce steam for a turbine, and an entrepeneur might add it as a key ingredient to a refreshing new treat. An Eskimo wouldn't give you a dime for it, but a thirsting prospector might trade you a handful of gold to get his hands on it.

If you meditate on it creatively, you soon see that a cube of ice contains rich possibilities limited only by your imagination. You achieve creative insight when you gain a full understanding of a phenomenon, carefully considering all its possibilities from a variety of points of view. Somewhat paradoxically, when you move from initial simplicity to a greater awareness of complex-

99

ity, you don't grow more confused—you begin to more fully appreciate the essence of an object, situation, or undertaking. In short, insight helps you solve problems by penetrating through their confusing symptoms to their very core.

Insight, which helps you spot and take advantage of strategic opportunities, is the first of two foundation skills. New Age executives unite insight with the second foundation skill, sensitivity—understanding and acting upon people's expectations and needs—to forge the strategy-culture alloy from which excellence is created. These two skills help you successfully manage the two basic components of corporate excellence.

Insight requires a mind capable of concentration, one that not only thinks creatively but is capable of adopting a variety of perspectives. Just as a photographer will take quite a few "shots" of a subject before deciding which pose will create the most effective portrait, an executive with insight will take several "shots" of a problem from varying points of view to determine which solution will produce the most desirable results. By doing so the insightful executive often discovers opportunities others never see and solves problems in ways that others never conceive possible.

Insight depends on physical and mental experience. However, since none of us lives long enough to experience everything, we can easily be trapped within a rigid set of habits, underutilizing our experience and greatly reducing our ability to spot opportunities, create advantages, and devise solutions to problems. Multiple perspectives free us to maximize our experience by letting us apply it in a different way for each point of view.

To gain insight you learn to ask a series of questions from far-ranging points of view. When insightful executives solve problems, they try to heighten their perceptions, going beyond the old, habitual, comfortable ways of experiencing the world. Like blind people, they ask questions that might never occur to their sighted friends. One executive we know urges his people to try a little experiment that involves tieing a blindfold over the eyes and then trying to perform ordinary tasks. "Include a relative or friend in the game," he says. "You'll appreciate having a sort of 'seeing-eye dog' to keep you from bumping into furniture and hurting yourself."

He claims that a rewarding side effect of this exercise is an increased sensitivity to one's dependence on others. "Too many executives feel at the center of any change in their organizations and pay too little attention to the fact that they must rely on the advice and insight of even the lowliest members of their team. Being blind for a couple of hours is a humbling experience."

For an hour or two people playing this game pay close attention to the world around them. They hear sounds that escaped them when their eyes were open. They smell aromas they usually ignore. Suddenly they feel the details of the fabric on the sofa, and when they pet the family dog or embrace their spouse, they pick up previously ignored odors, textures, and sounds. After a while they find their remaining senses heightened to compensate for the loss of sight, and they naturally start asking the right questions in order to cope with the handicap.

Joy Manufacturing, the billion-dollar capital goods producer, asked the right questions. Joy operates in the fields of petroleum equipment, coal mining machinery, air-pollution controls, and air machinery (fans and compressors), businesses that could lend themselves to a rigid traditional approach. However, André Horn, the company's chairman, never satisfied with thinking about the company in the same old way year after year, has deep insight. Despite the fact that Horn has been with Joy for twenty-seven years, his restless mind never stops asking questions. "Do we have the right economic perspective for looking at our company's future growth and development in the capital goods industry?" Horn asked himself. He then borrowed the "long wave" economic theory from the Russian economist Nikolai Kondratieff and changed the company's direction. In 1981, when Horn's "long wave" theory predicted a devastating recession, he began divesting the company of businesses where Joy did not compete effectively. He slashed the company's work force in half and sales dropped from $1 billion to $628 million. *BusinessWeek* accused Joy of overreacting to the economic situation, but Horn eventually proved them wrong. With insight, he had taken decisive action to trim Joy's operations months before competitors even thought about it. In 1982 the company enjoyed a 16.6 percent return on equity and remained well in the black through 1983 while most competitors suffered losses. In 1983 Joy's balance sheet displayed over $200 million in cash and its operations' break-even point had fallen by 25 percent. Now the lean and hungry company is pursuing acquisitions and could break the $2-billion barrier by 1990. If Horn's theory that until 1989 we are in a ten-year transition period between fifty-year growth cycles is correct, we will experience one more downturn that will hurt capital goods manufacturers before growth resumes around 1990. Therefore, Joy intends to stick to the businesses it knows best and acquire companies like WKM oil equipment. Such insightful moves could create lasting excellence for Joy.

Now that we've seen the importance of creative insight, let's look at what happens when a company doesn't have it.

Lack of Insight Causes Stagnation

From the mid-1950s to the early 1970s, Robert A. Magowan led Safeway Stores through dramatic growth. By the time he stepped down, the company had established itself as a world-champion food retailer, a position that remained secure until the mid-1970s when under the direction of William S. Mitchell, an accountant who surrounded himself with financial and legal professionals, the company stagnated. Given his experience in finance, Mitchell understandably tried to operate Safeway's twenty-nine divisions as if they were financial investments in a portfolio, an approach demanding caution rather than decisive leadership. After all, couldn't Safeway rely on past accomplishments to keep it at the forefront of its industry? The new management team imposed strict policies against actions that might possibly invite lawsuits, prompting abandonment of plans for health-food departments to avoid legal repercussions from unlikely but possible insect infestation. Afraid of being too visibly in the forefront, the company also stifled innovation, letting competitors come up with all the new ideas, and it stopped advertising loss leaders for fear of running out of items, then having to pay the legal consequences.

Safeway's management team did not capitalize on the company's strengths. The company learned the hard way that size alone will never protect a dominant position, because without constant training, a champion fighter can quickly get out of shape. Safeway also learned that maintaining a leadership position requires as much effort as creating one. The consequence of Safeway's lack of insight was a loss of key market shares. In Los Angeles, for example, the chain's market share dipped from almost 13 percent in 1974 to about 6.6 percent in 1980. Earnings began sliding in 1978, until return on equity dropped to 10 percent, a full 33 percent below the industry average. Could Safeway get itself back into fighting shape, or would it continue to flounder? In 1980, Peter Magowan, the son of the founder who had so successfully built the company, took over as CEO. Having studied his father's style and techniques, the younger Magowan immediately sought ways to win back market shares, expand superstores, promote nonfood merchandising, and reestablish a reputation as a lean and mean low-cost operator. It wasn't easy, but soon everyone in the company was looking for new ways to regain Safeway's title as the best-run food retailer in the country. The results have been an increase in revenues from $13.7 billion to $18.6 billion and a major recapturing of market share. In 1983 profits increased 15 percent and return on equity rose to 14 percent.

Without insight you see only confusing symptoms, not the causes of problems; with insight you can pierce to a problem's core. According to a landmark *Harvard Business Review* article, "Strategic Management for Competitive Advantage," by Gluck, Kaufman, and Walleck, strategic insight lies at the core of successful strategic management practices. In the article, one CEO advises his division heads, "If you can't tell me something about your business I don't already know, you probably aren't going to surprise our competitors either."

Creative Insight Discovers Opportunity, Advantage, and Strength

Thomas Drohan and Neil Harlan displayed great insight when their firm, McKesson, ran into trouble a few years ago. The nation's largest wholesale distributor had begun to stagnate with weak profit margins as client manufacturers increasingly distributed their own products. At first, Drohan and Harlan thought they should get out of the distribution business altogether. Wouldn't most smart executives simply cut their losses? But Drohan and Harlan meditated on the problem until they came to a different conclusion: since distribution was their business, perhaps they should simply be doing it better than anyone else. As a result of this insight, they made their entire operation so efficient that no manufacturers could possibly distribute more effectively and economically than McKesson. Drohan says, "The name of the game is adding value." But Drohan and Harlan didn't stop there; they're now using an advanced computer system to aid suppliers and customers, making McKesson an integral part of everyone's marketing effort. It's an entirely new concept of distribution, and it has won excellent results.

Creative insight precedes discovery. Opportunities, advantages, and strengths are so dynamic and volatile that you must maintain an insightful approach at all times. As previously discussed, the strategic thinker focuses on all three components to serve customers in new ways, finding new advantages over competitors, and exploiting new company strengths.

Insight penetrates the superficial attributes of the components of strategic thinking by attacking them conceptually. Consequently, the insightful executive thinks abstractly, weaving a fabric of generalizations from concrete data, experiences, and observations. When Ken Olsen, president of Digital Equipment

Corp., observed that DEC was losing sales and market share in areas where the firm had once dominated, he asked probing questions about why DEC's new personal computers weren't catching on. His speculations led to two generalizations: 1) customers and potential customers do not understand DEC computers as well as they should; 2) the firm's sales pitch wasn't putting the message across. Should DEC alter the way it conducted its business? When this general question led Olsen to the conclusion that DEC's sales compensation plan needed overhauling, he took his salespeople off straight salary and put them on an incentive commission plan. In just two months the freshly motivated sales staff won numerous new office automation and small business accounts.

Insightful executives never cease their curious probing. Volvo found its workers built better autos when a team worked on one car at a time rather than on the conventional assembly line. Wendy's hamburgers swept a market that had always defied competition, simply because, in the beginning, it promised a single attractive product: a delicious "old-fashioned" hamburger about which no customer could ask, "Where's the beef?"

Insightful executives are imaginative and innovative developers who can transcend old habits. They encourage disagreement and discussion among associates and subordinates. They make an abiding commitment to creativity, always setting aside the time and resources to nurture it. Steve Wozniak has insight. When Apple Computer's engineers were having trouble with a design, he came in and showed them how to reduce seventy integrated circuits to five. John Folkerth took the helm at Shopsmith when the firm found retailers unwilling to continue allocating sufficient floor space to his company's famous all-in-one woodworking machine. Folkerth's new direct mail marketing strategy helped Shopsmith flourish. Akio Morita, head of Sony, conceptualized the Walkman out of irritation with his children's blasting home stereo. Although few people are born with the creative insight of a Wozniak, Folkerth, or Morita, any willing executive can develop it by using meditation and conceptual frameworks to ask the right questions.

How to Become an Insightful Executive

Before you can set about acquiring creative insight, you must first learn to recognize it. Once you can readily recognize it, you'll be able to spot and remove the obstacles that block the path toward it. In the end, you will know how to ask the right questions.

Step One: Recognizing Insight

Recognizing insight in yourself or others begins with increased comprehension of the characteristics most insightful executives share. Don't look for once-in-a-lifetime brilliant flashes. Deep insight is a basic and abiding skill that continually guides the thinking of a strong leader.

Creative problem-solving derives from your ability to adopt multiple viewpoints and ask the right questions. If creativity makes people more independent, self-directed, and assertive and helps them allocate the right resources to cope with life's difficult situations, then insight may be thought of as a highly directed application of creativity.

Eugene Raudsepp, president of Princeton Creative Research and author of *How Creative Are You?*, has won acclaim for original research into creative problem-solving. We have applied portions of Raudsepp's "problem-solving behavior" test to help identify the characteristics of insightful executives:

- They prefer tackling problems that do not have precise answers, asking questions like, "In what ways can we create new needs in our customers, needs only we can meet?"
- They spend more time synthesizing information than gathering it, relishing the process of breaking information down into its component parts, then reconfiguring those parts to expose the essence of a problem.

- They can easily drop an approach to a problem that isn't working, forcing their way out of habitual methods of thinking or analyzing.

- They doggedly pursue difficult problems over long periods of time, never feeling frustrated when the solution isn't readily apparent.

- They don't worry about asking questions that might display their ignorance. Such "dumb" questions cut to the heart of the matter and open a new path of thinking.

- They pay more attention to information's content than to its source, never caring where insight comes from as long as it's based on accurate data or real perceptions.

- They do not apply strictly logical step-by-step methods to problem-solving, because they realize that each problem is unique and uniqueness resists easy formulas.

- They entertain offbeat ideas without automatically labeling them "crackpot": some of the best ideas seem idiotic in the beginning.

- They saturate themselves with all they can learn about a problem, preparing themselves thoroughly and with great enthusiasm.

- They love complex problems and enjoy struggling with thorny issues.

- They mentally experiment with solutions that would not even occur to others, considering every possible approach.

- They usually think up more ideas more rapidly than anyone else in brainstorming sessions because their disciplined but flexible minds thrive on such exercises.

- They picture situations and possibilities with vivid imagery that often colors their language, describing possible solutions in rich detail.

- They have made meditation a habit, not an occasional exercise, and set aside time each day for such activity.

In our own experience, insightful executives also routinely manifest their creativity by:

- Holding open discussions in which they encourage disagreement. Insightful executives spend a good deal of their time fostering honest exchanges of ideas among their associates and subordinates.

- Reading voraciously to satisfy a thirst for knowledge and the experience of others. Executives with insight constantly add new information and perspectives to their understanding.

- Enthusiastically entertaining new ideas. They help their associates and subordinates come up with innovative approaches.

- Asking penetrating questions. They ask more questions than they answer.

- Swiftly devising a number of scenarios for solving a problem. They visualize all possible viewpoints.

Of course, insightful executives don't view these activities as mere exercises but employ them to get results for themselves, their people, and their organizations. Recognizing the dynamic, ever changing nature of our New Age, they always focus on innovative decisions, encouraging their people to also adopt far-ranging points of view. They surround themselves with those who will promote distinctive orientations rather than simply acquiesce to authority. They enhance, rather than minimize, such differences. Rarely satisfied with the status quo, they pursue better methods for themselves or others to achieve results for the organization.

With these attributes in mind, you should be ready to test your own level of insight with the Executive Insight Self-Examination. A score of 40 marks you as a deeply insightful executive, while anything below 30 indicates a need for improvement.

EXECUTIVE INSIGHT SELF-EXAMINATION

		ALWAYS	OFTEN	SELDOM	NEVER
1.	You are stimulated by complex problems and situations that tax your thinking.	4	3	2	1
2.	You dislike the sort of rigid problem-solving that attacks every problem with a similar, mechanical approach.	4	3	2	1
3.	You encourage open discussion and disagreement among your people.	4	3	2	1
4.	You read voraciously to expand your experience.	4	3	2	1
5.	You entertain new ideas with enthusiasm rather than skepticism.	4	3	2	1
6.	You ask numerous questions, never worrying about whether they reveal your ignorance.	4	3	2	1
7.	You look at things from a variety of viewpoints before making a decision.	4	3	2	1
8.	You surround yourself with people who promote distinctly different orientations and points of view.	4	3	2	1
9.	You make decisions others call "innovative."	4	3	2	1
10.	You search for new and better ways of approaching work within your organization.	4	3	2	1

Stephen Pistner, CEO of Montgomery Ward & Co., ranks near a perfect 40. When he became CEO in 1981, Montgomery Ward had lost $163 million the previous year, proof that the old ways no longer created excellence for the large retailer. Apparently, Montgomery Ward just wasn't giving customers the products and quality they wanted. Pistner's penetrating insight into the company's plight prompted him to quickly make marketing a top priority, redirecting his company's focus to customer viewpoints rather thank traditional retailing views. Before long, Ward's dropped such product categories as tailored men's suits and carpeting in favor of brand-name merchandise such as Maytag and Sony. Pistner's relentless questioning set a new tone, putting Montgomery Ward back on the road to profitability. In 1983, the company earned $40 million, its first profit since 1979.

Step Two: Removing the Blinders

Before you can habitually ask the right questions, you must remove the blinders that inhibit insight:

Six Common Blinders

- *Resistance to and Avoidance of Change.* Many executives resist rocking the boat with change. Executives who cling to the status quo for safety are consciously or unconsciously resisting new insights.

- *Reliance on Rules and Conformance.* Other executives emphasize conformance over performance by policing adherence to rules, policies, procedures, programs, and structures. Such executives demand strict obedience to company policy.

- *Fear and Self-Doubt.* Some business leaders become paralyzed by insecurity, lack of confidence, negative conditioning, and fear of criticism. This blinder usually leads executives to cling to a safe point of view that has served them well in the past.

- *Overreliance on Logic and Precision.* Many leaders pay more attention to mechanics than results. Executives who expect problems and solutions to fit snugly into neat compartments cannot handle the sort of freewheeling and open-ended discussions from which new insights emerge.

- *Black and White Thinking.* Too few executives understand that simplicity can arise from complexity. The maturity that comes with experience tends to change previously black and white judgments to varying shades of gray, but many executives fear such shading in their corporate decisions, clinging instead to an either-or approach and reducing their options to a few oversimplified solutions.

- *Overreliance on Practicality and Efficiency.* Some executives refuse to "waste" time considering outlandish alternatives and ideas. Since they shoulder the practical responsibility for running an organization, they sometimes avoid all but pragmatic solutions to problems.

To help you remove these blinders, we have developed exercises that attack each one effectively.

Six Exercises for Removing Blinders to Insight

Exercise 1: New Ideas Daily. This exercise addresses problems of resistance and avoidance. Most people resist change because they fear it will take time and energy adapting to it, but too much such resistance can thwart insight. A & P, the once formidable grocery store chain, refused to follow its customers to the suburbs. When customers demanded both branded and private-label goods, A & P paid so little attention that their stores soon became outmoded, their prices uncompetitive. If only A & P had been open to new ideas!

Set yourself a goal of coming up with at least one new idea daily for at least one month. This may seem an unreasonable goal, but if you write one down at the end of each work day, you'll soon find yourself with a notebook full of new insights. A new idea can relate to work, home, play, or any other aspect of your life, but it must be genuinely new and you must consider some *action* on it, by implementing it, developing it, experimenting with it, or simply discussing it with your people. After you've filled a notebook with new ideas, you'll not only gain valuable insights into your organization's future, you'll find that new ideas keep flowing. Your secretary might confide to fellow workers at lunch, "People around here love the way the same old business seems new all the time."

Exercise 2: Breaking out of the Mold. To reduce your reliance on rules and policies, you must learn to view them as flexible guidelines rather than iron-clad requirements. Force yourself to break out of the mold. A 3-M employee invented the adhesive notepad, a major breakthrough, by going ahead long after the company had told him to stop working on it. Fortunately, he wasn't the sort of person who slavishly conformed to company rules.

Pretend for a day that all your rules and policies have been put on hold. Be adventurous, audacious. Spend an afternoon on the golf course or on the racquetball court, forget this month's meaningless report, suspend the policy that dictates your company's dress code. While rules and policies are not all bad, and a company could become alarmingly disorganized without them, your organization won't fall apart if you try living without them for a day, a week, or even a month. Once you feel comfortable with your rules and regulations as means rather than ends, practice "breaking out of the mold" in some way each week until it becomes a new habit. Once you have practiced breaking out for a few months, you will experience a change in your perspective and you may well hear a subordinate remark, "Hey, the boss has become more flexible lately. I like that!"

Exercise 3: Basic Creativity Training. Creativity training will help you conquer your fear and self-doubt and instill more independent, confident, and self-directed thinking. Albert Szent-Györgyi, the biochemist and Nobel Prize winner, said, "Discovery consists of looking at the same thing as everyone else and thinking something different." When you routinely look at things differently, you will see your creativity naturally grow. You might also read a book on creativity or attend one or more creativity training seminars. We recommend three guides: *How Creative Are You?* by Eugene Raudsepp; *A Whack on the Side of the Head* by Roger von Oech; and *The Art of Creative Thinking* by Gerald Nierenberg. If you choose a seminar, you'll find many good ones across the country; or you might contact Eugene Raudsepp at Princeton Creative Research in Princeton, New Jersey, or Roger von Oech at Creative Think in Menlo Park, California. Many executives have found their courses enlightening.

Exercise 4: Wild Thinking. You can grow less reliant on logic and precision by replacing any rigid and mechanistic approaches to problem-solving with freer and more creative ones. Alan Zakon, CEO of the Boston Consulting Group, suggests ways of thinking outside the normal channels. One method is called "geographical translation"—transferring a success from one part of the country or world to another. Zakon also recommends looking for historical successes that can be revived. At one time lavish movie theaters with plush seating showed first-run movies. Over the years these gave way to less luxurious theaters, but Sack Cinemas in Boston has recaptured the old vision with its Cinema 9, which serves croissants and espresso instead of popcorn and soft drinks. Yet a third approach Zakon suggests is looking at ways a business could change or evolve. Term insurance came about because someone dared to suggest separating the two traditional components of insurance—savings and protection. Now term insurance provides an alternative for people who want protection but not savings.

Whenever you find yourself bogged down with formal, technical processes for solving problems, pause for a little wild thinking. Since you're probably accustomed to certain kinds of structured approaches and meetings, you will probably have to force yourself to engage in the sort of freewheeling that never shies away from preposterous, outrageous ideas. Build some exhilarating wild thinking into your regularly scheduled meetings. Engage in such unfettered discussion for at least one hour a week for three months. After a few months, you will begin to feel a sense of liberation and may even overhear an associate exclaim, "I'm never afraid to say anything to the boss because I know he won't think it's off the wall."

Exercise 5: Making Things Complex and Ambiguous. We live in a highly complex world, so it's only natural to try to reduce complexity whenever possible. But executives who cannot see complexity or handle ambiguity tend to oversimplify problems. The American automobile makers once crowed, "If it isn't American-made, Americans won't buy it." The world turned out to be more complex than that statement implied, however, and GM, Ford, and Chrysler suffered as a consequence.

Instead of relying on the tried and true perspective on a problem, force yourself to see two or more strikingly different solutions. Before making any decision, step back to view the full richness of a situation. Look for multiple meanings and possibilities. Once a day for a month, pick at least one situation or problem to make complex and ambiguous. Look for hidden possibilities and attributes you may have ignored. Remember, you want your associates and subordinates to say, "The boss sees angles we never even contemplated."

Exercise 6: Evaluating Later, Not Sooner. An overreliance on practicality and efficiency convinces you that an arduous search for new insight wastes time and resources if it does not produce practical results. Basic creativity training can cure severe cases of this disease; you can also treat it effectively by withholding evaluation of an idea until it has been toyed with, explored in all its ramifications, and thoroughly thought through. No matter how troublesome a problem, it took some time for it to become so pesky, and a little delay now won't matter much. Hasty evaluation can destroy insight. Unwilling to abandon their quest for flight, Orville and Wilbur Wright took off a thousand times. Had they abandoned the endeavor on the basis of earlier defeats, they would not have won their place in history.

At least once a week for three months, deliberately postpone a new idea, discussion, strategy or culture plan by reserving judgment until it becomes unavoidable. Don't think you're procrastinating. Rather, allow a little further discussion, initiate an experiment, or demand a follow-up report.

Now that you can remove some of the roadblocks to creative insight, you are finally ready to ask the right questions.

Step Three: Using Meditation and Conceptual Frameworks to Ask the Right Questions

In *The Inner Game of Tennis*, Tim Gallwey describes the importance of "letting it happen." A Zen master posed this question to a group of Westerners: "What is the most important word in your language?" The audience responded with "love," "truth," "beauty," and so on, until the master stopped them by saying, "No. The most important word is 'let.' *Let* it be. *Let* it happen." The master went on to explain how you can surpass your previous achievements by tuning into the fundamental rhythm inherent in life. Too often Westerners approach the mastery of a skill, whether it be tennis or business management, with an aggressiveness that produces more stress than insight.

In business, "letting it happen" means letting your intuition, your years of experience, your awareness of competitors, your sensitivity to customers, and your understanding of cold, hard facts flow together in a calm and natural way. Most of us seldom tap the full reserve of our knowledge and experience. When we encounter problems, we suffer anxiety because problems pose dangers as well as opportunities. In our anxiety, we forget to trust our most valuable intuitive resources. Insight, like great poetry, music, or art, arises from the quiet depths of the unconscious, from a source that lies beneath words, deeds, thoughts, and figures. Dr. Abraham Maslow calls such moments of insight "peak experiences." People experiencing such moments describe them similarly: "I feel more integrated"; "I feel at one with the experience"; "I felt at the peak of my powers"; "it felt effortless"; "I found myself free of blocks, inhibitions, cautions, fears, doubts, controls, reservations, self-criticisms, brakes." Have you ever experienced similar feelings? If so, try to keep them in mind while you read the following pages on how to apply meditation to asking the right questions.

Intense meditation helps you attain the state of mind that *lets* your sometimes hidden inner reserve of knowledge and experience float to a conscious level. Like most of the hundreds of executives we've trained, you may at first resist meditation as a frivolous undertaking, but if you give it a chance you'll probably discover knowledge you didn't know you possessed.

You learn basic meditation by first applying it to an area less complex than your organization's strategic opportunities. First, pick an *object* of the meditation, perhaps an apple. Next, determine the *purpose* of the meditation, in this case drawing upon your knowledge and experience of apples to recreate in your mind the full richness of an apple's appearance, feel, sound, taste, and smell, as well as your feelings about those qualities. Notice how all five senses, and another sense, your emotions, come into play. Finally, establish an expected *result* of the meditation: a deeper understanding and fuller appreciation of the apple.

Before you actually begin to meditate on an apple, construct the right environment: a quiet space where no one will disturb you for at least thirty minutes. Perhaps you will visit a library or a remote outdoor location. Your office or den will suffice, provided you can unplug your phone and instruct your secretary or spouse that you are not to be disturbed.

Since you want to make meditation a daily habit, pay special attention to selecting the right time, but don't try to force it into your hectic schedule. Rather, make sure you do it regularly and at a time when you can get the most out of it. Many busy executives like to begin or conclude a hectic day with meditation, while others prefer to use it as a refreshing change of pace in their schedules. Regardless of your own ideal time, make sure it's one during which your frame of mind permits you to devote your full attention, free of stress and anxiety, to the meditation.

Now you're ready to begin. Sit or lie in a relaxed position. Direct your attention inward, blotting out the surrounding environment and focusing instead on the inner screen of your mind's eye. It helps to close your eyes and visualize your body, beginning with the feet and leisurely moving up to your head. Listen for the sound of your breathing, your heartbeat.

You are trying to reach a relaxed state called "alpha rest." Psychologists and physicians who routinely measure brainwaves with electroencephalographs have found that the alpha wave changes from an excited line to a smoother curve when the mind and body are at rest. Personal biofeedback equipment can measure your state of rest and even help you achieve it. Scientists have used such devices to prove that Zen masters and others who routinely employ a sort of self-hypnosis can achieve alpha rest at will.

A counting procedure can help you reach this restful state. A popular method involves slowly counting down from seven to one, picturing a color associated with each number (for example, seven, red; six, orange; five, yellow; four, green; three, blue; two, indigo; one, orchid). Regardless of the technique you use, remember that you want to *let* yourself relax into a state of calm and heightened sensory awareness.

When you attain such a state, turn your attention to the blank screen of your mind. Visualize a clear screen, then place the object of your meditation on it: a firm, red apple. Turn it over in your mind's eye, painstakingly exploring it with each of your senses. How does it look? Imagine its shape, the contours of its surface, its stem, its spots, its vivid color. How does it feel? Is it cool, firm, smooth? Touch each curve, each bump, each depression. Toss it in the air and catch it, then roll it in the palm of your hand. Now take an imaginary bite out of it. What sound does that make? How does the apple taste? Relish the bite, carefully chewing and tasting each morsel, recreating in your mind the delicious crunch into a perfect red apple on a cool autumn afternoon. Enjoy the smell of the bitten apple. Ask yourself how you felt about the best apple you ever ate.

You may take less than a half hour to explore your knowledge and experience of a red apple, but when you feel you have exhausted its possibilities, count yourself back up from one to seven. Now you should feel relaxed, and you should have brought much hidden knowledge and experience of a red apple to a conscious level. Once you feel comfortable meditating on such a simple matter, you might tackle gradually more complex ones, perhaps beginning with your view of one other competitor in your market and moving onto competitor strategies in general. Before long you should be able to apply the technique to more challenging issues, such as the different conceptual framework you must consider in order to achieve new insights.

Successful strategy formulation involves choosing the best strategy from many possibilities. As you saw in Chapter 2, strategic planning made an important contribution to management science by providing conceptual frameworks. The left-hand column in the table on page 119 lists a number of these devices.

A conceptual framework creates a state of mind that enables executives to move to the heart of the strategic issues facing their companies, while at the same time sidestepping mountains of minutiae and irrelevant data. While it would take a whole book to explore all the available conceptual frameworks, we've reduced a number of important types into the following table. Notice how some of them closely parallel the viewpoints in Chapter 2.

Meditating with the help of a conceptual framework allows you to weigh a range of different perspectives on a given problem or situation.

COMMON TYPES OF CONCEPTUAL FRAMEWORKS

Type	*Issues Raised*
Market Share Grids	"What market share does our product or service enjoy? What growth of market share do we desire?"
	The answers help you decide which products or services should grow, generate cash, or be liquidated.
Investment Priority Portfolios	"Which products or businesses should receive the most investment? How do we establish investment priorities?"
	The answers help you assess the strength and competitiveness of a product or business. For organizations with several products or businesses, they help set investment priorities.
Competitive Interaction Matrices	"What strategy should we pursue to gain advantage over competition? What can we do that is different and better? How do we stop competitors from copying us?"
	The answers help you focus on the interaction among competitors in the market, identifying three, four, or more competitive strategies available to any business in any market. They lead toward a strategy that avoids head-on competition.
Market Position Alternatives	"Should we be creating new products or should we let our competitors do it? If we let them go first, how can we gain an advantage? Are there ways to gain advantage other than by being first?"
	The answers help you identify fundamental postures, from innovator to follower, that a business can assume within a market. They help organizations add value to products

and services or to position existing products and services to greater advantage.

Driving Force Options

"What is the driving force in our organization? What really determines how we make our final decisions?"

The answers stimulate thinking about activities critical to the success of the organization. They bring insight into activities of overriding importance.

Diversification Scenarios

"Should we diversify? If so, how should we do it? What difficulties can we expect to encounter?"

The answers isolate the benefits and risks of various diversification decisions, providing insight into what kind of diversification may be most appropriate in a given situation.

Industry Characteristics Grids

"What is unique about our industry? Is the road to advantage over our competitors different in this industry? How is the industry changing? Can you win an advantage over competitors in different ways in different industries?"

The answers produce insight into opportunities and limitations in different kinds of industries and makes clear how that affects strategies.

Value Added Charts

"What do our customers value most about our products? What do they value in our competitors' products? Where can we add more value?"

The answers identify where, how, and why a product or service provides value to different customer segments. Insight into value helps you profitably exploit it.

Implementation Risk Matrices

"How should we implement our new strategy? What is the probability of its

	success? Where will we experience the most difficulty?"
	The answers focus on problems associated with carrying out a particular strategy, adding insight into the risks and benefits of various strategies.
Strategy Formulation Processes	"What strategy-formulation process do we use? What are the important steps we should consider?"
	The answers help you determine the steps involved in formulating strategies. They help you combine and implement various strategies.

Let's put what we've learned into practice by viewing a situation based on a very real business predicament. Jane Alexander (not her real name) is the CEO of an $80-million snack foods company, a job she inherited twenty years ago when her father died; but over the years she has proven her own ability to run the company effectively. While Jane's company produces a variety of snacks such as potato chips and pork skins aimed primarily at markets in the South and Southeast, during the past five years her company has suffered increasingly intense competition from a national rival. With the exception of this one competitor, Jane's industry is dominated by regional operations like her own. When the national competitor began making inroads into the regional market, Jane decided to ignore it and continued to focus on being the best regional competitor in the South and Southeast. For two years her strategy seemed to work, but the national competitor gradually eroded her dominant position until Jane could ignore it no longer.

She attended a strategy-formulation seminar, read a number of popular books on contemporary strategy, and hired a consultant to help. When the consultant identified productivity as the company's primary problem, Jane fired him. She knew her company suffered some productivity problems, but they did not fully explain the declining market share. At this point what would you have done if you were Jane?

A. Hire another consultant.

B. Keep looking for a solution.

C. Go back to the old strategy.

D. Sell the company to your competitor.

E. Hire a new marketing manager.

Jane chose option "B" and kept looking for a new way to approach the problem. In the strategic management seminar, she had read Kenichi Ohmae's book *The Mind of the Strategist* in which she had seen an intriguing conceptual framework. Could it change the direction of her company?

COMPETITIVE INTERACTION MATRIX

| | Business/Product Offered | |
	Old/Existing	New/Creative
Compete Head-on (Wisely)	1. Intensify Functional Differentiation	3. Ask "why-whys"
COMPETITIVE POSITION		
Avoid Head-on Competition	2. Exploit Competitor's Weakness	4. Maximize User Benefit

---

Let's briefly review how this matrix works. It offers four choices regarding which route you should take to obtain an advantage over competitors. These four choices appear inside the cells of the matrix and each one represents an alternate route to competitive advantage. The first choice, "Intensify Functional Differentiation," becomes the wisest in situations where you directly compete against a rival with old or existing products. To gain competitive advantage you must focus on one aspect of an operation that is most likely to win a substantial advantage over competitors. IBM's concentration on customer service offers a good example.

The second choice, "Exploit Competitor's Weaknesses," comes into play in situations where a company is attempting to *avoid* head-on competition with old or existing products. To gain your competitive advantage in such a case, you must isolate some relative superiority that contrasts with a competitor's weaknesses. For example, Savin Corp. emphasized smaller, more reliable copying machines over Xerox's fancier, more expensive ones.

The third choice, "Ask why-whys"—keep asking "why?" even when you think you have all the answers—makes sense when you are competing head-on against your rivals with new or creative products. To gain competitive advantage in this situation you must pursue aggressive initiatives in new areas that result in advantageous innovations. Apple Computer's innovative and unique MacIntosh was developed as an answer to the question, "Why can't we develop a different, easier to use computer?"

The fourth choice, "Maximize User Benefit," helps you avoid head-on competition against rivals who have developed their own new products. You gain advantage in this case by always enhancing existing products to maximize their benefits to customers. Dozens of companies pursue this strategy; Kodak, Polaroid, Canon, and a host of Japanese rivals all try to outdo each other with new bells and whistles that make picture-taking simpler and more enjoyable.

These four choices represent four different avenues to competitive advantage, but a company can only expect to successfully travel one route at a time.

The competitive interaction matrix and meditation allowed
Jane to free her thinking about her national competitor and
discover actions she could take to avoid head-on competition.
She selected the second choice in the matrix—"Exploit Competitor's Weakness"—as the best avenue for her company. Her
smaller firm could fare well against a large competitor by be-
having in ways a larger company couldn't. All she had to do
was avoid head-on competition with old and existing products
and focus on a strategy involving her own organization's relative
superiority. That way she could exploit the competitor's weaknesses. After concentrated meditation, Jane determined that
her company's advantages over her national competitor were
greater flexibility in producing different varieties of snack
products and greater sensitivity to the tastes and preferences
of regional customers. She also discovered three important
weaknesses in her national competitor: a lack of focus on certain
snack categories, a failure to serve certain regional snack preferences, and a dependence on national products that produced
high volumes. She was finally asking the right question: "How
can we focus on our strengths and exploit our competitor's
weaknesses?" It seemed too simple until she remembered that
the best ideas are simple ones developed after full consideration
of the complexity of the situation.

After more meditation, Jane began directing her company
to emphasize snack products neglected by the national competitor, and she reemphasized catering to regional taste preferences in the South and Southeast. She also began introducing
a line of new snacks and snack supplements each fall and spring
because she knew the national competitor could not respond
quickly and would not even attempt to respond in areas where
a given product could not achieve large national volumes. Her
company's first batch of new products included a larger pork
skin product, a barbecue dip to go along with the pork skins,
and a "hot-style" barbecue-flavored potato chip. Jane's company
could profitably create excellence with lower-volume products
that didn't compete head-to-head with the national competitor's
brands. The result? Jane's company regained its lost market

share in eight months and wrestled away four additional market share percentage points in a little over a year.

The Potency of Insight: A Summary

Insight, the first of the two foundation skills, enables you to create successful strategies. Insightful executives mull over all facets of problems, situations, and information because the more facets you study, the greater the chances for your new strategy's success. Executives with insight discover opportunities, advantages, and strengths others ignore or never see. Those who lack it lead their organizations to stagnation rather than excellence. Because one unwary moment can lead to failure, continuing insight spurs the excellent organization to maintain its leadership position. In the words of Alan Kay, former director of research at Atari, now at Apple, "Point-of-view is worth 80 IQ points." Although that extra brain power can make anyone look like a genius, effective management takes more than intelligence—it takes careful attention to an organization's most valuable asset, its people.

• CHAPTER 6 •

Sensitivity:
Doing Unto Others

It is the unique privilege of the leader to strengthen men. Nowhere else in contemporary industrial society does that privilege come to grips with opportunity so directly as in the organizations in which men work. To exercise the privilege demands sensitivity to subtlety and forthrightness of action, that creative fusion of aggression and affection which summons forth the highest human talents. The man whose leadership is the product of such fusion in the service of an ideal is aptly called the exceptional executive.

—HARRY LEVINSON

The employer generally gets the employees he deserves.

—SIR WALTER BILBEY,
19th-century British economist

Sensitivity Initiates Strong Cultures

Sean Duffy had worked for an East Coast power company almost all his adult life; in fact, having been born and raised not far from the power plant, he worked with people he had grown up with. So it was understandable that Sean, after taking a newly designed early retirement at age sixty-two, returned to his employer a week later to ask if he could go back to work. He was bored and lonely at home; he just wasn't ready to retire yet. The company said no, because it was more cost-effective to hire younger people without Sean's seniority and benefits package. Sean begged, pleaded, offered to take a wage cut, anything, if the company would only make room for him. The company refused. In six months, Sean Duffy was dead. His wife said he died of a broken heart. While this story may sound

127

dramatic, such insensitivity to an employee's needs occurs every day in companies that put policies, rules, requirements, and short-term profits ahead of people's needs. What these organizations don't realize is that people, not policies, produce profit over the long haul, and when peoples' needs are not met, they operate at levels well below their capacities, eventually eroding profits.

On the other hand, consider Warren Publishing Corp., located in Boston, where Virginia Coulter, age seventy-nine, works two days a week under Warren's flexible retirement plan. She's been on the job for sixty-two years. Her sister Winifred Church, eighty-two, still runs the company's mail room five days a week. She's been running it for forty years. In fact, almost 25 percent of Warren's employees are eligible for social security. In an *Inc.* magazine profile of Warren Publishing, Tim Warren, Sr., president of the company, stated, "Why should we tell anyone that they have to stop working at any given age when we can provide a flexible environment that supports them?" He went on to say, "We get tremendous value out of our older workers." In fact, the benefits to the company are great, including effective training of younger employees, a rich corporate culture, great models of the "work ethic," and an unmistakable message to all company employees: "This company really cares about its people!" The difference between Sean Duffy's company and Warren? Sensitivity. If employees don't perceive it, they might put in their hours but they'll never really give their hearts to the company.

Everyone has heard the old saying, "Don't judge a man until you've walked a mile in his shoes." That could serve as a working definition for sensitivity, the second core skill. The Japanese call it *haragei*, from *hara*, stomach, and *gei*, art. The art of getting inside another person. "Do unto others as you would have them do unto you" is a simple concept, yet difficult to practice because true sensitivity doesn't merely involve crawling inside another person's head, it includes *acting to fulfill the needs and expectations* you find there.

Perhaps it seems obvious that a strong corporate culture can't exist without sensitivity on the part of the organization and its executives to employees at all levels, but, as with insight, harnessing sensitivity requires a great deal of time and concentration. Just listening to a security guard's confession of a drinking problem or sympathizing with a secretary's need to balance child care responsibilities with her job isn't enough. Sensitive executives not only consider such problems, they *act* on them. While it may be easy to listen and sympathize, it's not so easy to nurture an environment that continually meets the needs and expectations of many unique and fallible human beings.

All people want their needs and expectations fulfilled by the organizations they choose to work for. Otherwise, they bide their time or resign. In either case, morale plunges and productivity declines. Turnover in personnel and deteriorating productivity are sure signs of organizational and executive insensitivity.

Insensitivity Is Unhealthy

In his book *High Output Management*, Andrew S. Grove, president of Intel, the highly successful chip manufacturer, described a philosophy of management based on three simple ideas: output-oriented approach, managerial leverage, and peak individual performance. In describing the output-oriented approach, Grove compared an organization to a machine on a production assembly line. Like such machines, organizations must crank out high output. By managerial leverage he meant that managers must increase the output of their teams by emphasizing those tasks that will allow management's own efforts to cascade through the team, increasing its productivity. Finally, peak individual performance comes from powerful motivation. Grove insisted that people are more highly motivated in a competitive environment where they race against each other. However, not long after Grove's book appeared, *BusinessWeek* reported that an alarming number of Intel employees were "jumping ship." Intel had begun losing the very resources that had made it such a dynamo, its people.

Corporate morale took a turn for the worse on January 17,

1983, when seventeen Intel employees resigned to start their own firm. One employee bemoaned the fact that the environment at Intel had changed; another claimed everyone at the company was "casting about for another job." On February 1, Ted Hoff, Intel's top scientist and designer of the first microprocessor, abandoned Intel for Atari. To some, his leaving suggested that Intel did not know how to manage and keep the right people. Not long after Hoff left, Vaemond Crane, head of the company's systems business, also resigned in the aftermath of a struggle over "turf." To make matters worse, management asked all employees to accept an across-the-board salary cut and pay freeze for one full year, due in large part to the fact that the year before the company had added some three thousand new employees in anticipation of an upturn that never materialized. Grove felt the company had done a good job of "selling the idea" of salary cuts, but employees reportedly disagreed.

After a number of employees left to start Xicor and Seeq Technology, Intel's technical prowess suffered enough of a setback that the company no longer sported its previous phenomenal fifty to sixty percent annual growth. Intel's sales fell 8 percent in 1981, when profit margins also dipped from 10 percent to 3 percent. While Intel achieved increased sales and profits in 1983, some observers have questioned whether this short-term performance, with Grove's push for a "125 percent" effort on top of an already standard fifty-hour work week, can continue over the long term. Grove's book does seem to reveal a less than wholehearted concern for the needs and expectations of his people. The once strong culture that certainly existed in Intel's rapid-growth days, when growth could spur employees toward the reward of a brighter future, appears to be bouncing back but still suffers from a degree of insensitivity.

Sensitivity Motivates

Employees of Hallmark Cards regularly encounter their CEO, Donald Hall, in the company cafeteria carrying his own tray, and they almost always see him at anniversary celebrations for long-time employees. The company, with 17,000 employees, boasts an attractive benefits package that includes a handsome profit-sharing program, child adoption assistance, interest-free loans, and physical exercise programs. Employees feel secure because Hallmark approaches firing someone with extreme caution and only after weighing all other alternatives. Hallmark's employees enjoy the respect and appreciation that executives show toward them, and they feel part of a family whose members care deeply for one another. No wonder folks in Kansas City think Hallmark is the best employer in town. And no wonder it ranks as the largest greeting card company in the world, with $1.25 billion in sales and stunning profits.

True sensitivity motivates people. When you take care to identify, understand, and act upon the needs and expectations of others, they tend to pay you back tenfold. The past decade has brought new emphasis on the importance of increased sensitivity in our personal and social lives, so why shouldn't we apply its power to our corporate lives as well? Popular books and magazines contain an increasing number of articles on the need for clear communication and more intimate understanding between men and women, different races, and parents and children. It's time we paid similar attention to intimacy, the kind of intimacy that allows people to share themselves openly with mutual trust, in our organizations.

A recent trend has seen emphasis move away from hierarchical structures toward more informal networks. By networks we mean people sharing ideas, information, and resources. Since organizations inevitably contain a variety of formal and informal networks, executives must learn to manage them effectively. Those who merely sit back and let the networks develop without their involvement, or who try to control them with formal management mechanisms, will suffer morale and productivity crises. Fortunately, however, anyone with the desire and the willingness to invest time and effort can gain the genuine sensitivity to individual needs that boosts morale and enhances productivity.

The Japanese have used *haragei* to achieve such goals, but

we need to do something more than merely imitate the Japanese. Employees today expect more and need more. If New Age executives want to satisfy higher expectations and more demanding needs, they must forge uniquely American cultures. You can't fulfill the needs of employees by issuing memos, establishing policies and procedures, or implementing Japanese techniques. Rather, you must learn to couple networking and intimacy to provide the nourishing environment in which employees can thrive.

The company that brought us vitamin B-12, streptomycin, and many lifesaving drugs knows the value of networking and intimacy. Merck, the fourth most admired company in the country according to *Fortune*, has demonstrated an overwhelming commitment to producing drugs that reduce human suffering, a commitment that also dictates the way Merck treats its people. Working for Merck is like working for an important and lifesaving cause. Through surveys and open discussions, management keeps itself constantly aware of employee attitudes and concerns. Company publications debate issues in an open, straightforward manner, proving management's genuine concern for employee needs. Employees receive careful training and development, and they take home fatter paychecks than anyone in the industry. Merck's profits have tripled since 1972, and in 1983 the company reported profits of $451 million on sales of $3.2 billion, an impressive 14 percent increase.

In another interesting case Herman Miller has used innovative office furniture design and manufacturing to revolutionize the way offices look and function. Miller, located in Zeeland, Michigan, tries to design open office systems that satisfy the needs of people working in contemporary settings. This simultaneous commitment to innovative satisfaction of a customer's comfort and a company's demand for peak efficiency also governs the way Miller's management handles its employees, who share responsibility for determining their company's direction and priorities. Everyone at Miller participates in the resulting productivity gains. This approach starts in the office of president Max De Pree, who is famous for his sensitive handling of people. He recognizes that each individual has unique gifts and he understands that his company must create an environment in which those gifts can prosper. You'll frequently hear words like "trust," "mutual respect," and "shared commitment" throughout the Herman Miller organization. The company's 1983 annual report quoted a production supervisor in one of its plants: "I was with a very well-known firm before this, a national company, and it was very cold and hard and businesslike and bottom-line oriented. When I came to Herman Miller, it was just a tremendous change. I guess it fits me, and I know fitting me is not one of the company's goals, but the company fits me and I fit the company because of the way I feel about things like that." This happy worker made only one mistake. His company *has* set "fitting him" as a major goal, and the results speak for themselves. Herman Miller's sales have risen from $30 million in 1974 to $300 million today.

The moral of these stories is clear. When executives treat their employees the way they themselves would like to be treated, the employees return the compliment in the form of a strong and productive culture. A culture not based on such sensitivity is like a marriage without love and respect. It's bound to fall apart.

Every excellent company displays sensitivity. Without it, employees feel underutilized and poorly motivated. Face-to-face communication, ongoing training and development, creative incentive programs, and job security are all aspects of sensitivity, but sensitivity must begin in the executive suite.

How to Become a Sensitive Executive

Before you can harness sensitivity, you must learn to recognize it.

Step One: Recognizing Sensitivity

In his masterful work *Human Intimacy: Illusion and Reality*, Victor L. Brown asserts that the realities of human intimacy include love, trust, openness, sincerity, service, and sacrifice, while the illusions of human intimacy trap us into self-obsession, manipulation, personal gratification, superficiality, and a false belief that violating the realities of human intimacy will not bring damaging consequences. According to Brown, successful human relationships grow from kindness, empathy, and commitment, and he warns that illusions about human relationships arise when people relate to "fragments of human beings," "deny the consequences of human behavior," and "deal in indulgence, not discipline." Despite the fact that contemporary society enjoys the virtually unlimited technology to create material comfort, people in our society tend to move from one superficial, unfulfilling relationship to another. Only through deep commitment and hard work can people win lasting pleasure and enduring security. But it does take work to talk to, touch, and in other ways cultivate intimacy with others.

Before you test your own level of sensitivity, take a look at an executive who offers an instructive model. The Olga Company is a New Age corporation that maintains a high level of sensitivity to its employees' expectations and needs. The $60-million company dominates the women's undergarment industry, with sales growth and income as a percentage of sales twice that of its direct competitors and the apparel industry as a whole, and a return on invested capital four times greater than competitors and twice the apparel industry average. During forty years of operation, Olga has set new annual sales and income records thirty-six times. *Women's Wear Daily* ranks Olga's quality number one, but more important, Olga's own employees rank their company the best place to work in the world. The company follows the five basic principles of what has been called a common venture enterprise: the dignity of all people; the use of resources for the common good; leadership through service; the business organization as a concerned community; and the right of employees to share in the profits of their production. Jan Erteszek, Olga's chairman, believes that investors may supply capital, but employees supply talent, competence, experience, and effort, investing the best parts of their lives in the success of the corporation. Consequently, they should share in the rewards. Since the *total* employee goes to work for a company, the company must serve the total human being. Erteszek's view on leadership and management is: "A position of leadership is not a passport to personal privilege or power. The duty of the leader is to serve the needs of those who are led."

Over the years we have often observed five blocks that make the journey to true sensitivity a difficult one. If you learn to spot these blocks, you'll be in a better position to avoid them.

- Assuming you know others' expectations and needs without discussing them.

- Treating all employees the same regardless of differences.

- Viewing employees as tools or production units.

- Seeing employees as they once were, not recognizing changes or improvements.

- Believing employees should respond the way you would respond in the same situation.

When executives assume, without asking, that they understand the expectations and needs of their people, they risk making poor decisions about such important factors as working environment, employee recognition, incentives, and communication methods. To overcome this, you must listen carefully when employees discuss their expectations and needs. Most executives spend 80 percent or more of their time listening to people, but unfortunately half the time they don't really hear what's being said.

When an executive treats every employee the same, serious problems arise. Treating everyone the same communicates the message, "I don't care enough about you to find out what makes you unique." To remove this block you must identify and understand the differences among individuals. This does not mean you develop a different set of policies for each employee, but it does mean you recognize and respond to the differences among your people.

Executives who view their employees as tools or production units deserve ten years of hard labor as a tool or production unit. On the other hand, those who try to induce in their organizations the intensity and intimacy of their family relationships win the same sort of satisfaction and security they enjoy at home, not just for themselves but for their employees as well.

Locking employees into a past perception ignores the fact that people change, at times quickly and in major ways. Regardless of deep-seated idiosyncrasies and personality traits, tomorrow's employee may differ as much from today's as today's differs from yesterday's. People acquire new technical knowledge, learn new skills, increase their experience and judgment, improve competence, and evolve interpersonal relationships. Track employee progress and backsliding with a keen radar. If an employee achieves a major improvement in any area, give public recognition to that achievement. If an employee seems to have lost something, figure out why.

Do you expect your people to respond to a given situation the same way you would? Even if you say, "Of course not," don't be sure. Most of us can't help projecting our own attitudes and approaches on others. Even if you have successfully crawled into another person's head, you have to be constantly on guard against projecting your own ideas onto that person's decision or solution to a problem. Fortunately, if an employee's decision concerns the organization's commitment, competence, or consistency, a strong corporate culture will narrow the range of acceptable courses of action, but many decisions do not concern cultural factors. Some executives push so hard for conformance to a cultural model that they thwart innovative, independent thinking, creating "yes" people instead. Such people do not support strong cultures. To remove this block, you must avoid projecting your own skills or style when you evaluate employees' actions. Detach yourself and rely on the tenets of your organization's culture rather than letting your biases determine your judgment.

Now that you are able to recognize sensitivity, you can delve into the individual components of your own sensitivity by taking the following test. Circle the number for each question that best describes you. Each "always" or "often" answer identifies a sensitivity problem of which you should be aware. A score below 30 deserves your serious attention.

EXECUTIVE SENSITIVITY SELF-EXAMINATION

	ALWAYS	OFTEN	SELDOM	NEVER
1. Do you deal only with people's particular immediate needs (a more comfortable chair, a small raise) rather than their deeper long-range needs (career advancement, satisfaction beyond a paycheck)?	1	2	3	4
2. Do you find yourself denying the damaging consequences of superficial human relationships?	1	2	3	4
3. Are you self-focused when you interact with others, considering what's in it for you?	1	2	3	4
4. Do you avoid getting personally involved with your employees, peers, or superiors?	1	2	3	4
5. Do you perceive subordinates as serving you and your needs, rather than you serving them and their needs?	1	2	3	4
6. Do you assume you know your peoples' expectations, needs, and wants without discussing them?	1	2	3	4

7. Do you treat your employees the same, regardless of individual differences?	1	2	3	4
8. Do you view your people as tools or units of production?	1	2	3	4
9. Do you see individual employees the way they used to be, ignoring improvements or changes?	1	2	3	4
10. Do you expect your people to respond the same way you would in a given situation?	1	2	3	4

Of course we feel Olga's Jan Erteszek would score a perfect forty. Regardless of your own score, you can take certain steps to improve or maintain it.

Step Two: Mastering Five Levels of Sensitivity

True sensitivity springs from a deep understanding of the basic needs and expectations of people. Two of the most well-known, widely used theories are Abraham Maslow's hierarchy of needs and Frederick J. Herzberg's motivational theory. Maslow identifies five levels of needs: physical well-being; safety and security; social affiliation; self-esteem; and self-actualization. When your physical needs such as those for food, clothing, and shelter are satisfied, the needs of the next level become paramount. Then, when the needs for safety and security are met through an assurance that your job situation frees you from having to worry about your physical needs, you concentrate on social affiliation needs, which are fulfilled by belonging to a group with shared beliefs, values, and concerns. Once these needs are satisfied, the need for self-esteem rises to the fore. You fulfill this need by feeling good about yourself as a result of recognition and praise from others. Finally, once you develop self-esteem, you focus on the need for self-actualization, which you attain through growing and developing into the sort of individual you believe you can or must be.

Herzberg's motivational theory isolates two groups of needs, motivators and dissatisfiers. The motivators include interesting work, challenging work, personal achievement, recognition, and the opportunity for increased responsibility. The satisfaction threshold for motivators has no limit and can reach ever increasing heights. By contrast, the dissatisfiers are organizational policies, working relationships and conditions, supervision, and compensation. Although you can achieve satisfaction in these areas, satisfaction does not increase your motivation. For example, an organization's poor policies will cause dissatisfaction, but good policies will only create satisfaction, not motivation. Dissatisfiers cause varying levels of dissatisfaction but not varying levels of motivation. Your satisfaction threshold—for instance, your idea of a good salary—rises over time, making dissatisfaction a strong possibility in the future.

Let's apply our understanding of needs hierarchy motivational theory by first considering five levels of sensitivity.

- **Sensitivity to security expectations and needs** requires that you dedicate yourself to your people's physical well-being, environment, working conditions, compensation, supervision, and benefits. Demand that your managers do the same.

- **Sensitivity to belonging expectations and needs** involves scrutinizing the social interaction, group dynamics, community feeling, participation in decision-making, and sense of family your people experience. Do you feel like a family member yourself?

- **Sensitivity to recognition expectations and needs** entails thoroughly evaluating how and when your employees win formal and informal recognition via oral and written praise, promotions, bonuses, awards, honors, and other means. No two people are exactly alike and the kind of recognition craved by one may not satisfy another.

- **Sensitivity to quality-of-work expectations and needs** requires you to define the sort of work people find interesting and challenging. What makes people feel inspired and excited? What calls forth their most creative effort? Individual differences become even more crucial at this point.

- **Sensitivity to self-actualization expectations and needs** helps you to look inside the hearts and minds of your people. Do you comprehend their dreams? What do they really wish to become? Do they feel that their dreams lie within their eventual grasp? Spend thoughtful time with each worker.

Now that you understand the five levels of sensitivity, examine where you stand in relationship to each. To assist you, we've designed a chart that helps you determine your current level of sensitivity. In the chart you will find suggestions about how to improve your mastery at each level.

SENSITIVITY CHART

	Sensitivity Rating		
Levels of Sensitivity	High (Always)	Medium (Frequently)	Low (Seldom/Never)
Security	This is the lowest need level, but it's a good start.	Design a regular employee-attitude survey.	Conduct an employee-attitude survey immediately.
Belonging	Assuming security remains high, you're ready to tackle recognition.	Find out who feels a sense of belonging and who doesn't, then work on the ones who don't.	Start thoroughly observing how employees relate to one another.

Recognition	If security and belonging remain high, move on to quality of work.	As you identify what works, try to improve it.	Experiment with new and creative recognition approaches.
Quality of Work	Assuming the three preceding levels are still high, move on to self-actualization.	Once you have an initial reading on what interests and challenges people, monitor it quarterly.	Conduct a series of interviews to discover what interests and challenges your people.
Self-Actualization	If all previous levels are high, you have mastered the sensitivity it takes to forge a strong culture.	Commit yourself to regular one-on-one sessions with each employee, preferably away from the office.	Take the people who report to you on a three-day retreat and get to know them.

Successfully heightened sensitivity depends on your interest in and willingness to change. While consulting with two strikingly different executives in two different organizations, we identified serious sensitivity gaps in both. One executive thanked us for our analysis and asked for help in improving his level of sensitivity. The other, recently divorced after fifteen years of marriage, asked for help, but he didn't really want to change. In fact, after several weeks he confessed that he really believed increased sensitivity was a waste of his time. He had agreed to work with us only because his CEO insisted that he do so. Needless to say, he did not gain heightened sensitivity. To him management meant getting people to conform to policies and programs for the greater good of the corporation and for his own promotion. In parting he said, "All this sensitivity stuff is okay for schoolteachers, mothers, and ministers, but not for a hard-nosed, bottom-line executive like me."

The other executive sincerely believed his increased sensitivity could spur his continued growth as an executive as well as his company's bottom-line performance: "I have a happy marriage and four successful kids. If only I could help my firm the way I've helped my family." In the weeks that followed, he worked hard. When he used the chart to evaluate his sensitivity, he scored medium in security and belonging, but low in recognition, quality of work, and self-actualization, so he embarked on a year-long program to improve his marks. First he tackled security, retaining a human resources consultant who had worked for the company before. Together they discussed ways to monitor employee attitudes on a regular basis. They didn't expect a survey to elicit all the answers, but they did hope it would provide clues about employees' perceptions of organizational policies, supervision, working conditions, compensation, and benefits. The survey revealed that almost 65 percent of the employees felt they didn't fully understand how their specific tasks fit into the overall picture of the company's product lines and that they thought of themselves as performing perfunctorily within a well-oiled machine. Although they felt secure in their jobs and enjoyed the camaraderie of their fellow workers, they didn't feel any creative effort would win strong recognition from management. The employee survey seemed to mirror the executive's scores on the self-administered sensitivity chart, so he immediately took two decisive steps: monthly meetings with separate groups during which he painted the overall picture of corporate goals and encouraged discussion about the relationships among the separate groups, and a "Plus-10 Club" incentive program that would put into an employee's pocket 10 percent of companywide savings or increased productivity derived from his or her creative idea. Within three months, all workers better understood where they fit within the organization and twenty people had been inducted into the Plus-10 Club. Sales in dollars and units per employee increased by 10 percent and 7 percent respectively, the best three-month performance in the company's history.

At the end of the three-month period, the executive took his key managers on a three-day retreat where they spent four hours daily discussing an agenda structured around sensitivity, two hours in deep, private meditation, and the rest of the time playing and informally talking about everything from their families to politics and religion. In the weeks that followed, the executive took each manager aside for a one-to-one encounter away from the office.

From one such meeting emerged the idea that a manager deserved special recognition if three or more of his people made the Plus-10 Club. At the end of six months, two managers had won places in the new "Plus-30 Club," receiving not only a plaque but a 10 percent salary bonus. Another manager volunteered to revamp the company's internal publication to include a "People" section profiling members of the Plus-10 Club and detailing new incentive holidays for those who made the club twice. The executive began a monthly column that detailed the importance of previously unsung groups within the organization.

By the end of one year, the executive scored himself high at every sensitivity level. To top it off, profits had increased 20 percent for the year and were up to an impressive 14 percent of sales from 10 percent a year before.

Now that you have seen how to master the five levels, you need to closely study the fundamental rule of sensitivity.

Step Three: Doing Unto Others

We're not going to preach the old Dale Carnegie line about treating others the way you would like to be treated. We're talking about creating excellence, not just becoming a nice person, and we don't accept the usual application of the Golden Rule that implies other people would like to be treated the way *you* want to be treated. All of us know unselfish people who struggle desperately to satisfy the needs of others but turn out to be terrible executives. Why? Aren't they truly sensitive? Their failure stems from their inability to recognize that others seldom respond just the way *they* do. They're so busy asking, "How would *I* like to be treated?" that they miss the point of sensitivity, namely, identifying and understanding the unique expectations and needs of entirely different people.

To clarify its true and original meaning, we've added a few words to the Golden Rule: "Treat others the way you would like to be treated, *assuming you had their unique set of expectations and needs.*" Given this expanded definition of the Golden Rule, try exercising your sensitivity with these cases:

Exercise 1: Future Line Manager. Put yourself in the following situation. You are the executive vice-president and chief financial officer for a $2-billion consumer and industrial products manufacturer with thirty-nine different operating divisions. Five years ago you hired a bright young manager who now directs one of your most important corporate staff departments, Business Analysis and Planning. Before she joined your firm, she spent two years at the "Big 8" accounting firm Peat, Marwick, Mitchell & Company. She holds an MBA from Wharton and a BA in economics from Stanford, and is one of a handful of key managers who will probably be running the company ten years from now. She desperately wants a line management position in one of the divisions, but she has served as director of Business Analysis and Planning for only eighteen months. Attuned to her talent and sensitive to her desires, you have held several discussions with her and feel fully aware of her expectations and needs. Her goals include becoming a line manager over a functional area such as marketing or production, then a division manager, and eventually a corporate officer. However, because she has only gained staff experience, has occupied her present position for only eighteen months, and is a woman, you know you'll hear some static from division presidents if you propose the idea that she assume line responsibility in one of their divisions. Furthermore, since she is the best director of Business Analysis and Planning you have ever had, you'd hate to lose her just now. Perhaps she could do more for the company if she stayed where she is for three to five years. By then she might even have won a staff vice-presidency. On the other hand, if you don't do something to meet her needs you may lose her to another company. What would you do?

A. Tell her that she is not ready for line management and needs to wait at least two years. Only then will you discuss the matter again.

B. Convince her she will have more impact on the company by remaining in her current position, communicating your belief that it's also in her own best interests, that it's what you yourself would do in her shoes.

C. Move her into a line management position in one of the divisions as soon as you can.

D. Offer her a staff vice-presidency in three years if she agrees to stay where she is.

E. Tell her there are no currently available line management positions suited to her experience and background, then hope she changes her mind about leaving staff management.

F. Work out a career development plan with her that will maximize the benefits to the company and to her.

G. Increase her salary and ask her to stay where she is.

Which one did you pick? From our point of view, options B, C and F represent the most logical directions. But which will get the best results? What would a truly sensitive executive, aware of the full range of expectations and needs, do? Understanding that sensitivity does not necessitate giving employees everything they want when they want it, the sensitive executive nonetheless strives to fulfill the expectations and needs unless they 1) sharply contradict the best interests of the company; 2) clearly do not serve the best long-term interests of the employee, given his/her expectations and needs; or 3) are out of line with the employee's performance, commitment, or competence. Therefore, the sensitive executive would have selected option

B, with option C as a back-up. Of course F makes sense in all cases. First, he would have communicated the feelings, perceptions and judgments represented in option B, then he would have asked his bright young manager to carefully weigh his words before their next session a week later. If, at the second meeting, the manager still expressed a strong desire to move into line management, despite her boss's recommendations and judgment, he would implement option C. Given her overpowering desire to move into line management and believing her to be competent to succeed, further attempts to dissuade her would only diminish her superior performance, weaken her commitment to the company, and eventually drive her out of the organization. Although you can partially mold another's expectations and needs, at some point you must decide either to meet them or to reject them. If you want to build a strong corporate culture and keep your good people committed, you'll apply the fundamental rule of sensitivity, doing all in your power to meet expectations and needs as if they were your own.

Exercise 2: The Worrier. Pretend you are in a situation where a manager who reports to you is highly competent but worries excessively about everything. The worrying gets so intense at times that *you* begin to worry that his anxiety may affect his colleagues. However, of the six managers reporting to you, the worrier displays the highest competency, the most dedication, and the most promise for advancement. One recent incident especially concerns you. During a staff meeting with your managers, the worrier began to raise unnecessary objections, based on fear, to a major decision the group had made a month earlier. He nagged at the point like a terrier with a bone until the meeting turned sour and ended on a note of keen frustration. After the meeting you sat in your office contemplating what to do with this manager. Unfortunately, his behavior made you so uncomfortable you never took the personal time to really get to know him. What would you do?

A. Ask the manager to stop worrying or leave the company.

B. Send the manager to a psychologist for help.

C. Communicate to the manager that you find his worrying disruptive. If he can't avoid it, he should keep it to himself.

D. Get close to the manager, trying to find out what prompts the worrying. Determine whether unmet expectations and needs contribute to his problem.

E. Don't worry about it, let it go. Hope that it will go away.

F. Help the manager find another job outside the company.

This one is easy. The sensitive executive would pick option D. While he recognizes that getting close to the worrier will not be easy, he can accept no other alternative. Of course, a time could come further down the line when terminating the manager would be a sensitive act: if the problem began to constantly endanger the expectations and needs of others within the organization, the sensitive executive would have to take that painful step. But termination should only follow an exhaustive attempt to solve the problem.

A sensitive executive works much like the conductor of a large orchestra. Each musician may be a strong-willed artist, but each must play his or her instrument in harmony with the rest of the ensemble. Inept musicians or poorly tuned instruments can spoil the total effect you wish to achieve. Train the musicians well and teach them to properly tune their instruments. If they continue to play badly, don't sacrifice the quality of the group in a vain effort to help those who may never rise to the challenge.

The Magic of Sensitivity: A Summary

Sensitivity helps you look inside another person in order to understand that person's expectations and needs. Such understanding helps you act to meet those needs and expectations as if they were your own. Sensitive executives motivate people in the most effective, lasting ways. Those who lack sensitivity, no matter how insightful their strategies, offer nothing but cold, heartless plans, and their efforts at rallying the troops to support a vision of the company's future will probably fail.

CHAPTER 7

Vision: Creating the Future

Executive recruiters, asked what qualities their client companies are seeking in a candidate for a top job, report that they're hearing our old friend "charisma" a great deal more than they used to. "Vision" also seems in increasing demand; while the headhunters aren't sure precisely what the term means, they sense that it has to do with new and much sought-after skills in motivating people.

—*Fortune*

The best way to predict the future is to invent it.

—ALAN KAY

Clear Vision Creates the Future

We all have dreams and fantasies about the future. Most of us picture ourselves more successful, wealthier, and happier than we are now, but we will not reach those goals by idle dreaming. Major events loom on the horizon, among them technological breakthroughs in artificial intelligence, that we can view either as threats to our humanity or as opportunities for advancement. Our individual and corporate success will depend, as never before, on our ability to anticipate and participate in such changes.

Unlike dreaming or fantasizing, vision, the first of two integrative skills, helps New Age executives position themselves and their organizations to create and take advantage of future opportunities. Vision is both an offensive and a defensive skill, on the one hand helping you chart a course that creates change, and on the other helping you respond to external changes. It links the foundation skills to the adaptive skills (versatility and

149

focus) and it joins the second integrative skill, patience to allow leaders the necessary time to create lasting excellence. Visionary executives integrate creative insight and sensitivity to forge the strategy-culture alloy, and they patiently use versatility and focus to maintain excellence over the long term.

Executives with clear vision invent excellent futures for their firms; those who lack it set their companies adrift in dangerous waters. The dramatically different fates of two retail giants, F. W. Woolworth and S. S. Kresge, are instructive. In the fall of 1982, the Woolworth Company closed 336 Woolco discount stores, eliminated the jobs of 35,000 people and posted a $325-million after-tax write-off. By stark contrast, its arch-rival Kresge propelled its two-thousand-store K Mart discount chain to $17 billion in sales that year. Why did one of these enterprises crash while the other soared to excellence? Hoping to exploit a hot concept that seemed to promise enormous growth and profitability, both Woolworth and Kresge started discount store operations, Woolco and K Mart, respectively, at about the same time. Both giant parents enjoyed sufficient resources to expect success; both had demonstrated retailing expertise in the past; both had displayed strong bottom-line success; and both expected to extend their success far in the future. What led them to such different results?

From the very beginning, Kresge charted its course in the discount store business as if the company knew exactly where its future lay, while Woolworth never could make up its mind. Kresge boldly launched a string of stores, heavily discounting everything from clothing to bed sheets to tires and refrigerators and achieving respectable profits with quick turnover. Before long, K Mart had chalked up record growth and profitability, with over 150 new stores opening their doors every year.

Woolworth, lacking clear vision, hesitantly opened only half the new discount stores planned for California, then scrapped the rest. The existing stores had to shoulder sole responsibility for heavy advertising and other expenses they could have shared with the aborted stores. Says one Woolco official, "We couldn't decide which way we wanted to go, variety, discount store, or medium-price, right from the start." To make matters worse, Woolco consolidated both its variety and discount store buying into one organization, thereby blurring what should have been distinct identities. Customers not only found prices higher than those of the competition in some places and lower in others, they couldn't distinguish Woolco from new, emerging specialty discounters such as Caldor and Target. Commented one competitor, "Woolco had a lot of potential that was never exploited. I can remember people at K Mart considering them a sleeping giant. But the giant never woke up." Though Woolco's failure derived from poor strategy, operational blinders, and organizational ineffectiveness, the real root of the problem lay in a lack of clear vision.

What do we mean by vision? Essentially, *vision is a mental journey from the known to the unknown, creating the future from a montage of current facts, hopes, dreams, dangers, and opportunities.* Just as the mental journeys of Thomas Jefferson and Karl Marx guided nations, such journeys can dictate the success of businesses; and just as nations must adapt their original visions to changing conditions, so must corporate leaders mold their visions to keep pace with a rapidly evolving world.

In the words of Jack Welch, chairman and CEO of General Electric Company, "Said simply, are we as a nation ready to accept that what was good enough ten years ago, just isn't good enough today?" If we accept the fact that American productivity has declined in recent years, we must also accept the fact that the same old management tools, techniques, and skills that propelled a company to success in the past just don't cut it anymore.

How can we recapture vision? Didn't the old vision of hard-nosed, bottom-line management serve us well until recently? Doesn't some of it still serve us well? We don't have to start from scratch, but if we are to successfully lead our companies into an ever changing future, we must shape the old vision in imaginative ways. As visionary leaders guide their companies through change, they will be able to transcend the facts and figures at hand.

The so-called "high-tech revolution" illustrates such transcendence. America's explosive electronics and computer companies either did not exist at all before World War II or were unknown and inconspicuous then. Before the war, IBM made cash registers; Steve Jobs and Steve Wozniak, the founders of Apple Computer had not even been born. But in thirty years IBM has become synonymous with computers, and in less than ten Apple has ignited a giant new market for its machines. Behind both of these successes were the guiding hands of visionary leaders capable of not only predicting but creating change.

Someone must assume responsibility for renewed vision. Psychologist Warren Bennis studied ninety top leaders in an effort to isolate the qualities shared by visionary leaders and came to realize that top leaders share a common trait: all have a compelling vision and a dream about their work.

Harry Gray of United Technologies, who came to the then United Aircraft Company in 1971, is the sort of leader who can create a new vision for a company. Gray spent his first few years at the United helm correcting existing problems, but all the while he was envisioning the future. Finally, in 1973, he announced that the company would from then on focus on electronics, communications, transportation, energy, and environmental systems. He also made a clear commitment to competitive leadership, the basis of which would be "market dominance, excellence in technology management and transfer, willingness to invest to become the technology leader, and the determination to share corporate UTC capabilities in electronics, services and R and D." From then until now, Harry Gray has religiously implemented his vision, strategically weaving together acquisitions in each of the areas of emphasis, developing the organizational capabilities of the companies based on his "bottom line technology" philosophy, and ensuring that strategy and culture carefully and consistently blend together. The result? Gray systematically transformed United Technologies from a mature government-dependent military supplier into a more highly diversified industrial company with competitive positions in a variety of related technology-based businesses. In 1971, when Gray took over as president of United Technologies, the company lost $44 million on sales of $2 billion. In 1983, the company made a $509 million net profit on nearly $15 billion in sales.

Clear vision results from a profound understanding of an organization and its environment. The executive needs a practical knowledge of the dynamics of industries, markets, and competition and must recognize the potential of the corporation to influence and exploit those dynamics. It takes a craftsman's, not a technician's, skill. The craftsman can see exactly what the end product will look like and exactly what work must be done to achieve it. He then puts his tools and materials to work shaping the product, adjusting and adapting as he goes, keeping in constant mental view the look and feel of the goal. By contrast, if you simply follow a set of instructions without vision, you'll never create superior results.

New Age executives with vision spend a great deal of their time mentally residing in the future. No matter how complex their undertakings, the future lies a small step from the here-and-now for visionary managers.

Vision Determines Success or Failure

To explain the success of Japanese companies, American business executives cite such things as the efficiency and productivity of the Japanese worker, superior management techniques, and Japanese culture itself. However, some, such as Paul Tippett, chairman and CEO of American Motors Corporation, see it another way: Japan's success in the U.S. markets stems from its governmental and political treatment of industrial growth and foreign trade, targeting key industries with high export potential and domestically protecting and nurturing these industries until they are strong enough to compete abroad. Tariffs prohibiting foreign competition, quotas on foreign investments, and other restrictions maintain a "home-market hot-house" environment. In addition, selected companies can fix prices and establish beneficial supplier relationships. When these companies finally do enter foreign markets, the government offers them such advantages as accelerated depreciation, tax and antitrust exemptions, subsidized loans and R and D funding. Obviously, this strategy has helped Japan make its powerful vision a reality for three decades.

Is it easy to create such a powerful vision? New visions often suffer ridicule and laughter. Merrill Lynch prompted guffaws when it introduced a "useless" cash management account in Colorado in 1978, but after many years of investment and losses, these "useless accounts" now amount to $15 billion in cash and an estimated $35 billion in securities.

By contrast, formerly dominant companies such as B. F. Goodrich, National Cash Register, and RCA have lost major markets and millions of dollars to more visionary competitors:

- National Cash Register lacked the vision to move from electromechanical cash registers into new electronic products. In the early 1970s, competitors developed new technology that made NCR's products obsolete. Even though NCR had the resources and expertise to come up with the necessary technological innovations, it didn't, and wrote off $140 million in outdated, electromechanical inventory.

- B. F. Goodrich became the premier maker of bias-ply tires in the United States in 1976 by pushing the company and its suppliers to come up with improved raw materials, tire cords, and designs. But by 1979 bias-ply tires were almost extinct, and Michelin's radial tires had swept the market to become standard equipment on American cars. By perpetuating the past, Goodrich failed to create the future.

- In 1955, RCA Corp. headed a list of the ten major vacuum tube manufacturers in the United States. When solid-state technology emerged, RCA tried halfheartedly to get into it, but it was a matter of too little, too late. By 1975, RCA was no longer in the vacuum tube or the semiconductor business. Neither were the other nine producers of vacuum tubes.

Such fates have befallen numerous once dominant American firms. When powerful visions die, so do the companies they guided. In their place spring up new enterprises that have clear corporate visions. Consider Sony, Lotus Development, and Siecor:

- Sony's Corp.'s recent introduction of a line of cameras with electronic imaging (an electronic image of the picture you wish to take allows you to decide whether to keep or reject it before it becomes a still photograph) exemplifies the Sony vision. Kodak, which pioneered chemical processing technology, will be scrambling to catch up.

- One of the hottest software companies of the 1980s, Lotus Development Corporation, successfully implemented founder Mitchell Kapor's vision of user-friendly, "all-in-one" software with Lotus 1-2-3. Before long, Lotus was outselling VisiCalc two to one. Now the company has launched Symphony, an even more powerful tool that surpasses the company's own current bestseller.

- Dow Corning and Siemens of West Germany formed a brilliant new joint venture, called Siecor, to exploit optical fiber technology. This innovation will enhance worldwide communications as well as Dow's bottom line.

Vision Unites Strategy and Culture

The rejuvenation of American productivity depends on our ability to marry the often warring concepts of hard-nosed, bottom-line strategy and corporate culture building. And a successful marriage requires a powerful corporate vision. Despite the tremendous effort involved in gaining vision, the hard work can pay off in the form of an American corporate renaissance.

Hewlett-Packard's vision, developed years ago, binds market strategies and corporate culture together by giving individual managers the autonomy and freedom to be entrepreneurial and innovative. While H-P's competitors have chastised it for holding onto an entrepreneurial culture in an industry they think requires more coordination and integration of products and systems, H-P's vision continues to keep the company near the head of the pack. At H-P, strategy and culture work beautifully together. John Young, president of Hewlett-Packard, describes the company's objectives: "They are a kind of glue, the basic philosophy, the basic sense of direction, sort of a value set, that draws everyone together."

Another company that has successfully wed strategy and culture is Corning Glass Works, which accomplished the feat in a unique way. Though Corning recognized the need for new ideas and technologies, the company also realized that its reliance on marketing and production had produced a culture somewhat resistant to technological innovation. Rather than grafting a new culture onto the old, they engaged in joint ventures with emerging, entrepreneurial companies, such as Genencor, Inc. and Nutrisearch, that already enjoyed cultures and strategies geared toward technological innovation. It worked because Corning understood that innovation-oriented strategies and staid corporate cultures don't mix well.

Vision joins strategy and culture together to achieve corporate excellence. Without vision to bind them, corporate strategy and culture tend to drift apart, as they have within such large companies as Exxon and RCA, which are pursuing strategies their corporate cultures cannot effectively implement. When Exxon entered the computer business, it ran into trouble because it tried to run its high-tech operation the way it had always run its oil companies. RCA, whose once pioneering vision helped create an entire electronics industry, disrupted the union of strategy and culture by entering such diverse businesses as car rental and financial services. The result was musical chairs in the executive suite, confused and disgruntled employees, and severely sagging profits.

How to Become a Visionary Executive

With our definition of vision in mind, we can tackle the important task of first acquiring vision, then using it to create a successful future. But before you acquire it, you must learn to recognize it.

Step One: Recognizing Vision

First, you must learn to distinguish between executives with vision and those without it. Since it's easy to feign vision, this is not as simple as it seems. Some self-styled visionaries are really dreamers who let their imaginations paint interesting but impractical pictures of the future. Such fantasies may inspire people for a period of time, but when they fail to materialize, they bring disillusionment in their wake.

John Kotter, Harvard Business School professor and author of *The General Managers*, has shed interesting light on the nature of effective executives by filming a "day in the life" of two very different senior executives, one closely resembling the "visionary executive," one falling considerably short. The visionary executive, a skillful strategic player, works quite differently from the nonvisionary one, who is merely trapped in a role. Consider the differences:

- The visionary executive smilingly admits he has only a few crucial appointments scheduled on his calendar. In contrast, the nonvisionary executive couldn't squeeze in another appointment. His overloaded schedule has strapped him in a straitjacket.

- The visionary executive spends considerable time walking around the organization, warmly greeting and chatting with employees. The trapped executive spends the bulk of his time in large, formal meetings, during which he directs the actions of his subordinates.

- The visionary executive frequently talks about his philosophy, the corporate direction and values he thinks will keep the company successful. The nonvisionary executive never talks about philosophy and, in fact, does not appear to have one. "I'm too busy to fool around with abstractions and fantasies," he says.

- The visionary executive urges his employees to bring both their brains and hearts to work because, in the critical path of life, you cannot separate the two. The other executive, who frowns a lot and rarely smiles, takes executives aside between meetings to criticize their work.

- During his work day, the visionary executive spends a lot of time in the plant discussing new products. He hosts spontaneous and informal lunches with key personnel, after which he delivers inspirational speeches to small groups of key employees. The nonvisionary executive, who wastes most of his time in meetings, devotes a lot of time to such unproductive undertakings as reviewing a sales training film script, reading it aloud, word by word, to the district managers.

The two types of executives can by defined by the following traits:

Nonvisionary Executive

- Solves daily problems and makes decisions.
- Meets formally with immediate subordinates.
- Is aloof, rational, critical, and "cold" (people and ideas prompt a reserved response).
- Pays attention to weaknesses.
- Talks about current business activities.

Visionary Executive

- Articulates philosophy.

- Makes contact with employees at all levels.

- Is receptive, expressive, supportive, and "hot" (people and ideas ignite him).

- Pays attention to strengths.

- Talks about future goals.

Obviously, vision distinguishes the strategic player from the trapped executive. Though strategic players do more than merely create visions for their organization, their visions reside at their very core and rule every action. By contrast, trapped executives do what they do because they're too busy to see where they are going, have no concept of what's really important, and experience rather than invent the future.

In a study of fifty outstanding chief executives, Warren Bennis identified certain common characteristics. The successful CEO:

- Develops a compelling vision of the firm's future.

- Translates the vision into a reality by concentrating on the keys to success.

- Remains deeply involved at the very heart of things, spurring the actions necessary to carry out the vision.

- Motivates employees to embrace the vision.

- Constantly articulates the vision so that it permeates all organizational levels and functions, taking the organization where it's never been before.

In yet another effort to understand the differences between executives with vision and those without, Abraham Zaleznik of the Harvard Business School distinguished between leaders and mere managers. In his famous *Harvard Business Review* article, "Managers and Leaders: Are They Different?," Zaleznik argued that mere managers tend to adopt impersonal, passive attitudes toward goals, viewing them as means of getting the job done. Such managers attempt to solve problems by continually seeking compromise among people and ideas. They view themselves as conservators and regulators of an existing order that they personally identify with and from which they gain rewards. They worry more about people's roles than about the people themselves. These managers enhance their self-worth by perpetuating existing processes and orders. To maintain controlled, rational organizational structures, they generate bureaucratic red tape and display little directness and warmth.

In striking contrast, true leaders adopt a personal and active attitude toward goals, viewing them as basic reasons for being. Leaders work in the opposite spirit from managers, attempting to develop fresh approaches to pesky problems. They view work as an artistic act. They worry about ideas and how ideas affect people, and they relate to people in intuitive and empathetic ways, asking themselves, "What will these events and decisions *mean* to our people?" Seeking opportunities for change, they wish to profoundly alter human, economic, and political relationships. Since their sense of identify does not depend upon titles or work roles, leaders foster organizational structures that often appear turbulent, intense, and even at times disorganized, but their organizations motivate individuals and often produce outcomes greater than expected. We can now begin to see what an executive with vision really looks like. The visionary leader:

- Searches for ideas, concepts, and ways of thinking until clear vision crystallizes.

- Articulates the vision into an easy-to-grasp philosophy that integrates strategic direction and cultural values.

- Motivates company employees to embrace the vision through constant persuasion and setting an example of hard work.

- Makes contact with employees at all levels in the organization, attempting to understand their concerns and the impact the vision has on them.

- Acts in a warm, supportive, expressive way, always communicating that "We're all in this together, like a family."

- Translates the vision into a reason for being for each employee by continually relating the vision to individual cares, concerns, and work.

- Concentrates on the major strengths within the organization that will insure the success of the vision.

- Remains at the center of the action, positioned as prime shaper of the vision.

- Looks for ways to improve, augment, or further develop the corporate vision by carefully observing changes inside and outside the organization.

- Measures the ultimate success of the organization in terms of its ability to fulfill the vision.

To measure your visionary ability, take our "Executive Vision Self-Examination." Circle the number in the column that best describes you. A perfect score of 50 marks the truly visionary executive. Anything below 30 indicates some need for improvement.

EXECUTIVE VISION SELF-EXAMINATION

	ALWAYS (WITH GUSTO)	ALWAYS	OFTEN	SELDOM	NEVER
1. You consider new ideas and angles until your vision becomes clear.	5	4	3	2	1
2. You translate the vision into a simple philosophy that employees can readily grasp.	5	4	3	2	1
3. You motivate employees to embrace the vision.	5	4	3	2	1

4. You make contact at all levels within your organization.	5	4	3	2	1
5. You are warm and supportive.	5	4	3	2	1
6. Your vision is an all-important cause for you and you instill this belief in others.	5	4	3	2	1
7. You concentrate on major strengths of your people and your organization.	5	4	3	2	1
8. You remain at the center of action.	5	4	3	2	1
9. You look for ways to improve your vision.	5	4	3	2	1
10. You measure the ongoing success of your vision.	5	4	3	2	1

John F. Welch, Jr., chairman and CEO of General Electric Company, would undoubtedly achieve a perfect score. With his vision, he has transformed many of GE's more mundane and mature businesses, such as electric lights and plastics, into profitable growth enterprises, consistently achieving earnings growth at rates well above sales growth. Welch's style of leadership in these turbulent, changing times has won wide attention for its simplicity, forcefulness, directness, and, most of all, its vision. GE, Welch believes, must be the industry leader, it must be "number one or number two in everything the company does." He warns that companies that refuse to think likewise, who hang on to losing or stagnant operations, won't survive the 1980s.

Now that you have learned to recognize vision, you are ready for the sometimes painful job of taking a cold, hard look at your organization.

Step Two: Organizational Introspection

It takes courage and a hard-won objectivity to take a hard look inside yourself and your organization. Like a spouse or a child, an organization may possess certain flaws you've learned to overlook. Nevertheless, you cannot acquire or use vision without stepping back and casting a cold eye on your business and all the factors that affect it. We call this process organizational introspection. To succeed with it you must again exercise the art of meditation, objectively weighing every possible factor that can influence your future. The more factors you can isolate and analyze, the deeper and more disciplined your creative thinking becomes. Remember, you're not fantasizing or desperately seeking a flash of blinding insight. You're striving for clear vision. Simply knowing yourself is not enough; to achieve clear vision, you must come to know the full complexity of your organization and its environment.

When Roy Ash first brought his well-known name and promises of a rosy future to the marginally profitable Addressograph-Multigraph Corporation, his strategy seemed brilliant. He immediately replaced 80 percent of the company's management, then plunged into high-tech fields by acquiring a dozen young companies. The booming expansion and glowing promises turned out to be too good to be true, and as the new AM International, Inc., teetered on the brink of financial collapse, Ash lost his job. Nevertheless, Ash still insists that his strategic decisions were not only correct but were the only avenues that could insure AM International's survival. Even though his subordinates valued his abilities as a brilliant conceptualizer, and although few found fault with his strategy's basic direction, many strongly disagreed with its implementation. When Richard B. Black took over as the new chairman, he conducted a ruthless organizational examination which revealed that the former management had not been in touch with reality. Ash had allowed his vision of a rosy future to cloud his view of the company's growing financial predicament. Though Ash had been unable to push any new venture solidly into the black, he had steadfastly believed the company to be winning the battle.

Contrast Roy Ash with Robert Van Tuyle, who has mastered the art of organizational introspection and has developed a compelling vision in the process. Robert Van Tuyle is CEO of Beverly Enterprises, the largest nursing home chain in the U.S. His company operates in an industry most people would consider extremely risky, yet Van Tuyle has converted a series of dangers into opportunities. Since not even the smallest detail escapes Van Tuyle's inspection, Beverly Enterprises flourishes. Says Van Tuyle about his initial assessment of Beverly's position in the nursing home industry, "The industry was hopelessly fragmented and I figured if we were worth a damn we could build a good empire."

From the beginning, Beverly Enterprises seemed to have a remarkable ability, based upon a profound understanding of the dynamics of the environment, to accurately read the nature and needs of the industry. Understanding both its limitations and capabilities, the company established a centralized quality-assurance staff of seventy-five trained nurses to control its medical services around the country. It led the way in nurse training programs and wrote a useful manual which the whole industry has adopted as its standard. Similar precedent-setting activities (from an 800-number hotline to headquarters for patient complaints to an adopt-a-grandparent program in which local school children make weekly visits) have rocketed Beverly Enterprises to a premier position. Revenues have increased twelvefold since 1976, and sales, at $816 million, grew 68 percent in 1983, making it *Fortune's* second-fastest-growing service company. Profits also leaped to a level of $26 million, a 62 percent increase. Beverly expects to be at $1.1 billion in sales in 1984 with 75,000 beds in 643 nursing homes.

Where can you learn the art of organizational introspection? Despite its importance, you won't find it in the traditional business school curriculum. Mainstream business education in

America has emphasized rational, logical, and analytical techniques but has sadly neglected the meditative process that allows the mind to roam the many realms of knowledge and experience, ultimately reaching the sort of penetrating understanding that leads to a clear vision of the future.

When you tackle something as complex as the future of a large business you should try to break the problem down into its parts, perhaps meditating on one component (your key people, customers, trends, or competitors' strategies) per session over a period of days or even weeks. Try to begin each session by posing one crucial question, the answer to which will help shape your vision. Such questions might include:

- What are the critical dynamics of our organization's environment? How do things really work? How do we make money?

- What trends are changing the nature of our industry? What represents the state-of-the-art in the industry? Does it pose opportunities or threats?

- What are our competitors doing? Are they gaining competitive advantage at our expense? Are we seeking new ways to gain our own advantage?

- What do our customers really want? How do they value what we offer? Can we add greater value?

- Who are we as an organization? How do our people feel about who we are? How do they view our purpose?

- How is our organization distinctive and unique? What opportunities does our distinctiveness afford us?

- What are our most important and dominant capabilities, skills, and relationships? Can we further exploit them? Do we sufficiently understand them?

- What is our potential as an organization? Where can we be five, ten, twenty years from now?

- If I could rewrite the history of my own achievements or of those of our industry, our organization, or our people, what would I change?

- Why have we succeeded in the past? Do I really understand the nature of and reasons for those successes?

- Why have we failed in the past? Do I really understand the reasons for those setbacks?

Reach a state of rest, then place your question on the mind's screen. Since you are now considering something more complex and less tangible than an apple (as discussed in Chapter 5), you will tap more than your senses, concentrating on all the knowledge and experience that relates to the question.

It's important to keep your meditation as nonjudgmental as possible. At this stage of vision-shaping, you want to bring all your hidden knowledge and experience to a conscious level where it will increase your depth of understanding. Don't evaluate, criticize, or try to make important decisions yet. Keep your past feelings out of the picture by pretending you have been asked to objectively answer the question as an outside observer rather than as a leader enmeshed in all the daily crises of your business.

Look for handles, firmly grasping any new thought or feeling that excites or stirs you. Be alert for key words, phrases, ideas, metaphors, images, and symbols. Whatever absorbs your attention, label it, so you can get a firmer grip on it. Imagine you're assembling a five-hundred-piece jigsaw puzzle. As you identify and label a piece, try to fit it together with other pieces until a clearer picture gradually emerges. For example, one executive at this stage in the meditation process felt a new idea about the distinctive competence of his organization arise out of his attempt to get a handle on what had brought his company its initial success. In the past he had always assumed the employees' advanced computer science training had formed the core of the company's innovative software, but as he reviewed early accomplishments, he began to see another pattern emerge. Yes, he had hired the brightest young engineers but it was their youthful *exuberance* more than their technical training that had sparked important breakthroughs. How could he maintain that "we can do anything" spirit as the young engineers got older?

Continue asking yourself questions about the handle. Where did it come from? What other new insights relate to it? What caused it? Where is it going? Does it represent a danger or an opportunity? But how do you know when you've exhausted each angle? As with the apple, you should come to a point where the exercise bores you or even frustrates you. Move on, keeping stress and anxiety at bay. If you think you are experiencing a breakthrough, don't abandon the exercise until you've been able to state it simply and eloquently.

Three years ago our software company executive had replaced the firm's slogan, "We Can Do Anything" with one he thought better typified his vision: "The Technical Edge." Had that been a mistake? As he mulled over phrases that might recapture the old vision in fresh language, he considered "Think Young," but then he realized that the phrase might offend some older employees. Then it struck him: "Outrageous Thinking." He might have to fine-tune it, but it did express what he wanted from his people.

Let the deeper understanding wash over you. After you count yourself back up from one to seven, consider in what ways, if any, your deeper understanding should help shape your vision. A week after his meditation, the software executive pinned a button to his jacket: "Outrageous Thinking Keeps Us Ahead." Soon, the slogan fired up even the senior staff, who seemed to enjoy this new call to youthful exuberance.

Clear visions take time to develop; they don't come after a few meditations, and they often start out fuzzy, only later resolving into clear pictures. Tom Watson's vision for IBM developed over several years before it culminated in his decision to bet the company's future on the System/360 computer. Harry Gray kept quiet for two years at United Technologies before unveiling his new vision.

Donald Burr, CEO of People Express, fell in love with both airplanes and business as a young boy. Later, after graduating from the Harvard Business School, Burr went to work for an investment company that specialized in airline and aerospace securities and venture capital. After years of thinking about the best way to run an airline and gaining some practical experience as chief operating officer at Texas International, Burr decided to make his dream of a different kind of airline come true. Together with two associates, Burr liquidated his personal assets to incorporate People Express. Today the company reports six-month revenues of $116 million and net income of $6.3 million, while many of its competitors are fleeing into bankruptcy. Unlike its rivals, People Express provides stock to everyone in the organization, thereby avoiding the usual barriers between owners and employees, and its low-fare package has given the airline the industry's best seat utilization and load factors, as well as the lowest operating expenses per available seat. How did Burr, Gray and Watson do it? After painstaking evaluation, they built strong scenarios.

Step Three: Scenario Building

Once you have meditated on the crucial questions about your organization and its environment, you can take the next important step, mentally creating the future before you create it physically. At some point during your meditations, you will leave the world of introspection for the world of *projection*. Because projection provides a means for testing your vision before you fully commit your company to it, it begins even before a fuzzy vision resolves into a clear picture. Obviously, the more mistakes you can avoid during testing, the better your chances for ultimate success. Mentally creating the future through scenario building clarifies initial fuzziness and minimizes costly trial and error.

Don't confuse scenario building with planning. We abhor over-analyzing or overplanning because our experience with hundreds of companies has convinced us that an "action orientation" and "experiment with it" attitude gets quicker and more lasting results than the time-consuming and too often artificial "analyze it and plan it first" orientation. Xerox is a case in point. It devoted millions of dollars and years of effort to the development of a personal computer. It hired many of the most brilliant minds, people who would eventually make microcomputer technology possible. Why couldn't Xerox make the breakthrough? Overplanning and overanalysis. According to Alan Kay, Xerox's former director of research now at Apple, Xerox had a sure-fire micro product ready long before Steven Jobs and Steve Wozniak started to shave, but unlike the Apple Computer founders, who waged a "quick-and-dirty" war, Xerox got bogged down planning the Invasion of Normandy.

Scenario building is a creative thinking process; there are four key stages in its development.

Four Stages of Scenario Building

- Defining the Vision. A thorough yet simple description of the vision, including its philosophy, strategic direction, and cultural values.

- Determining Opportunities and Dangers. A careful identification and quantification of all the positive and negative potential outcomes of the new vision, including analysis of the best and worst possibilities.

- Listing Key Success Factors. A thorough evaluation of all the factors involved in implementing the new vision, with special emphasis on a handful of key factors that will ultimately determine success or failure. Such factors include people, money, resources, and expertise.

- Sequencing Major Events. A logical progression of milestones that should occur during vision implementation and the likely impact any one event will have on other events.

Let's observe how a fictional CEO, John Derrick, president of a diversified company on the West Coast, goes through these four stages. Derrick's company exceeded $500 million in sales last year and netted $18 million in profits from table-top laminate manufacturing, leasing and rental property, commercial real estate development, glass contracting, banking, and computer retailing. Over the past two years, John has sought a way to pull these diverse operations together under some kind of conceptual or philosophical umbrella that would allow the company to take advantage of synergies, shared resources, and a common corporate culture. After months of soul-searching meditation, he developed the following scenario to test his developing vision:

- *Defining the Vision.* Each of the divisions in our company offers superior service, which allows us to gain competitive advantage. In our strictly service-oriented businesses, such as banking and leasing and rental, service has always won satisfied customers, but it has also distinguished us from our competitors in the laminate, glass, development, and computer businesses. My vision? A service-minded corporation, with each unit providing exceptional service profitably. Superior service would become our motto, our philosophy, our vision, facilitating synergy among units, making it possible to share resources, and providing a strong foundation for a common corporate culture.

- *Determining Opportunities and Dangers.* The upside? Increased competitive advantage and profit margins. We would increase market share from 10 percent to 50 percent in each of our businesses over the next three years, resulting in increased sales of $100 million to $300 million. Most of our units could attain increased margins because their improved services would return much more than they cost. Increased profit margins could reach as much as $10 million, but no less than $3 million.

  The downside? Increased costs of communication, training, and advertising, which could be $1 million to $3 million over a three-year period. If the vision proves ineffective, the biggest downside will be wasted time and opportunity. We could lose three years at a minimum, costing the company lost sales of potentially $300 million, with lost profits of $10 million. Can we quantify the cost of lost opportunity?

It could run as high as $500 million, especially if we forego other growth opportunities in the process.

- *Listing Key Success Factors.* The key factors that will determine success are, in order of decreasing priority: 1) motivating employees to deliver superior service; 2) persuading customers of the value of our superior service (allowing us to command higher prices); 3) setting superior service standards in each of the businesses. First, we must imbue all employees with a deep and continuing commitment to our goal. Second, we must package and deliver our superior service in such a way that we convince our customers to pay for it. And third, we must establish the highest possible service levels without eroding our profitability targets.

- *Sequencing Major Events.* Implementing the vision involves five steps which do not necessarily need to be implemented in this order: 1) target which customer segments want higher levels of service; 2) set levels of service for each of the businesses; 3) establish an informal contract with the employees to get them fired up; 4) implement an internal and external advertising program communicating our commitment; 5) measure customer reaction and continue tracking it. Because milestone 3, motivating employees, has the most impact on the others and will take time to accomplish, we'll start there and monitor the situation closely. We can hold off on numbers 1, 2, 4, and 5 until we see how our people respond, then proceed in numerical order.

I don't expect this vision to be fully implemented for three years. I'm prepared for that. The cost is acceptable, even if the actual business expenses (not including opportunity cost) triple my estimate. I see the risk as relatively small because our businesses are already using service to compete and distinguish themselves. Revising the vision will most likely occur as we monitor our people's ability to embrace the vision and our customers' response to our new service levels. As things progress we can consider what kinds of revisions to make.

Remember, scenario building increases the probability of your vision's success, so be sure you account for every possible opportunity or danger. Only then will you really learn something from mentally "test-driving" your visions.

To help you judge the effectiveness and usefulness of your own scenarios, take our Scenario Effectiveness Test. If you can answer "yes" to each of the following questions, your scenario will probably work.

Scenario Effectiveness Test

1. Does the definition of your vision make sense to a person unfamiliar with your company and industry? (One executive we know tests his definitions on his fourteen-year-old daughter.)

2. Have you identified all of the potential benefits and liabilities associated with your vision? Be sure you include both tangible and intangible opportunities and dangers. Studying case histories of failed companies can reveal dangers you may have overlooked.

3. Have you quantified each opportunity and danger? Attach a dollar value to even the most intangible danger, such as bad reputation.

4. Does your scenario identify every key factor that will determine success or failure? Include less obvious psychological and environmental factors. Even the weather can affect the implementation of a vision.

5. Have you arranged the key success factors in order of decreasing priority? Be sure you can explain how each relates to the others.

6. Have you properly sequenced all major events? Sometimes less critical events occur early, and in some cases events can take place concurrently.

7. Do you understand the impact each major event will have on every other event? You should be able to describe

how changes in one event will affect each of the other events.

8. Have you weighed all the risks and costs of carrying out your company's vision, allowing for the unthinkable worst case?

9. Does your scenario accommodate change? A good scenario contains specific plans for evolving conditions and determines at which points change is most likely to occur.

10. Can You commit your scenario to paper for future review and development? (Some executives like to enhance their scenarios with computer graphics.)

If your scenario passes this test, you are well on your way toward formulating the kind of vision that catapults companies into the ranks of the best-run corporations of the world. Like meditation, scenario building should become a continuing habit. Before long, you'll begin to think in scenarios, and your scenarios will make you a creator, rather than a victim, of the future.

The Challenge of Vision: A Summary

Vision is not just one of the six New Age skills, it is the pivotal skill, providing a bridge between your strategy-culture alloy and the changes which that alloy will bring to your organization's future. The scenarios you build with vision help put your future in focus, allowing you to convert potential dangers into opportunities.

Visionary executives not only position their organizations to make the most of impending changes, they attempt to influence those changes by causing rather than merely reacting to them. Executives who lack vision are doomed to suffer a future they had little influence in creating, while their visionary counterparts will capitalize on change with versatility and focus.

• CHAPTER 8 •

Versatility: Anticipating Change

By involving itself in a diversified, complicated and demanding environment, a company hastens the development of knowledge within itself and increases the likelihood that it will be able to adapt to a variety of situations.
—RICHARD NORMANN

In every economy...there is one crucial and definitive conflict...the struggle between past and future, between the existing configuration of industries and the industries that will someday replace them.
—GEORGE GILDER

Versatility Converts Threats into Opportunities

It took thousands of years of technical progress and the combined commitment of hundreds of brilliant scientists to unleash the power of the atom, yet in thirty short years we have built enough nuclear weapons to destroy the world many times over. In 1946 the first computer, ENIAC, weighed thirty tons, towered two stories high, and covered fifteen thousand square feet, yet today, a Radio Shack TRS-80, which fits inside a suitcase, can add and subtract twenty times faster than ENIAC. Tandy didn't ship its first TRS-80 until 1978, one year after Apple Computer was incorporated, but together the two firms have shipped over two million machines, more than IBM has ever shipped.

At the turn of the century one would have seen hundreds of textile factories crowding the shores of New England's Merrimack River, but the smokestacks have now given way to the steel and glass headquarters of Wang Laboratories, Digital Equipment Corp., and dozens of booming high-tech companies. On the other side of the continent, bulldozers have pushed aside the orchards of the Santa Clara Valley to make room for Intel, Apple, Memorex, Fairchild, and IBM. From Massachusetts to California, our entire landscape has changed dramatically.

Few of the largest and most successful firms of fifty years ago still depend on, or are even still involved in, their original lines of business. Thirty years ago IBM made typewriters and calculators. Union Pacific Corp., once concerned only with the operation of railroads, now derives half its income from minerals development, oil, and gas. Oil companies make textiles, textile manufacturers distribute pharmaceuticals, and toymakers sell computers.

Change. No other single word so completely captures the essence of contemporary society and its enterprises, and no other characteristic of the New Age poses more demanding problems for executives. Tried-and-true approaches no longer work against the force of accelerated change. Technical innovations, global communications, and fierce competition can bring changes overnight that once took decades or even centuries to manifest themselves. Product and service life cycles have grown dramatically shorter because, according to a *Fortune* article, rapid technological change plus easy credit, mass communications, and advertising have put business on a rollercoaster. As never before, corporate and executive success, even survival, depends on an ability to control the ride.

New Age executives take advantage of accelerated change with versatility and focus. They use versatility to anticipate change, focus to successfully implement it. If the foundation skills (creative insight and sensitivity) help you lay the groundwork for excellence, the adaptive skills (versatility and focus) help you make the changes required for maintaining it.

By versatility we mean the capacity to embrace and participate in an ever changing world. That may sound obvious and easy to accomplish, but most people resist change because any major change, from a marriage to a new job, brings with it new conditions, adapting to which takes time and energy. Since we almost instinctively react to change as a threat rather than an opportunity, we cannot learn to master it unless we learn to welcome rather than fear it. You must help evoke and control change rather than simply suffer through it. To better anticipate changes, versatile executives seize opportunities to incorporate change into their personal and professional lifestyles. Unfortunately, it's easy to fall into accustomed habits, reacting to new situations with previously successful responses. But only when you change a habit can you begin experiencing the world with a fresh perspective, the sort of outlook that spots a trend, foretells an innovation, or anticipates shifts in consumer behavior, competitor strategies, products, and opportunities. If you become intimately aware of change in one aspect of life, you automatically become more acutely aware of impending changes in other areas. By creating change at one level, you can better control it at all levels.

Versatile Robert Smith, executive vice-president of Security Pacific National Bank, pioneered his firm's move into the discount brokerage business. Smith not only anticipated the changes rushing toward the banking industry on the heels of deregulation and diversification, he poised his company to take advantage of the inevitable opportunities. Although banks cannot (yet) underwrite securities or buy and sell from their own portfolios, they can use their trust departments to buy and sell securities for their customers and offer them investment advice. Smith set up the first bank-based discount brokerage service at commission rates lower than those available from the big retail brokerage firms by forming a partnership with Fidelity Brokerage Services of Boston. As the strategy grew increasingly successful, Security Pacific established its own national brokerage system and wound up selling its services to other banks around the country. Interestingly, Security's wholesale service to other banks is twice as profitable as retail banking. If Smith is right when he predicts that five-thousand other banks will eventually be buying his bank's innovative service, he will have put his organization in a perfect position to dominate the market niche. Does versatility affect the bottom line? You bet it does. Security Pacific enjoys a 17 percent return on equity while the rest of the industry gets only 13 percent.

Versatility has put another bank, Norwest, on the frontier of nontraditional financial services. After fire destroyed Northwest Bank Corporation headquarters in Minneapolis in 1982, the nation's eighteenth-largest bank ($20 billion in assets) began moving in new directions. With their headquarters in ashes, CEO John Morrison and executive vice-president David Jarvis decided to convert their catastrophe into an opportunity by aggressively establishing a national presence in a few key areas. What less versatile executives might have treated as a threat to their company's existence, Morrison and Jarvis saw as an opportunity to create excellence. They changed the company's name to Norwest, acquired Dial Finance's thirty-eight-state network, and started Residential Funding Corporation to buy, repackage, and sell home mortgages as negotiable securities. The new Norwest broke from fifty-five years of traditional banking and positioned itself with over seven hundred financial offices in forty-three states. When deregulation allows interstate banking, it's poised to dominate its industry. Operating earnings from Norwest's consumer finance activities grew by forty-three percent to $53 million in 1983, making the company one of the leading consumer finance organizations in the country, and it increased its mortgages by 66 percent to $12.1 billion in 1983, firmly establishing it as America's largest mortgage banking concern. While net income jumped 40 percent to $125 million in 1983, earnings dipped in 1984 as a consequence of the company's costly expansion, but according to a managing director of Salomon Brothers in a recent interview with *BusinessWeek*, "By being in front, they've [Norwest] been able to grow exponentially." That growth should improve the bottom line in the years to come.

Without Versatility, Response to Change Is Too Slow, Too Late

Toshiba Corporation, the Japanese electrical equipment maker, has had trouble adapting to change in the early 1980s. Once an aggressive innovator that produced Japan's first washing machine, light bulb, and transistor radio, the company grew lethargic and unresponsive, unable to take advantage of high-tech opportunities and letting competitors assume its preeminent position at home and abroad.

As with so many other traits of excellent organizations, versatility begins in the executive suite. Although Toshiba's new CEO, Shoichi Saba, seems to grasp the problem, he faces a huge struggle to solve it because late response to change has become so deeply ingrained in the company's culture. Despite the fact that Toshiba introduced Japan's first word processor, it quickly lost its market share to Fujitsu's better, cheaper model, and its line of Beta rather than VHS video cassette recorders has put the company out of step with current trends. Finally, whereas other Japanese companies have long recognized the need to develop joint ventures with foreign companies to reach specialized foreign markets, Toshiba is just now working on its first joint medical electronics research venture with U.S. hospitals.

In our own country, Chase Manhattan Bank has also adapted too slowly to changes in its industry and markets. By not taking advantage of opportunities to acquire existing banks in states where Chase was not already operating, it has fallen behind its rivals in consumer banking. Its "day late, dollar short" attitude caused it to fumble in Florida. When Biscayne Federal Savings and Loan, a failing thrift, became available for acquisition late in 1983, Chase made a bid, but the bid expired when Biscayne's net worth fell below a level set by the court. Chase failed to submit its second bid before Citicorp beat Chase to it. Why did

Chase react so slowly? Observers blamed reluctance and hesitancy.

With differentiation and diversification running rampant in
the banking industry, has Chase made any innovative efforts
to keep up with its competitors? Unfortunately, with its Drysdale and Penn Square fiascos, Chase displayed a marked inability to manage diverse operations. Penn Square cast a shadow
on the bank when energy-related loan activities originating in
one department were not checked by petroleum experts in another, causing Chase to swallow $232 million in loan losses when
Penn Square went under. Since Chase's treasury experts did
not get involved with Drysdale, Chase ended up with staggering
and unnecessary liabilities. When a company like Chase fails to
capitalize on rollercoaster changes in an industry like banking,
a lack of versatility usually lies at the core of the problem.

Versatility Ingrains Adaptability

Resistance to change can become as ingrained a habit as that
baggy old sweater you wear until it disintegrates. Fortunately,
you can assume a welcoming stance to the new and as yet untried. Once you've learned to welcome change, adapting to it
becomes a lot easier than resisting it.

We've relied heavily on banks for examples in this chapter
because, unlike the high-tech fields where innovation and change
are a way of life, banking is an old traditional industry that has
only recently undergone tremendous changes. Among banks,
Citicorp shines as one of the best-run companies in the country
and, not coincidentally, this biggest and best of banks ($142
billion in assets and net income of $860 million, twice that of
any other U.S. bank holding company) is also the most adapt-
able, innovative, and versatile. How has Citicorp achieved such
success? By ingraining versatility in workers at all levels within
the organization, establishing a continuing track record of innovations. Its rivals fear and respect it in much the same way
IBM's competitors fear and respect Big Blue. Citicorp's striking

innovations include negotiable certificates of deposit developed in the 1960s, 550 automated teller machines blanketing New York City, and industrial banks, savings and loans, and consumer finance operations throughout the United States that skirt interstate banking laws. Citicorp issues the most bank credit cards, and it is the world's largest private lender to foreign countries. But it does not rest on past accomplishments. At Citicorp, experimentation is a way of life, plunging the company into more unusual financial services than any other bank and putting it in an ideal position to exploit deregulation. When *The Wall Street Journal* asked Richard Braddock, a Citicorp executive vice-president, to explain why Citicorp enjoys such a dominant position, he said, "Having a lot of activity going on, and learning from it, is the best [thing] we can do." A lot of diverse action—that's versatility. Heightened activity always enhances adaptation. Poking a little fun at his former employer, one ex-Citicorp executive characterized the company's attitude as "Ready, fire, aim" rather than "Ready, aim, fire." How does Citicorp ingrain an action orientation in its executives and managers? For one thing, when an employee makes an understandable mistake, the company doesn't fire that person, provided the mistake involved versatility, innovation, or adaptation. You can't be both versatile and mistake-free because accelerated activity in many new and different areas inevitably leads to mistakes. That's when most learning occurs. People within versatile organizations learn more than people in organizations that cling to tradition and resist change.

We are barely beginning to comprehend the importance of versatility in helping us anticipate and adapt to changing environments. In his landmark research, Robert Miles of the Harvard Business School studied the effects of diversification in six companies over several years. While many companies have historically used diversification to enhance mature or declining business operations, invest excess cash, and spread financial risk over operations with different business cycles, Miles's research showed that diversification also helps organizations grow and learn. Miles asserts that companies that diversify learn as much about themselves, their strengths, weaknesses, resources, and competences, as they do about the new business, because diversifying creates an environment in which executives and their organizations have no choice but to anticipate and adapt to change. Diversification forces them to be more versatile and consequently improve their overall responsiveness to internal and external forces. In his book *Coffin Nails and Corporate Strategies*, Miles concludes that "strategies of diversification and globalization" have helped such companies as Philip Morris, R. J. Reynolds, American Brands, Liggett & Myers, and Lorillard adapt successfully. But isn't there a danger of over-diversification? Shouldn't you stick to what you know best? The answers to those questions are not simple. A 1984 *Fortune* comparison between conglomerates and nondiversified industrial companies in the Fortune 500 revealed that conglomerates outperformed nondiversified companies in 1981, 1982, and 1983. In 1982, for example, conglomerates achieved a 13 percent return on equity, while nondiversified companies achieved only 11 percent. Sticking to what you know best may be sound advice to a firm operating in a relatively stable environment, but in a world of accelerated change, survival may depend on learning to do something other than what you know best. Will the acceleration slow down or will it continue to gain momentum? You don't need a crystal ball to predict that we'll see more change by the year 2000 than we've seen during the past fifty years. To cope with these changes you'll need superhuman versatility, but how do you acquire it?

How to Become a Versatile Executive

Obviously, before you can use versatility to create excellence, you have to be able to see it in yourself and others, and you must be able to distinguish genuine versatility in a company from an array of undirected activity.

Step One: Recognizing Versatility

To put this skill in perspective, let's again consider what happens when a company lacks it. Digital Equipment Corp.'s lack of versatility blinded it to change in the computer industry. In 1960, DEC introduced the minicomputer to the world and shortly became the world's second largest computer manufacturer, behind IBM, filling a gap between little micros and huge mainframes. But despite its stunning rise to $5 billion in annual sales, the company lost numerous key executives after a sweeping reorganization, and DEC's unflagging commitment to the once innovative minicomputer caused it to miscalculate its entry into personal computers with overly fancy, overpriced machines. Profit margins dropped 37 percent, and DEC stock sank to half its former price. How could that happen to a company built on anticipation of change in a volatile industry? DEC simply didn't anticipate that lower-priced mainframes and more powerful inexpensive micros would squeeze the middle of the market. Like most organizations suffering a lack of versatility, DEC failed to see change coming, reacted slowly to it, and ultimately made a blundering response. These three danger signals should alert executives that their organizations are insufficiently anticipating change. Perhaps DEC has learned a lesson, because it is now positioning itself as the "systems" company, emphasizing its competence to link many machines into large networks, an apparent anticipation of a hot new trend.

A flurry of recent articles has touted high-output management, high-speed management, high-tech management, and other supposedly newfangled techniques for adapting to the New Age. A *Fortune* article claimed that executives facing market turbulence are learning vital lessons:

- To think constantly about new products.
- To back new product thinking with prompt investment.
- To stay close to the customer.
- To keep up with competitors' investments and costs.

- To more closely coordinate product design, manufacturing, and marketing.
- To move quickly.

These six lessons may offer clues to recognizing versatility, but we would add that versatile executives regularly and consistently:

- Develop and try new ideas, products, approaches and methods, never allowing complacency or inflexibility to settle in.
- Monitor the environment with acute attention to detail, quickly and thoroughly studying anything that might signal a trend or a change in customer or competitor behavior.
- Get into the habit of moving boldly but in a coordinated, orderly fashion, seizing opportunities with discipline.

In his book *The Leader*, Michael Maccoby articulates the development of a new "self-development or self-oriented" character in our society. Maccoby suggests that leadership by this new character can become the basis of a new society, one that fosters productive adaptation to a rapidly evolving world. The "new" self-oriented person says: "I can contribute more, if they listen to my ideas, if I am treated as an individual, neither as a child nor a machine, and the rewards are fair. Otherwise, I'll look out for myself." Clearly, this new character has two sides, one positive and one negative. The positive side includes:

- A flexible, experimental, and tolerant attitude.
- An interest in self-development, playfulness.
- A sense of fairness and a participative orientation.

The negative side includes:

- Self-centeredness, detachment from others.
- A self-indulgent, demanding attitude.

- Rebelliousness and manipulativeness.

If New Age executives can ingrain the positive traits in themselves and their people, at the same time minimizing the negative ones, they will be able to cultivate the new character. An assessment of the positive or negative new character traits in individuals and groups can help executives recognize versatility. If the negative traits outweigh the positive, versatility does not exist, but if the positive ones outweigh the negative, it does. The ratio between the two indicates how much need there is for improvement. To see how this works, consider the following situation. An executive orders an employee, who has been working within a six-member task force, to deliver a summary presentation to senior management, bringing it up to date on current progress and results. A person with the positive traits would enthusiastically accept the assignment, then immediately call the other five task force members together to discuss the best way to make the presentation. Everyone would freely discuss different approaches and decide as a group on the best one. All six members would prepare the content of the presentation. As new ideas came forth during the preparation, everyone would have a chance to react to them. It could be a deeply satisfying, shared experience, with the person designated as the spokesperson giving credit to colleagues during the presentation and sharing the experience with everyone afterwards.

By contrast, a person with the negative traits might enthusiastically accept the assignment, then retreat to a private office to determine how best to exploit this opportunity for personal advantage. To retain all the possible glory, he or she would not involve the other members of the task force. What an opportunity to shine in the eyes of management! No credit would be given to others during the presentation, and afterwards the spokesperson would keep details of the meeting as secret as possible.

You can also recognize a versatile executive by measuring whether or not he or she uses "adhocracy," a term first popularized by Warren Bennis in *The Temporary Society* and Alvin

Toffler in *Future Shock*, then later clarified in Peters and Waterman's *In Search of Excellence*: "By adhocracy [we] mean organizational mechanisms that deal with all the new issues that
either fall between bureaucratic cracks or span so many levels
in the bureaucracy that it's not clear who should do what; consequently, nobody does anything." In an atmosphere of adhocracy, bureaucratic red tape never delays seizure of
opportunities. Consider the new, revitalized Coca-Cola Company, which adopted adhocracy as a way of life. Five years ago,
Coke sat by complacently as Pepsi took bigger and bigger bites
out of its market share, but not today. Demonstrating its new
commitment to adhocracy, Coke recently launched a price war
to combat Pepsi's increasing market share, then it followed up
by introducing four new drinks in less than a year. On the other
hand, Seven-Up has still not discovered the secret of adhocracy. Problems have plagued Seven-Up for several years, and
its recent lackluster introduction of Like, a new cola drink,
indicates that more than sales are slipping through the cracks.
The versatile executive makes sure that sort of thing doesn't
happen.

Assuming you can now recognize it when you see it, you are
ready to evaluate your present level of versatility. If, after ad-
ministering this self-examination, you score above 30, you probably display a high degree of versatility, but if you score below
that, you should undertake a disciplined program for improvement.

EXECUTIVE VERSATILITY SELF-EXAMINATION

		ALWAYS	OFTEN	SELDOM	NEVER
1.	You see things coming and don't get blind-sided.	4	3	2	1
2.	You act on new developments rather than solely react to the actions of others.	4	3	2	1

3.	If your actions result in errors, they're minor, not major, ones.	4	3	2	1
4.	You initiate and try new products, approaches, and ideas.	4	3	2	1
5.	You monitor your organization's environment closely, paying attention to important events, issues, and conditions.	4	3	2	1
6.	You get your people in the habit of moving quickly on new plans in a coordinated fashion.	4	3	2	1
7.	You are flexible, experimental, and tolerant when people don't do things the way you would do them.	4	3	2	1
8.	You approach learning as self-development and seek adventure and enriched experiences.	4	3	2	1
9.	You are fair and participate in dealing with the new ideas and suggestions from others.	4	3	2	1
10.	You practice "adhocracy," the art of keeping things from falling between bureaucratic cracks.	4	3	2	1

Walter Wriston, chairman and CEO of Citicorp, scores a perfect 40. An aspiring executive could get a PhD in versatility under Wriston. According to Levering, Moskowitz, and Katz in their book *The 100 Best Companies to Work for in America,* Citicorp attracts a distinct breed: people who relish action, thrive on competition, and love pressure. Stuffy banker types need not apply. Obsessed with changing the nature of banking, Citicorp prefers people who thrive "in the eye of the hurricane." It all comes from Wriston himself, who has created an organizational environment in which people behave with versatility or get out. One of his most versatile protégés is John Reed, whom Wriston handpicked as his successor at Citicorp. Reed displays the innovative and risk-taking style Wriston has inculcated in his organization, and he will undoubtedly continue his mentor's tradition. Wriston's flexible organization offers abundant opportunities to move around and create special niches. Wriston likes it that way, telling prospective employees, "Each new job I've accepted (except for the one I now hold) didn't exist before I took it." A virtuoso of versatility!

Step Two: Pursuing Varied Activities

No one can acquire genuine versatility without regularly pursuing a variety of activities at both the personal and professional level. It's as much an attitude as a skill. If you don't weave varied activities into all levels of your life, you will never be able to anticipate and adapt to change. Executive Jack Baird, based on an actual entrepreneur, founded and ran a highly successful chain of computer stores. In a cutthroat competitive arena, Baird has managed to outdistance his competitors and establish a solid market position. In 1983 his company grew from twelve to forty-two stores, racking up sales of $35 million, profits of $2.7 million. In 1984 he expects the company to double sales and increase profits to $8.4 million. To what does he attribute his success? "I'm restless, always involved in some new escapade. I've recently mastered scuba diving and have taken up computer-assisted graphics as a hobby. It prepares me for the crazy market I'm in. I never know what to expect next, but 90 percent of the time I respond faster and better than my competitors because flexibility and change are part of my everyday life." To accomplish this, Jack Baird follows three simple rules we recommend to all executives seeking greater versatility:

Three Rules for Making Varied Activities
Part of Your Everyday Life

- Never allow more than thirty days to slip by without pursuing a major new personal or professional activity. These can range from hobbies not directly related to your work, such as skydiving and fly-fishing, to more professional undertakings such as developing a new marketing strategy, designing an innovative format for staff meetings, conducting an introspective management retreat, or formulating a new compensation plan. Executives too busy for new hobbies are too busy to learn, and people who stop learning about themselves stop learning about their businesses. Versatile executives gain valuable insights when their minds are busy learning chess or their bodies are busy mastering the balance required by skiing.

- Drop at least one old, worn-out activity every thirty days. An old, worn-out activity is one that has become an unquestioned habit after six months or so. If you've been playing racquetball every Thursday evening, spend next Thursday learning to paint landscapes. If you've been preoccupied for nine months with staff reorganization, turn your attention to new products.

- Avoid adding new activities that are similar or related to old ones. If you've pursued a new marketing strategy one month, you can't count a new advertising campaign as a new activity the next month. Build twelve-month cycles between related activities. Don't switch from racquetball to tennis but to something as daringly difficult as road racing or wood sculpture. Move from personnel to product innovation, from marketing to finance.

Observe how Baird applied these rules during the last three months:

- In February, he took up scuba diving during a week's business trip to Hawaii. In three days, he qualified as a certified scuba diver; then he arranged for two future scuba diving trips in April and June.

• In March, he instituted a new competitor-monitoring system that involved visiting his chain's competitors in five different markets, followed by meetings with his own people during which he shared what he had observed. He also held the first of a series of monthly management training sessions aimed at imparting his skills to new store managers.

• In April, he and his fifteen-year-old son began developing software for graphics designers after his son, a gifted artist, had opened up to him the exciting possibility of computer-assisted graphics design for home computer users. What began as a hobby could well become a handsome business opportunity. Both father and son grew closer as they worked shoulder to shoulder at the terminal, and they agreed to spend one day each weekend for six months developing a new product for which the son would obtain a copyright.

During this same three-month period, Baird dropped three major activities:

• In February, he eliminated weekly staff meetings with the chain store managers. The meetings had become rigid and formal, seldom solving problems or airing new issues. In their place, he designed one-on-one meetings designed partly to address a manager's specific individual needs, partly to allow him to get closer to his managers on a personal level. Every other week the meeting was held away from the office at some place where the two could both work and play.

• In March, he dropped his membership in the local Rotary Club. While the membership had been valuable at one time, it had become a burden, so Baird decided not to attend for mere appearance's sake. Instead he resolved to join the Big Brother program in a nearby community where he planned to increase his chain's penetration.

• In April, Baird dropped a line of computer products. It was a difficult decision, but he felt the company's focus had diffused across too many product lines. The manufacturer tried desperately to change his mind, but Baird held firm. Had he not been a versatile executive, he might have caved in to pleadings that did not promote his own long-range strategy.

New activities form an integral part of a New Age executive's life. Now that you understand how varied activities provide the right attitude from which to approach change, you are ready to find out how to preview change in a way that will make you seem clairvoyant.

Step Three: Previewing Change

This final step enables you to predict impending change and thereby prepare yourself and your organization to adapt to it. Anticipating change requires that you see change coming, before you begin planning and discussing alternative scenarios for adapting to it. Remember, you want to condition yourself for change so you can begin to create and control it rather than simply succumb to it.

We've designed a simple but effective methodology based on the assumption that all changes exhibit a similar life cycle with identifiable phases and different rates and magnitudes of change. The rate and magnitude of change in a typical life cycle of change is represented by a bell-shaped curve, beginning slowly with seemingly minor events, accelerating with more critical events, peaking with major events, decelerating with smaller events, and eventually leveling off.

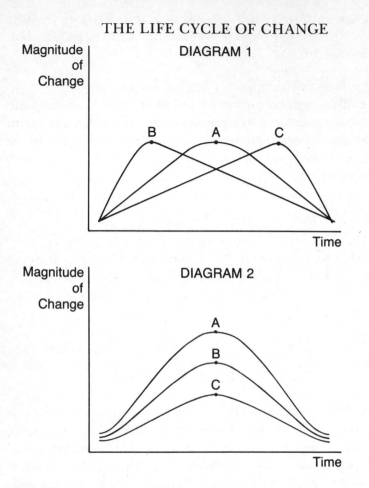

THE LIFE CYCLE OF CHANGE

As indicated in the two diagrams, once change begins, it accelerates, peaks, and declines. The rate of a change is depicted by plotting the curve toward the point at which it peaks, its magnitude by the height of the curve. While most change cycles follow a uniform bell shape, some exhibit variations of it. In Diagram 1 the B variation displays a change that happens like wildfire, while the C variation shows one that takes longer to build toward climax.

A normal change, like the one marked A in Diagram 1, occurred in the restaurant industry. Change began slowly in the 1960s as fast-food outlets, usually single location or small chains, cropped up across the country. Change accelerated and peaked during the 1970s with the firm establishment of companies like McDonald's. The 1980s have brought a deceleration of change.

A fast change, like curve B, occurred in the airline industry when deregulation brought about immediate change.

A slow change, like curve C, occurred in the automobile industry as smaller cars began entering the United States in the 1950s, and accelerated markedly only when the oil crisis hit in 1973.

In Diagram 2, we see three different magnitudes of change. A major change, like the one marked A, is currently occurring in the banking industry. Right now, change in the banking industry is still accelerating and has yet to reach its peak.

A medium change, like the one marked B, occurred in the computer industry when the minicomputer came on strong in the 1970s. Most would agree, however, that the microcomputer is turning out to be a major change for the industry.

A minor change, like the one marked C, occurred in the food retailing industry during the late 1970s, when new technology made improved pricing, inventorying, and checkout practices possible.

Regardless of the form a change takes, the trick lies in spotting slow, minor developments in the beginning of a change's life cycle, then using knowledge of them to predict or anticipate faster, larger changes as the life cycle inevitably peaks. The process involves six steps:

Six Steps for Previewing Change

- Set the boundaries of the change you want to observe, whether it be in a market, a product category, an industry, a group of competitors, one competitor, a customer segment, etc. For example, if you were concerned with new products entering the marketplace, you would set boundaries around the type of product you want to observe, and then look only at the changes relative to new product offerings. Tangential information will come to your attention, but don't get sidetracked—go back to it later.

- Identify every manifestation of change within the boundaries you have defined. Make a list of every change you see, especially small fluctuations that you may not have paid attention to before. For example, if you are observing competitor strategy changes, you need to look for all possible indications of a change in strategy—new distribution arrangements, new products, new advertising campaigns, new sales policies, etc.—anything that might suggest a change in your competitor's strategy.

- Group and label the changes you have observed, looking for relationships among them. Once you have established connections, define the nature of the change in each group as specifically as possible. For example, if you are observing changes in technology in your industry, you may find that several changes relate to new product design or features, while others relate to how the products are being produced and still others to how technology in other industries is affecting the use of your own industry's products. In other words, you will have identified three groupings of technological change: product enhancements, production process improvements, and advances in companion or auxiliary products.

- Determine the underlying cause of the change in each group. Since changes first reveal themselves through symptoms, dig beneath the surface for underlying causes. This step requires the meditation principles from Chapter 5. For example, if you are observing changes in customer buying habits, you may have identified one group of changes which indicate that customers are making quicker decisions to buy your product. As you study the data, looking for the underlying cause of the change in customer behavior, you may detect that greater customer familiarity with and acceptance of your product has shortened the decision time. This underlying cause could dictate how you will add to and promote your product line.

- Mark each of the causes of change you identify on the appropriate "life cycle of change curve." Be on the lookout for changes that are lesser or greater than their symptoms at first make them appear. For example, if you are observing the proliferation of new businesses entering your industry and have identified one of the causes as decreasing production costs, you may then determine that production costs will most likely continue their decline from half of what they once were to three fourths of what they are now. As a result you may place the change at the top of the curve, indicating that changes will continue, but at an ever decreasing rate and magnitude.

- Study the causes of change as indicators of further change. Pay close attention to causes that lie toward the beginning of the change life cycle. Project existing changes into the future by building the sort of scenario you learned to construct in Chapter 7. For example, if you are observing changes in raw material costs and determine that one of the causes, dwindling finite natural resources, has just begun, you will probably conclude that you'll see accelerating changes involving conservation, alternative raw materials, and synthetic substitutes. Your conclusion will help you place yourself in an ideal position to convert the danger into an opportunity.

Previewing change does not provide a crystal ball for peering into the future, but it does help you anticipate the probable nature, rate, and magnitude of impending changes. With that caution in mind, let's apply the six-step method in a complex business setting.

The Case of the "Big Eight" Accounting Firm

Imagine this situation. In November 1984, the ten partners of a Big Eight accounting firm's Denver office were enmeshed in a day-long strategy session to determine their office's direction for the coming year and beyond. 1984 had been a tough year, visiting tremendous changes on the firm, many of them unpleasant. The managing partner had kicked off the meeting with a summary of the office's current predicament: "We lost three bank clients last year to a national rival because of its specialization and focus on banks. We lost two oil and gas clients to regional and local accounting firms that did not even exist a year ago. On the other hand, we gained one of the best retailing clients in Denver on the coattails of our highly visible consulting engagements on the East and West coasts, and we won four new clients, each in a different industry, largely because we can provide them with more services than auditing. What mixed results! Today we must begin figuring out what's happening to us, so we can avoid further losses and increase our wins. The business is changing, but we're not doing a very good job of controlling that change to our advantage. Losing those three banks really hurt. And we seemed surprised at landing the new accounts. We cannot continue to be surprised, sitting back and hoping for the best." When the managing partner sat down, he invited discussion.

If you had attended that meeting, how would you have applied the previewing change methodology? Take a minute to mentally walk through the six steps before you continue.

Ready? Let's see what actually took place.

Since the ten partners had paid some attention to versatility prior to their strategy session, they followed the six-step process we recommend. First they set the boundaries of their discussion by limiting it to their competitors in the Denver metropolitan area. These included local and regional as well as national Big Eight competitors. Next, they spent two hours brainstorming and identifying all the changes that were occurring among their local competitors. The list included over sixty changes, ranging from new personnel with specialized backgrounds to advertising directed at special customer segments. Before breaking for lunch, the partners spent an hour grouping and labeling the sixty changes. To their surprise, they boiled all sixty down to four groups: specialization, intensified competition, national reputation, and consulting services. During lunch, the discussion caught fire as they spiritedly debated the causes of the changes. Three hours later they resumed the formal meeting with some agreement about the causes of change in each of the four groups. As they began assessing each change's position on the life cycle curve, the discussion grew fiery. At last they were identifying the indicators of further change and regaining some control over their destiny. By the end of the day they had reached the following conclusions:

• Specialization of services directed at different client segments will continue over the next five years. Change in this area will accelerate at a greater rate and magnitude in the future. Specialization will most likely center around client industries where accounting firms can become "experts."

• Intensified competiton came from a rush of new competitors into the market, but this change has almost run its course because the Denver market is becoming saturated. Future change will be minor with stability on the horizon.

• National reputation strongly affects certain key services and will grow in importance. The change is rapidly accelerating and, while it is just beginning to strike Denver, it has been happening for a few years in New York, Chicago, and Los Angeles. The change will peak locally during the next three years, which means national capabilities will have strong impact next year.

• Consulting services are becoming more and more critical. Acceleration increases daily. Even though consulting firms have proliferated throughout the country in the last decade, consulting in accounting firms, particularly the Big Eight, has not yet peaked. Consulting capabilities could increasingly attract clients looking for more than a mere public accounting firm. Since accountants get so close to clients during auditing, we can seize many opportunities to help them in ways other consulting firms can't.

The previewing-change methodology helped these ten partners anticipate onrushing changes and formulate a strategy to
capitalize on them. They no longer need to worry about having
more control over their future—they have already taken the
reins firmly in hand.

The Beauty of Versatility: A Summary

Versatility prepares us for the ever changing world in which
we live. If we approach that world with fixed ideas and positions, we will suffer, not prosper. But, if we embrace and participate in the changes, we will perform more creatively and
powerfully than we ever imagined possible.

Without versatility we become set in our ways, isolated in our
own world, unable to adapt to changes around us. And when
we are finally forced to change, control already lies beyond our
grasp.

With versatility we can learn to adapt to any situation, making
adaptation a part of our daily lives. In the words of Marilyn
Ferguson, author of *The Aquarian Conspiracy*, "Believing in a
world of fixity, we will fight change; knowing a world of fluidity,
we will cooperate with change."

Anticipating change and preparing yourself for adaptation
through versatility solves only half the change equation. The
other half involves actually implementing change in your organization. To successfully do so, you'll need to master the next
skill, focus.

• CHAPTER 9 •

Focus:
Implementing Change

When the group or civilization declines, it is through no mystic limitation of a corporate life, but through the failure of its political or intellectual leaders to meet the challenge of change.

—WILL and ARIEL DURANT

It is wonderful how much is done in a short space, provided we set about it properly, and give our minds wholly to it.

—WILLIAM HAZLITT

Focus Exploits Change

Think of accelerated change as an object hurtling toward you at tremendous speed. If you first spot it a mile away, its speed and the distance between you and it blur its nature; all you can see is an indistinct shape. As the object continues rushing toward you, you begin to discern a rough oblong shape, but you can't determine much else about it. Is it a threatening enemy missile or a friendly vehicle you might ride toward the future? Quickly, it bears down on you. As you peer at it closely, you suddenly see handles on its side. An opportunity, not a danger! If you have focused well enough and soon enough, you can seize it, letting it whisk you forward well ahead of those who failed to focus on it in time.

Focus, the second of the two adaptive skills, allows New Age executives to exploit change. As we saw in the previous chapter, versatile executives anticipate change. Focused executives successfully implement it. While versatility comes from full participation in an ever changing world, focus requires undivided attention to details. The Chinese character for crisis combines two seemingly conflicting symbols: one for danger, the other for opportunity. Picture versatility and focus as that sort of combination. While they may seem on the surface to contradict one another, they actually represent two inseparable skills. Such versatile men as Leonardo da Vinci and Benjamin Franklin maintained an intense focus that not only propelled them toward great achievements but also sustained their interest in and enthusiasm for a variety of endeavors. Their focus spurred their versatility and their versatility discovered new targets for their focus.

We define focus here as the ability to direct individual or organizational energy and resources toward one or a few details at a time. Suppose you have correctly anticipated an impending change. How do you adapt to that change without damaging the delicate balance between strategy and culture? By focusing on one step of implementation at a time, you can bring about the sort of permanent change that a brilliant strategy and strong culture can naturally accommodate. Successful organizations must be able to evolve, but if they try to change "too much, too soon" they risk losing their excellence. Remember U-Haul's attempt to abandon dealers in favor of moving centers overnight; Quaker Oats's plan to drive its food marketing culture into toys and restaurants; and Bausch & Lomb's struggle to transform a ragtag instruments group into a tight-knit unit with a swift reorganization? All three tried to do too much, too soon.

Another case in point is Johnson & Johnson, considered by many to be one of the best-run companies in America. J & J has begun to move from pills and lotions to technology-based products, a large shift in direction that will necessitate some fundamental changes, such as replacing one competence (marketing prowess) with another (technological leadership), stressing centralized cooperation over decentralized autonomy and leaving mature consumer markets for emerging high-tech ones. Clearly, the new strategy demands a new culture, but J & J will find it nearly impossible to become a leader in medical high-tech unless it starts focusing more than it seems to be doing. Since 1980 the company has acquired twenty-five high-tech companies. Can any organization, no matter how versatile its leaders, focus on so many enterprises at once? Apparently not. In 1983, J & J took a $38-million write-off on Extracorporeal Inc., a dialysis equipment maker, after the venture's products became outmoded in a changing market. Another J & J acquisition, Ortho Diagnostic Systems, has languished under revolving leadership and organizational turmoil, problems that have contributed to its failure to keep abreast of technological developments in its field. And then there's Technicare Corp., the maker of sophisticated diagnostic imaging equipment, whose overengineered products have, according to one stock market analyst, lost $110 million over a four-year period. Trying to do too much, too soon has hurt J & J. Fortunately, however, a $6-billion company can afford to make some mistakes, if it learns in the process. After all, that's versatility. But at some point J & J must move from experimenting with high-tech diversification to focusing on a few key areas where it can achieve lasting change with a more carefully combined strategy and culture alloy.

For contrast, consider Sears's cautious diversification. Drawing upon years of financial experience with Allstate and fifty-two million credit-card holders and relying on its expertise in selling through catalogs and stores, Sears brilliantly seized the opportunity to increase its offerings of financial services by focusing on two new areas: real estate and stocks. Sears thoughtfully forged a unique, almost unmatchable position as the only national retailing chain offering a full range of financial services. Ironically, many competitors saw danger, not opportunity, in the onrushing change and laughed at Sears in the beginning, but according to Phil Purcell, president and CEO of Dean Witter Financial Services Group at Sears and one of the architects of Sears's strategy, Sears got the last laugh: "For months we were treated to variations of the 'socks and stocks' routine, mostly from nervous competition. Still, the company was not deterred by this unsolicited flak. Within four months of completing the acquisitions, we announced our plans to test a new concept for the delivery of financial products and services in eight full-line Sears stores located around the country. Again industry observers predicted that the new financial service centers could not possibly succeed on the premises of a general merchandise store, especially one that appealed to the broad spectrum of the American public. Obviously, they did not foresee the enthusiasm with which these prototypes would be greeted by consumers everywhere. After all, Sears's fifty-two million customers have had more than a half a century's experience with buying insurance through our catalogs and stores. For us, broadening the product mix to include real estate and stock brokerage activities was a logical extension of that highly profitable Allstate experience." Sears had earlier demonstrated versatility by moving into the insurance business and building the world's largest credit-card customer base, tactics that prepared Sears for the focused implementation of its financial service centers. Sadly, some companies never progress from versatility to focus.

Lack of Focus Stifles Permanent Change

When the birth rate began to decline several years ago, Gerber Products Co., the baby-food maker, decided to seek growth elsewhere. Before long, the company that had cashed in on the baby boom had bought a trucking company, an insurance firm, and fifty-seven child care centers. Did Gerber focus? Hardly. In 1971 the company changed its slogan from "Babies are our business...our *only* business" to "Babies are our business...." The trucking company lost $1 million in 1983, while the insurance firm and child care centers are only marginally profitable. To make matters worse, the company lost almost $1 million in 1983 international sales. However, Gerber seems to be profiting from its mistakes as the new chairman, Carl Smith, refocuses Gerber's strategy back on babies, the company's traditional audience. He has guided efforts to add such nonfood items as toys, clothing, high chairs, strollers, car seats, and feeding paraphernalia to Gerber's product lines, a broadened package the company has successfully piloted in selected test markets. As sometimes happens, Gerber may quickly overcome the negative effects of an initial lack of focus by paying more attention to it in the future. In fact the company's new slogan is "Babies are our business...and have been for almost 50 years."

In another typical scenario, Kroger Company, the $15-billion food retailer, celebrated its one-hundredth birthday in 1982 with record earnings and the acquisition of Dillon's large chain of grocery stores. On top of the $600-million Dillon acquisition, Kroger created the new Foodland Distributors wholesale company, expanded manufacturing capabilities, and introduced superstores with new departments such as floral shops, financial centers, and hair salons. Predictably, the company's lack of focus led to six straight quarters of declining earnings in 1983 and 1984, with 1983 earnings 31 percent below the previous year's. Kroger had always been a successful innovator, but it couldn't handle so many new undertakings at one time. Not even the most superb innovator can juggle so many different balls without dropping one or all.

Gerber, Kroger, and scores of other American companies have yet to understand that only intense focus makes lasting excellence possible.

Intense Focus Generates Competence

Focus allows companies to make dramatic changes in their operations while keeping strategy and culture harnessed in the process. Although any dramatic change carries with it both opportunity for bold progress and the threat of too much change too soon, many situations do demand quick action. Emery Air Freight became the premier air freight forwarding company in the 1970s and might have held on to that position indefinitely had Federal Express not focused on two small details vital to the overnight delivery business, reliability and lightweight packages. As a traditional freight forwarder, Emery used scheduled airlines with scattered services to transport parcels, while Federal built its own fleet of aircraft and centered its operations in Memphis. When deregulation hit the airlines and airline schedules became less reliable, Emery suffered while Federal shone. Furthermore, Emery had geared itself to handling all sorts of freight that needed to arrive overnight, from business letters to heavy machine parts, but Federal focused on the light end of the market, designing a system that maximized the handling of letters and small parcels. As a result of paying attention to details, Federal flew past Emery to become number one in overnight delivery. To its credit, Emery learned some lessons from Federal, among them the importance of focus. Three years ago John C. Emery bet his company on his belief that focus could work for Emery, too. Over that period, he duplicated Federal's reliability by purchasing twenty-four Boeing 727s, leasing another forty aircraft and building an operations terminal in Dayton, Ohio, to sort packages; and he focused on his company's traditional specialty, packages weighing over seventy pounds. Determined to reestablish a position in an industry his firm once dominated, Emery implemented these changes with such concentration that the company achieved astonishing results in a very short time, with record revenues of $683 million in 1983 and profits up 145 percent to $25 million. Even though Federal Express still leads with over $1 billion in sales and $89 million in profit, Emery has turned the corner toward excellence.

Some sage once remarked that attention to detail separates the superlative from the spurious. That certainly holds true in business. Superlative results invariably come from focusing your energy and resources on those few crucial details that allow you to successfully implement change and enhance the strategy-culture match without letting yourself get swamped by trivia. In an environment of accelerated change, everything you do as an executive either stifles or facilitates change in your organization. If you focus your organization's energy and resources on one or a few changes at a time, taking precautions to blend that change into the strategy-culture mix, you will advance the sort of learning that leads to lasting competence.

When, sixty years ago, Kodak became number one in cameras, it decided to cement its status by focusing on selected changes. Despite enormous changes in the camera industry since then, Kodak has managed to retain its position with such innovations as its instant camera, disc camera, and all-in-one video camera-recorder. Each of these three changes represented major new thrusts for the company, but together they brought success because Kodak focused at the right time. Similarly, throughout the past sixty years, Sherwin-Williams has continued to dominate the paint industry, Gillette razors have held a sharp edge, and Singer sewing machines, Campbell soup, Goodyear tires, and Lipton teas have maintained lasting excellence by focusing on staying number one at all costs. But does focus mean just staying in the same business? Not at all. It means fostering appropriate learning and competence to keep products, people, and leaders on top.

Since no one organization enjoys unlimited resources to do everything it wants, leaders must apply focus to help them select the correct changes their resources will allow them to implement. Otherwise, they run the risk of overloading managers and high achievers in the organization with too much change in too short a time. Intense focus does not come automatically or accidentally, but, like all the New Age skills, can be acquired with time and effort.

How to Become a Focused Executive

Now that you appreciate the nature and power of focus, you are ready to begin acquiring it. As with the previous skills, you must first learn to recognize it.

Step One: Recognizing Focus

Some people have developed the ability to focus intensely on whatever activity or problem they tackle, and as a result, achieve desired results in a short time, thus buying time to pursue other tasks or problems with equal focus. Highly focused people have a hard time *not* applying focus to all phases of their lives. William F. Buckley, Jr., displays such a high degree of focus that novelist Kurt Vonnegut once called him "a man who has won the decathlon of human existence." Whether you like Buckley's politics or not, you have to agree that the founder and editor of *The National Review*, host of television's *Firing Line*, syndicated columnist for over 350 newspapers, author of bestselling books (both fiction and nonfiction), lecturer at more than fifty colleges each year, music lover, harpsichordist, sailor, husband, and father is a true Renaissance man, a New Age success in all his endeavors. In his autobiographical book, *Overdrive*, Buckley reveals that one of the secrets of his personal and professional success is an ability to intensely focus on the task at hand, which frees him to accomplish more in a year than most mortals accomplish in a lifetime. Significantly, he combines his ability to focus with an uncanny ability to swiftly shift focus from one area to another.

In the pages of Buckley's memoir, we find three attributes of focus that we think aptly define the focused executive:

- Pursuing every activity of life with full attention. For example, Buckley writes with such concentration that he can crank out a column in twenty minutes, buying him time for music or sailing. Likewise, focused executives can put such uninterrupted concentration into meetings that they can conclude in twenty minutes what might take several full-hour meetings for their unfocused counterparts. They buy time for meditation and action on other important matters.

- Limiting your activities to those in which you can achieve excellence. Again, Buckley doesn't engage in pursuits in which he has no interest or competence. He does not involve himself in the management of the family businesses, which is all too often a temptation to the less focused person. In like fashion, focused executives do not waste time designing the corporate letterhead or selecting office furniture when someone else can do so more efficiently and with more flair.

- Totally shifting from one activity to another when required. Buckley finalizes each issue of *The National Review* before moving to another project. By the same token, focused executives move from activity to activity at convenient breaking points, or they tie up loose ends before launching their focus in another direction.

Scientists, doctors, and researchers might not be able to explain the phenomenon that enables people to focus their attention on one activity while temporarily excluding others, but we think one word sums up the primary force behind focus, *interest*. When something truly interests you, it automatically attracts a certain degree of focus. Versatile executives find their attention drawn to a wide variety of interests, each of which they award with their full attention. To master focus, you must develop the ability to manage your interests, determining when and for how long you should award each your undivided attention. Although your interests develop over the years and are strongly influenced by tastes and preferences acquired as early as childhood, you can take four steps to manage them as focused executives do:

- First, identify and categorize your personal and professional interests, not just those activities to which you do devote time, but also those to which you think you *should* devote time. Try to rank your interests in terms of their importance. Which lead to excellence? When change requires you to focus on an area that does not interest you, you may be tempted to ignore the change. However, if the change will have a strong impact on your organization or industry, you can take one of two paths: delegate the responsibility for implementing a certain change to someone who does display interest in that area and therefore can achieve the necessary focus, or implement the change yourself in a way that coincides with your interests. Although versatility will broaden your range of interests, you can't force or fake interest in certain areas. For example, if your organization has anticipated the need for a change in marketing, but you are a financial type with little interest in marketing, don't try to feign your enthusiasm for marketing. Delegate the responsibility to someone who is interested in it. If you don't have anyone capable of assuming the responsibility within your organization, bring someone in from the outside.

- Identify and categorize the personal and professional interests of the people who report directly to you, paying attention to those they feel are most important. Sensitivity will help you do so quickly and accurately. When you're sensitive to the interests of your people, you can better manage those interests, maximizing their great potential by applying them in areas where focus will help your organization exploit change. For example, your organization may need more sophisticated financial controls to insure careful monitoring and control of the costs of your expanding product line. To bring about the change successfully you must find people who will fully embrace the need for better financial procedures. Never assign people who aren't enthralled with financial controls to implement such a change.

- Always review your own and your people's interests with respect to a given change. Knowing that interests change, focused executives also know how to instill interest in both themselves and their people. Meditation and freewheeling discussions can reveal interesting facets of a previously mundane or boring problem. The more interest you can build, the more likely you are to achieve focus. For example, implementing change always requires more than one person to make it happen, and some people in an organization will probably not be interested in the proposed change. What do you do then? One organization answered this question by spending six months communicating to its employees why its proposed acquisition of a pharmaceutical distribution company would aid in the sale and distribution of its hair and body care products. By communicating the advantages of this acquisition in great detail over an extended period of time to all employees, the company heightened their interest and they consequently became committed to make the acquisition a success. When the time came to integrate the acquisition into existing operations, people were eager to make it happen.

• Sustain interest in an area long enough to allow your focus to successfully implement change. When you lose interest you also lose focus and set yourself up to become a victim rather than a master of impending change. How many times have you seen a new program or approach introduced, only to be scrapped a few months later because of a lack of sustained focus? If a change takes tremendous time and effort, consider a rotating assignment of personnel to make sure the interest level remains high. One high-tech company in San Jose uses task forces to come up with technological innovations, constantly shifting the composition of the task forces to maintain high interest levels. It makes sure each task force keeps abreast of the innovation efforts of all other task forces, so when team members move from one task force to another they get involved quickly and effectively.

Focused executives also understand the nature and use of two essential preconditions to change. First identified by Gene Dalton, chairman of Brigham Young University's nationally recognized Organizational Behavior Department, during breakthrough research at B. F. Goodrich, these two preconditions are: a *felt need* and a *respected other*. By *felt need* we mean that before meaningful, lasting change can occur, a need for it must be felt throughout the organization. By *respected other* we mean some individual or group of individuals respected within or outside the organization who must advocate the change. When these two preconditions for change exist, an organization has an excellent chance of making a lasting and profitable change. A few years ago, IBM experienced a strongly felt need throughout the organization to get into the personal computer business, a move that meant some major changes in the way IBM sells its products. We think it applied the necessary focus to make the PC line of computers an eventual success. Scandinavian Airline System found a respected other in Jan Carlzon, the company's president. Carlzon told SAS employees they needed to change from an aircraft orientation to a customer orientation. Trusting his judgment, they believed and followed him. As a result, the company went from a $10-million loss to a $70-million profit in just eighteen months.

Finally, focused executives outline the specifics involved in implementing a change long before the actual change will take place. Insight and vision help them isolate all relevant variables that will affect or be affected by the change. Each detail requires special action. One of the best examples of a masterful change plan was the downsizing of General Motors cars in the mid-1970s. While General Motors certainly took its time to respond to the challenges of competitors who were producing small cars, when it did respond and make the change, it did so superbly. The powerfully felt need was the competitive threat from foreign car makers and the highly respected other was chairman Richard Gerstenberg. Once Gerstenberg made the decision to reduce the size of GM cars, the organization began to shift in an orderly fashion that belied its size as the second largest company in America. Gerstenberg created a "project center" that coordinated engineers from all the divisions. This organizational mechanism immediately produced cooperation among divisions you would have expected to fight over turf. Furthermore, GM drew upon its expertise with small cars abroad by bringing Pete Estes back to the United States from his assignment as head of overseas operations. Because Gerstenberg recognized the value of persuasion during a major change process, he stressed the importance of management by diplomacy. He demanded GM's focus, and he got it. GM accomplished its downsizing two years ahead of its domestic competitors, and its cars went from being the industry's worst gas guzzlers to being the most efficient fuel users.

We've assembled the attributes of focused executives into a composite picture against which you can test yourself. A score of 30 or less indicates need for improvement.

EXECUTIVE FOCUS SELF-EXAMINATION

	ALWAYS	OFTEN	SELDOM	NEVER
1. Do you approach activities with your full, undivided attention?	4	3	2	1
2. Do you restrict your focus to activities at which you can excel?	4	3	2	1
3. Can you shift focus quickly and completely from one activity to another?	4	3	2	1
4. Do you list and rank your interests in order of importance?	4	3	2	1
5. Do you list and rank your people's interests in order of importance?	4	3	2	1
6. Do you get your employees extremely interested in a project before you attempt to implement change?	4	3	2	1
7. Are you able to remain interested in a project, keeping your focus intense over a long period of time?	4	3	2	1

8. Do you make sure there is a
    "felt need" among your
    people before you embark
    on change?   4   3   2   1

9. Do you identify a "respected
    other" advocating the
    change before you proceed?   4   3   2   1

10. Do you lay out all the
    specific details of what will
    affect and be affected by the
    change before you
    implement it?   4   3   2   1

Chrysler's Lee Iacocca could score a perfect 40. Iacocca brilliantly led the crippled Chrysler from near bankruptcy in 1979 to a whopping $701 million in 1983 profits, an astronomical percentage inprovement. Of course, the stunning turnaround took all six New Age skills, plus more, but at its center lay Iacocca's ruthless focus on controlling costs. Obvious? Wouldn't any executive have focused on that? Perhaps, but not to the degree Iacocca did. Beginning in 1979, he cut Chrysler's payroll in half, shut down one-third of the company's plants, and sharply boosted productivity until, today, Chrysler's break-even point is half of what it was three years ago. Only after Iacocca had made this central change did he shift his focus in 1983 to the development of new models. Undivided attention to one area bought him time to concentrate on others in the future.

Step Two: Eliminating Unfocused Activities

Once you can recognize focus, you can begin eliminating activities that don't contribute to your foundation of strategic thinking and culture building. Since everything you say and do as an executive affects change efforts, any activity that does not contribute to achieving your goals will jeopardize your future.

To eliminate unfocused activities, you must ruthlessly avoid thoughts and actions that do not further your attempt to cause and control change to your organization's advantage. Ask yourself daily: "Is this particular activity helping us maintain focus?" Your answers should turn out to be "contributive," "partially contributive," or "noncontributive." The following case, based on a true story, illustrates how to determine into which category various activities fall:

The Case of the Entrepreneurial Hospital Corporation

The top management of a hospital corporation that operates fourteen major medical centers, eleven community hospitals, five alternative care clinics, and three surgical centers wanted to infuse entrepreneurship into its organization. Competition was heating up and the whole industry was in the throes of unprecedented change resulting from new technologies, insurance programs, and government legislation. After careful consideration, management decided to adopt an organizational structure and philosophy that would give managers more autonomy and freedom to respond to volatile opportunities in the market. Although such an approach meant a major shift from traditional practices in the field, key people in the organization believed it could insure not only continued growth, but survival itself. To help them adjust, they hired a consulting firm that specialized in health care marketing. The firm had gotten good results in similar situations, so management felt confident that the results would be worth the price, even if some of the recommendations would be tough to follow.

The change effort initially focused on the basic unit of organization. Previously, the company had been organized by type of medical service throughout a wide geographical area. One organizational unit governed all medical centers, one ruled all community hospitals, another managed all alternative care clinics, and still another ran all the surgical centers. The new approach would assemble all services and facilities within regions under five different regional vice-presidents who could respond to all medical service opportunities and threats in that area.

The new structure would give regional vice-presidents the authority to add or subtract services and facilities to better serve their communities and gain competitive advantage over rivals. The managers of individual service centers, whether hospitals or outpatient clinics, would also have the authority to add to or subtract from their own services and facilities to better meet patients' needs. For example, if the manager of an alternative care unit desired to add a surgical center to his services, he could do so if he could justify the market need and meet corporate financial return goals. If the regional vice-president wanted to take a service from one medical center and house it in another new specialty facility (for example, a psychiatric hospital), he could make that decision if it followed corporate guidelines for revenues and profits. Under the old structure these kinds of decisions had been made only at the top by the CEO and board of directors after laborious analysis and deliberation.

After the company effected the reorganization, the consultants followed up by analyzing the activities of the CEO, to whom the new vice-presidents reported, and they found that he had 1) held an emergency meeting with all the administrators of the company's medical centers to discuss further cost-cutting measures, 2) called a special board meeting to deliberate on the building of a new surgical center in one region, 3) met with corporate staff planners to finalize a new company-wide strategy for alternative care clinics, and 4) held a management retreat to discuss the new autonomy and entrepreneurship the new company structure and philosophy should make possible. How would you evaluate the CEO's activities—as contributive, partially contributive, or noncontributive to the overall focus?

- The meeting with the company's fourteen medical center administrators did not contribute to increased focus because it simply perpetuated the old system and undermined the new. Since the company's five new vice-presidents, each responsible for one of the newly created regions, attended that meeting, they felt confused by the CEO's implicit message that he didn't trust them to carry on the same discussions in their individual regions.

- The special board meeting to approve a new surgical center was also noncontributive because it signaled that the CEO still felt no important action could be taken without board approval. This piece of red tape could only inhibit entrepreneurship because it promoted hesitancy, forcing would-be entrepreneurs to try to nail down every variable in unnecessary detail to avoid higher-level second-guessing. For bold change to work, the five vice-presidents had to be free to make major decisions on their own. The CEO and board should have limited their endeavors to broad strategy and philosophy guidelines, not specific decisions.

- The meeting with corporate planners to discuss a company-wide strategy for alternative care clinics partially contributed to increased focus because the new geographical divisions did need the benefit of corporate guidelines to influence their own unique regional decisions, but it was noncontributive insofar as the vice-presidents were not involved in it. Eliminating their participation in and responsibility for overall strategy could only stifle their entrepreneurship. The recommendations of the five vice-presidents should have been part of formulating company-wide alternative care strategy.

- The management retreat to discuss the new autonomy and entrepreneurship of the regional divisions contributed to the company's focus because it increased understanding of the new approach and enhanced the chances of successful changes.

Once you have identified activities as contributive, partially contributive, or noncontributive, what do you do about partially and noncontributive ones? You face three alternatives: eliminate, modify, or add. In the case being considered, the meeting with the fourteen medical center administrators should have been eliminated because the CEO could have done nothing to make it contributive to the new focus. The special board meeting on a new surgical center should have been modified to exclude board members and include that region's vice-president: the CEO and board might develop a corporate-wide surgical center philosophy and strategy, but they should leave decisions about individual surgical centers to the division vice-president and CEO. To make the meeting with the corporate planners fully rather than partially contributive, the CEO could have added the regional vice-presidents to these finalizing strategy discussions.

Once you have eliminated, modified, or added to your activities, you are ready to tackle implementation.

Step Three: Implementing Change

The implementation of any change involves five steps:

- Define the change, specifically relating it to your organization's strategy and culture.
- Determine which people, skills, organizational structures, operating systems, and management orientations need to change.
- Quantify the level of effort and resources needed to bring about each of the changes identified in Step 2.
- Develop a focus allocation plan and timetable for shifting focus to elements involved in the change effort.
- Begin steadfastly implementing the change, monitoring progress closely and making necessary adjustments along the way.

Let's look at these steps more closely. First, in order to define the change and specifically relate it to your organization's strategy and culture, consider in what way your organization's strategy and culture will have to evolve in order to accommodate the change. If your organization has pursued a low-cost producer strategy, with a culture competent in cost-cutting and efficiency, and it now decides to become more of a marketer, you'll have to take into account all the existing elements that need changing. Before you continue your change efforts, you'll have to decide whether such changes are realistic. Your estimation of what needs to change may be so overwhelming that you decide to pursue another strategy. If you decide to continue with the change, move to step two.

Second, to determine which people, skills, organizational structures, operating systems, and management orientations you need to change in order to accomplish a successful implementation, make a list of existing people, skills, systems, and orientations. Compare the list to one containing all the new people, skills, systems, and orientations you will need. For example, your organization may possess an existing skill in the production of high-quality products, but, due to the increasing quality of a competitor's attractively priced products, the change requires producing lower-cost products with the same high quality. In that case you may have to decide if your current people can achieve that goal or if someone new must come aboard to do it. Once you have determined all that needs to change, you must once again decide whether to continue or reconsider your plans for change. If you decide to continue, proceed to step three.

Third, to quantify the level of energy, resources, time, and dollars needed to bring about the changes identified in step two, you should attach values to each item that will have to change. Identify as accurately as possible what costs for new personnel assignments, training programs, promotional campaigns, and lost opportunity you will incur. For example, you may have chosen a new product-oriented organizational structure to implement the needed change, calculating that it will take 25 percent of your personal time to find the new managers (who will cost 10 percent more than existing managers) and ten three-week seminars at $1,000 a head to train existing managers. You face an 8 percent increase in your organization's salary budget, and the entire marketing and sales organization will suffer such a state of confusion for at least six months that you'll lose up to 12 percent of last year's sales-to-date. Even before you announce the new organization you must invest at least 15 percent of your own time to create a sense of need for the change. Again, you should assess whether you can afford to continue at this point. If you can, take step four.

Fourth, to develop a plan and timetable for shifting focus, carefully assign the tasks over a period of time. Drawing from the facts and figures that result from step three, you should be able to rank the level of effort required to achieve changes in people, skills, systems, etc., as high, medium, or low. As you assign the tasks of reorganization, follow a simple rule of thumb: never ask your organization to implement more than two high-effort changes at a time. With this in mind, chart all the changes to be made, allowing ample time for the change to become a permanent part of your organization. For example, an organization may have identified two skills, one system, and one management orientation that must change in order to achieve successful implementation. The management orientation requires high effort, the two skills medium effort, and the system low effort. A proper allocation of focus would probably combine the high and the low in the same time period, with the two medium-effort changes combined in a later period. Never overload your organization's focus. However, you can increase available focus by strongly matching people's interests with the current focus at each stage of change. If everything still looks realistic, and the modifications to your organization's strategy-culture mix are acceptable, you are ready to implement your change.

To begin implementing and monitoring progress toward change, you must act boldly but alertly. Be prepared for surprises because the best-laid plans never unfold exactly as intended. Measure focus levels and check for evidence of permanent change. If an area of medium-effort change now seems to require a higher level of effort, be prepared to delay another medium- or low-effort task for the time being. Act decisively but be flexible. Any battle plan is only as good as its ability to evolve under the heat of fire. It always takes time for a worthwhile change to become part of the fabric of an organization. At one company, for example, change required that branch-office managers become more marketing-oriented. Signs of permanent change only became evident after six months when branch managers who had never communicated directly before began calling each other to get marketing data and ideas for their own branches.

The Power of Focus: A Summary

Focus makes successful, lasting, and profitable change possible. It requires your undivided attention to the details that have to change. Lack of focus thwarts permanent change. Unfocused executives may temporarily take advantage of a change over which they exerted little influence but if they do so with superficial approaches they will seldom get their organizations to adapt to change in a lasting way.

Focus, since it helps you increasingly control whatever attracts your attention, builds competence. And when competence grows, you stand a better chance of turning accelerated change to your advantage. You can't build competence in marketing, R and D, sales, distribution, or finance without intense focus, and you can't successfully exploit change without replacing old competence with new.

We turn now to the final skill you need to develop. Just as vision integrated insight and sensitivity to lay the foundation for excellence, the last skill, patience, integrates all the New Age skills by helping you employ one or more of them at the right time and in the right proportion.

• CHAPTER 10 •

Patience: Living in the Long Term

By the time it came to the edge of the Forest the stream had grown up, so that it was almost a river, and, being grown-up, it did not run and jump and sparkle along as it used to do when it was younger, but moved more slowly. For it knew now where it was going, and it said to itself, "There is no hurry. We shall get there some day."
—A. A. MILNE

I know why there are so many people who love chopping wood. In this activity one immediately sees the results.
—ALBERT EINSTEIN

Patience Leads to Lasting Excellence

Jim, founder of a fast-growing American software development company, had arrived in Tokyo the night before an important meeting at which he hoped to finalize negotiations for a cooperative venture with a Japanese computer manufacturer. He was eager to win a favorable agreement that could triple his annual sales. Arriving fifteen minutes early for his appointment the next morning, Jim sat fidgeting in a chair outside Mr. Yamamoto's office, alternately glancing at his watch and shuffling papers in his briefcase. Finally, a secretary ushered him into Yamamoto's office at precisely ten o'clock.

"Good morning, Mr. Adams." Yamamoto rose and bowed. After the two men exchanged business cards, Jim shoved Yamamoto's into a shirt pocket without even looking at it, while

221

the Japanese executive studied and caressed Jim's as if it were a gift. Eventually he looked up and smiled at his visitor.

"Tea, Mr. Adams." It sounded more like a statement than an invitation.

"No, thanks."

The secretary poured tea into two small cups. Anxious to impress his potential partner, Jim immediately launched into a technical description of his company's new database management program. His own tea grew cold. He couldn't understand why Yamamoto just sat there smiling and sipping his tea. Why wasn't he paying attention? Didn't the program impress him?

When Jim paused uncertainly, Yamamoto nodded. "You have seen the blossoms in the Imperial Garden?"

Blossoms? Jim had come to Japan to talk software, not horticulture. He plunged ahead with his pitch. "No, our program facilitates simultaneous access of up to three million...." Feeling desperate now, Jim spoke louder and faster. When he finished, Yamamoto raised his hand.

"Your first visit to our country? Perhaps I may be of service in helping you find suitable points of interest."

Shocked that the deal was slipping away, Jim outlined his lowest price-quantity offer.

Yamamoto's smile broadened. "Mr. Adams. I like your program. And your price. I'll have agreements drawn up."

Wiping the perspiration from his forehead, Jim heaved a sigh of relief. He had won the negotiation. Or had he?

A few weeks later when he attended a seminar on doing business with the Japanese, he listened as the seminar leader explained how the Japanese value silence and patience. It didn't take long for Jim to realize he had actually lost the negotiation, but even if he had known the importance of the business card ritual, the tea ceremony, and the need to establish a relationship before conducting business, he still would have had to struggle with his own impatience. His anxiety had driven him to give a desperation offer from which his company would derive much less profit than if he had matched his opponent's patience.

Sadly, American business people, who so often emphasize

quick inventory turnover, short-term return on investment, and fast-track careers, seldom prize patience. But New Age executives must rise above shortsighted emphasis on immediate results and commit themselves instead to the long-term view. This does not mean abandoning immediate goals, but it does mean evaluating their relationship to a more distant future. If you have developed a thoughtful strategy and have fostered the kind of culture you need to implement it successfully, you must be patient enough to see your vision through to its conclusion. Otherwise, you probably lack faith in your vision.

Do patient executives simply stick it out during bad times, waiting for the inevitable good times to return? Certainly not. At the beginning of Chapter 7 you saw how the lack of vision brought about the demise of Woolco. Although Woolworth executives stuck patiently with Woolco over the years, their patience with an inadequate strategy-culture mix was misplaced because they were merely waiting to suffer the future. Quite simply, we define patience as a persistent commitment to approach all management tasks with the future firmly in mind (and therefore under control), employing the New Age skills at the right time, in the right proportion, and for the right duration. Because it allows you to take the time to create excellence, patience integrates the other skills, fostering the ideal environment in which they all can flourish. Let's take a closer look at how this actually happens.

In 1976, John J. Byrne left Travelers Insurance to save Geico Corp., then the nation's seventh-largest auto insurer, which was teetering on the brink of bankruptcy. Geico, founded in 1936, had long been a leader in the auto insurance industry, following a success formula based on selling insurance directly to drivers, avoiding agents' commissions. By focusing on safe drivers, Geico could offer low prices and still make a profit on underwriting as well as on investment of premiums, traditionally the major source of earnings for insurers. Then, in 1973, a new management group changed the old formula for success by pushing for sales growth without carefully tracking costs or maintaining the safe-driver underwriting standards. When its ratio of premiums to capital available to pay claims reached twenty-six to one (the industry shoots for three to one), Geico could barely meet its claim obligations.

Enter New Age executive Jack Byrne. In a recent *Fortune* magazine profile, Byrne compared himself to A. A. Milne's storybook character Winnie the Pooh. Says Byrne, "Pooh is among the greatest managers of all time." Why? Because Pooh is what Byrne calls a relaxed realist, one who patiently faces, accepts, and deals with reality, always keeping his mind on the "honey." Byrne's patience, however, does not stop him from making tough, quick decisions.

In the first several months after Byrne came to Geico, he functioned like a turnaround manager, bringing his focus to bear on what the company had to do to get on its feet again. But his patience let him recognize that he would not be able to implement any long-term strategy and vision until the company was healthy enough to survive such medicine. After persuading the industry to reinsure 25 percent of Geico's policies, Byrne then sold new equity to raise $76 million. Geico increased rates enough to reduce premiums by 23 percent and thus bring the ratio of premiums to capital available to pay claims closer to industry standards. With the turnaround complete, Byrne drew upon his creative insight to establish four rules that would govern the company's strategic direction: 1) keep a good balance sheet and an acceptable premium-surplus ratio; 2) hold underwriting profits at 5 percent before tax; 3) become the low-cost producer; and 4) invest the assets for a maximum total return. The strategy has worked brilliantly, because Geico has indeed produced underwriting profits and has averaged a 36 percent return on equity since 1977.

While Byrne was mapping out his insightful strategy, he sensitively built a strong corporate culture that fosters a common commitment within the management team—a third of which are new to the company—to being the low-cost producer. To do so Byrne consistently trusted subordinates to set their own goals by consensus. Byrne's knack for motivating his people helped him to rally the troops around the four strategy elements. Encouraging employees to speak their minds, and then listening to what they have to say, he remains constantly approachable, often wearing a cardigan sweater that he considers to be a management tool. His straightforwardness lets his people know where they stand with him at all times.

He even used his consensus style to forge a vision of Geico's future. Assembling the company's top executives, including twenty-eight "planning center" managers and other key staff and line executives, he conducted sometimes cumbersome marathon sessions to arrive at a consensus regarding the definition of Geico's mission. Although the group ultimately agreed to stick with the auto insurance business, Byrne knew his company's vision needed something more. As early as 1979, less than three years after he had joined the company, Byrne had recognized that the 5 percent rule of profit on underwriting was hampering sales growth. Could he turn this apparent danger into an opportunity? Could he help Geico become more versatile? Perhaps, but patience let him listen to his sensitivity, which said that an immediate change in the 5 percent rule would shock his people. Any authoritarian directive could destroy Geico's emerging culture, which was more important than short-term growth. Sure, Geico needed to change, but change without consensus could be a threat. So Byrne focused his efforts on slowly building an awareness of the need for change. It took four years, but Byrne's patience triumphed when his own people finally insisted that the 5 percent rule had to go. Recognizing the need for change, they were now ready to dedicate themselves to a new vision of going much more aggressively after new business with lower prices. From now on the 5 percent rule would apply only to policies in force for more than three years, thus allowing the company to lower prices to attract new customers and increase market share. By the end of 1982, sales growth jumped to 30 percent, and the company's cost-cutting efforts put Geico in a good position to offer lower prices than State Farm, its principal competitor.

All great leaders know the value of timing. Creative insight, sensitivity, vision, versatility, and focus all played a role in the

Geico success story, but Byrne's patience directed the show because it helped him decide when and for how long to put a skill
or combination of skills on stage. The bottom line? The company's stock price jumped from $2 a share in 1976 to $55 in
1983, with revenues passing $600 million and profits continuing
to grow at an annual rate of 16 percent.

Impatience Compromises Perennial Performance

In the late 1970s, Dart Industries, a consumer products conglomerate, committed itself to becoming one of the great corporations in America. In the mid-seventies Tom Mullaney had
come aboard as president and chief operating officer after a
stint at PepsiCo's Wilson Sporting Goods division, which he had
run with superior results for several years. Mullaney brought
Phil Matthews, also from PepsiCo, to Dart as executive vice-
president and chief financial officer. Together they had charted
a course that would divest the company of losers such as Vanda
Cosmetics and Dart Resorts and acquire new winners such as
Duracell batteries; and they had hired one of Mullaney's former
employers, McKinsey & Company, to help develop a long-term
strategy.

From the beginning, Mullaney and Matthews had begun
building a strong culture committed to effective business planning and strategic management. As their plans materialized,
Dart seemed destined for excellence. It was just a matter of
time. But Justin Dart, founder of the company and still chairman and CEO, was impatient. Nothing ever moved fast enough
for Justin. Although his aggressive entrepreneurial spirit had
built an empire, he couldn't accept the fact that his company
had entered a new stage of development that required consolidation, shoring up, and solidification of the company's diverse
operations. Ironically, Mullaney and Matthews at ages forty-
four and thirty-nine, had the patience that Justin Dart in his
seventies lacked. Dart's impatience led him to the bargaining

table with Kraft Inc., where he proceeded, against Mullaney's recommendations, to conclude the 1980 merger of Dart Industries and Kraft Inc. into Dart & Kraft. Mullaney resigned, with Matthews close on his heels. A few years later, Justin Dart, having pulled together a $10-billion conglomerate, died a happy man. Unfortunately, the vision of excellence had departed with its architects, because today, Dart & Kraft languishes as a lackluster performer, unable to figure out what it is and where it's going. Profits have stagnated, and sales dropped 5 percent in 1983 to under $10 billion. After the merger, return on capital fell to 11 percent and has only climbed back to 13 percent today. Kraft had agreed to the merger because it felt that adding nonfood products to its lines of food products would put the company on a faster track, but it quickly grew disillusioned.

Is it too late for Dart & Kraft to adopt a longer-range view? Perhaps not. Although observers had expected Dart & Kraft to acquire Esmark, it declined to make a higher bid than Beatrice because it had apparently begun to look inward at taking advantage of its own strengths. Now the company is focusing on adding new products to extend existing product lines and to buoy up sagging brand names. As a final irony, it appears that Dart & Kraft has begun doing just what Mullaney and Matthews had envisioned all along.

In Chapter 1 we cited three major obstacles to excellence: short-term orientation, shallow thinking, and quick-fix expectations. Impatience runs like a vein through all of them. While one must master all the New Age skills to overcome such obstacles, patience, more than any other, "lets it happen." Remember Gallwey's advice to *let* it be. Without patience, the other skills don't have time to work their magic.

Patience Produces Staying Power

Companies come and go, but the best ones remain on everyone's list of excellence year after year because they have staying power. Nowhere is such power as important as in the chemical industry. On June 12, 1979, American cyclist Bryan Allen set a record by pedaling the bicycle-powered Albatross aircraft twenty-two miles across the English Channel to Cap Gris Nez, France, battling turbulent air every inch of the way. Allen had staying power, but he had to give some credit to his sponsor, Du Pont, which supplied three crucial materials for the aircraft—Mylar, Delrin, and Kevlar. Allen used Du Pont's new Kevlar, a fiber developed as a steel substitute, for the Albatross's propellers, wing framework, and control cables. Stronger than steel but extremely lightweight, Kevlar allowed Allen to build a ninety-six-foot-wing-span aircraft weighing only fifty-five pounds. Others have used Kevlar as cable to anchor oil rigs in the ocean and as a key ingredient in bulletproof vests. It's what *Fortune* calls a "miracle product," and its history proves its manufacturer's patience and staying power.

During experiments with a new type of molecular structure early in the 1960s, Du Pont researchers created a strong new fiber with great strength, but it remained nothing more than a curiosity until 1965, when researcher Stephanie Kvolek selected one of its many variations for continued research. In the years that followed, the fiber survived test after test as Du Pont patiently sought the best raw materials with which to produce it, the best synthesizing method, the best way to insure its safety, and the best way to make it commercially viable. After Du Pont completed its tests in 1970, the company applied for a patent and launched extensive experiments to determine how to manufacture Kevlar in large quantities for widespread application in commercial products. It tested Kevlar in tires and soon realized its potential to form lightweight panels in skis, boats, and missile bodies. In 1973, Du Pont finally constructed a machine to manufacture Kevlar, and in 1976, the company began offering it to industrial customers on a limited basis. Still, Du Pont management did not decide to really push the new material until the end of the 1970s when researchers finally felt confident enough to recommend that the company back it to the hilt. Having spent $250 million and twenty years of research on Kevlar to this point, Du Pont put another $250 million into a plant that began producing the fiber in 1982; then it pumped in another $200 million to increase production capacity. That billion-dollar investment will undoubtedly be rewarded as Kevlar's reputation grows, aided in no small way by Byran Allen's achievement, the sort of inspired publicity of which Elisha Otis would be proud. Such stories, which are simply business as usual at Du Pont, account for the fact that it enjoys prestige as the largest and most admired chemical company in the country. Since *Fortune* began its survey of the best corporations in America, Du Pont has ranked number one among chemical companies every year.

Such staying power enables a company to accept challenges and hurdle obstacles along the path toward realizing corporate vision. Consider the two different paths Philip Morris and Liggett & Myers took when they reached a fork in the road for the tobacco industry. While the former exhibited patience, the latter engaged in a frenzy of impatient short-term thinking and impulsive behavior.

In the mid-fifties, Liggett & Myers was twice the size of Philip Morris. In 1959, both firms began to diversify, but Philip Morris began slowly, at first investing heavily in cigarettes, especially overseas, then acquiring Miller Brewing Company and, more recently, Seven-Up. These diversifications sprang from a vision of a superior consumer marketing and distribution company with dominant competence in market segmentation, advertising, and promotion, skills that could inform a strong corporate culture. Focusing intensely on the success of each new acquisition to make sure it fit securely into the strategy-culture mix, the company also practiced versatility by quickly selling an acquisition the instant it turned sour. In contrast, Liggett & Myers diversified like a feeding shark, gobbling up businesses whether they capitalized on the company's strengths or not, and then continuing to digest them long after it would have made good business sense to cough them up. At the same time, it overharvested its cigarette business by continuing to pay high dividends to shareholders. Lacking insight into the nature of its markets, it could not envision a future beyond the next year.

Today, Philip Morris is eight times larger than Liggett & Myers and is the most profitable major tobacco company; Liggett & Myers's market share has sagged from 20 percent to less than 3 percent. Whether or not you use or approve of its products, you must admit that Philip Morris has effectively and patiently exploited change.

How to Become a Patient Executive

With this proof of the value of patience in mind, you can begin to learn the art of patience, mastery of which will help you use all your other skills with exquisite timing. As with the other New Age skills, you must be able to recognize patience before you can acquire it.

Step One: Recognizing Patience

In their recent book, *Decision Making at the Top*, Gordon Donaldson and Jay Lorsch, both Harvard Business School professors, summarized their research into the complexities of corporate decision-making. Their goal was to discover why so many organizations make decisions that cause them to disappear during times of economic turbulence. Since turbulent times characterize the New Age, we found Donaldson's and Lorsch's answers extremely valuable.

Obviously, it takes a strong leader to guide an organization through major changes involving strategy and culture, and Donaldson and Lorsch identified two leadership qualities that are essential to success: patience and persistence. Remember our definition of patience? It includes a *persistent commitment* to a clearly formulated vision and to the use of the New Age skills. As we discussed in Chapter 3, it takes time to develop new ways of doing things, and you can't take the necessary time unless you have patience. Donaldson and Lorsch identified these characteristics of patient executives:

• A capacity for personal reappraisal that allows the executive to rise above the pressures of day-to-day activities and evaluate his or her role in the broader scheme of things. When one executive, who had been intimately involved in the development and implementation of a new marketing strategy, backed off to reappraise her role, she was amazed to discover that her tight hold on the reins actually prevented others from embracing her new strategy. She immediately began working *through* rather than over others.

• A commitment to corporate assessment that leads the executive to analyze the sources of the organization's difficulties and to address them in terms of the organization's existing and future strengths. This characteristic, while similar to the first, goes beyond individual analysis to the organization as a whole. For example, after one executive meditated on his company's serious product distribution problems, he gained the insight that independent, rather than company-controlled, distributors might feel more highly motivated to serve the company's rapidly growing and diversifying institutional food business.

• Confidence in a vision of the organization's future. Confident people are patient people, and patient people marshall strong confidence behind their visions. Those who lack faith in themselves, their visions, and their organizations are always impatient. For example, Ruben Mettler, TRW's chairman, finds his firm at a crossroads, with its eastern operations depending on heavy, old-line manufacturing, its western operations relying on sophisticated high-tech ventures. Mettler wants two radically different strategies to remain competitive and viable, but he must wed two disparate corporate cultures into a tighter unit before that will happen. Doing so will take so much time that Mettler has embarked on an "evolutionary" management approach that encourages new ways of looking at products, markets, and the entire organization's structure. Because he has confidence in his vision, he's prepared for the fact that it will take years to effect lasting changes.

Patience helps you make good decisions in the proper place, at the right time. As patience plays its integrative role in creating excellence, it functions as a timer to make sure events unfold in logical sequence. Chester Barnard recognized this long ago in his classic 1938 work, *The Functions of the Executive*, in which he described four characteristics of good decision-makers: "The fine art of executive decision consists in not deciding questions that are not now pertinent, in not deciding prematurely, in not making decisions that cannot be made effective and in not making decisions that others should make." In other words, patient executives know when *not* to decide. The pace of accelerated change has blinded many executives to this time-honored advice. Barnard goes on to assert that four rules can help executives make good decisions:

- Make decisions that are pertinent now. That means having the patience to put off a decision that your financial officer is pleading with you to make right now but that in your judgment need not be made until certain events and circumstances have occurred. When someone insists that you must answer yes or no *right now*, you should usually answer no. When Bill Agee, ex-chairman of Bendix, made a bid to take over Martin Marietta, the target company became hostile. Making a decision that would have been better left until later, much later, Agee pressed forward while Martin Marietta tried to turn the tables by purchasing stock in Bendix. The result? Allied Corporation entered the fray and snatched up Bendix and the Allied-Bendix merger added little value and may have marked the decline of once strong Bendix.

- Never make decisions prematurely. That doesn't mean patient executives don't act quickly or experiment with solutions to problems, but it does mean that they don't act hastily or experiment prematurely. When Osborne Computer, the company that successfully introduced the world's first portable personal computer, the Osborne-1, prematurely announced the follow-up Osborne Executive, customers stopped ordering the Osborne-1. Flagging sales for the pioneer machine contributed to the company's eventual bankruptcy.

- Make decisions that can be carried out. Executives who make decisions their organizations can't support are not only impatient, they are foolish. Patient executives carefully pursue strategies their cultures can implement, focusing on changes they know their people can successfully make. Coleco Industries, the Hartford-based toymaker, decided to get into computers after a stunning success with its Colecovision home video game system, but the company has yet to reap any rewards from the decision. It found out that a culture geared to marketing Cabbage Patch Kids could not easily transfer its skills to more sophisticated products, especially products the company hastily rushed through production. Flaws in the machine and a lack of software turned CEO Arnold Greenberg's promise of stellar growth into a large 1983 loss.

- Never make decisions others should make. In emergencies and crises, impatient executives can't resist making decisions for their subordinates, but when you make a decision someone else should make—even a strategically sound one—it adversely affects the culture. Ted Brophy, chairman of GTE Corp., hired Tom Vanderslice from General Electric to turn GTE around and position it in telecommunications. Although Vanderslice did a good job, substantially increasing productivity, profits, and revenues, Brophy stepped back into the picture and said he would not retire as expected. Since Vanderslice had anticipated the top job, he resigned. Brophy had let Vanderslice succeed in changing the culture at GTE but then wanted to regain control instead of letting the architect of the changes see them through. Such a move can deal a crushing blow to any budding new culture.

   In another classic work, *The Exceptional Executive*, Harry Levinson identifies six common managerial errors: "encouragement of power-seeking, failure to exercise controls, stimulation of rivalry, failure to anticipate the inevitable, applying pressure on men of limited ability and misplacement." Levinson divides these six errors into two groups. The first three relate to inadequate management of aggression, while the last three involve shortsightedness. If you look closely at the two groupings, you will see that impatience lies at the heart of both. Impatient executives encourage power-seeking because they think it makes subordinates attack their tasks with great lust. They fail to exercise controls because controls might slow the tempo, and they stimulate rivalry because they feel competition spurs high output. Impatience also leads to shortsightedness, because some think ignoring the inevitable might make it go away. An atmosphere of impatience applies pressure on those of limited ability because it sets unrealistic goals even a talented individual cannot reach. And impatient executives frequently misplace people because they mistakenly assume that careful consideration of employee capabilities is only a waste of time.
   A few pages back you read how Geico's Jack Byrne called Winnie the Pooh a great manager. In *The Tao of Pooh*, Benjamin Hoff uses Milne's classic to elucidate the Taoist point of view that life is sweet and that sourness and bitterness come from the interfering and unappreciative mind. Compared to his friends, Pooh remains unfrazzled, down to earth, calm, and, above all, patient. Owl constantly pontificates, showing off his wisdom, but never solves problems or makes things work; Rabbit is an impetuous activist, always calculating and clever, but always out of touch with reality; Eeyore, the donkey, frets and complains but never brings himself to action. Pooh, on the other hand, doesn't force things or try too hard, because he knows if he remains relaxed, sensible, and in touch with what's important, doing everything he can do in a situation, things will

work out. Hoff concludes his book with the following advice: "Within each of us there is an Owl, a Rabbit, an Eeyore, and a Pooh. For too long, we have chosen the way of Owl and Rabbit. Now, like Eeyore, we complain about the results. But that accomplishes nothing. If we are smart, we will choose the way of Pooh. As if from far away, it calls to us with the voice of a child's mind. It may be hard to hear at times, but it is important just the same, because without it, we will never find our way through the forest."

Now, let's put everything we've learned about recognizing patience into a composite picture of a patient executive. The resulting Executive Patience Self-Examination gives you the opportunity to test your own level of patience. If you score below 30, you'll have to work on developing the patience you will need to find your way through the forest.

EXECUTIVE PATIENCE SELF-EXAMINATION

		ALWAYS	OFTEN	SELDOM	NEVER
1.	During times of change, are you patient and persistent?	4	3	2	1
2.	Can you reexamine yourself and your vision during the process of change?	4	3	2	1
3.	Do you have confidence in your vision?	4	3	2	1
4.	Do you make decisions on only pertinent issues?	4	3	2	1
5.	Do you avoid making decisions prematurely?	4	3	2	1
6.	Do you make only those decisions that can be carried out effectively?	4	3	2	1

7.	Do you avoid making decisions others should make?	4	3	2	1
8.	Do you control your response to aggression?	4	3	2	1
9.	Do you make a habit of mentally residing in the future?	4	3	2	1
10.	Once your vision is in place, do you act calm and relaxed instead of worrying about the consequences?	4	3	2	1

Of course, Geico's Jack Byrne could score a perfect 40. He even compares himself to Winnie the Pooh. Once Byrne's vision is in place, he keeps his mind on it, just as Pooh keeps his mind on the honey.

Step Two: Increasing Your Patience Level

Experts espouse many methods for increasing patience, but not all of them will work for you. In fact, finding a successful method for increasing your patience poses quite a challenge. For this reason, we've developed nine different approaches to increasing patience. Once you have found a good method, employ that method over and over and over again. It takes patience to become patient.

Nine Ways to Increase Patience

- Keep an "impatient moments" journal, recording every impatient moment you experience during the course of the day. Briefly evaluate the moment in writing, commenting on why it happened, what you could have done to prevent it, and how you will improve your response to similar situations in the future. The more often you write in the journal, the faster you will increase your patience. One executive we have dealt with for a number of years tried this method and found that within a month he had identified five different types of situations that consistently ignited his impatience. Once he identified these situations, he was able to anticipate and control them.

- Practice the "relaxation response." Dr. Herbert Benson, a Harvard Medical School professor, introduced this technique in his book of the same name. He suggests that you 1) find a quiet, calm environment with minimum outside distractions; 2) get into a comfortable position which minimizes muscular tension; 3) shift your mind from rational, externally directed thinking to a constant focus or stimulus (a word, a sound, a phrase, an object) to eliminate all mental distractions; 4) assume a passive attitude in which you do not evaluate or worry about anything, particularly how well you are performing the technique. This relaxed state is similar to the "alpha rest" we mentioned in Chapters 5 and 7. Use this method when moments of impatience arise. One investment banking executive we know uses the relaxation response every morning and evening as he commutes to and from Wall Street and has found that it eases his transition into and out of the clamor of his business.

- Meditate on the source of your impatience. Try to understand the cause more deeply than you have before. Since you don't want to stop until you reach a new insight, allow for several meditation sessions. Once you have thoroughly contemplated the source of your impatience, you will be better prepared to address and correct it. Oftentimes, the source of impatience is a legitimate business concern that demands attention, but sometimes it derives from a more deep-seated emotional problem. One executive who had initially isolated the source of his impatience as his boss's lack of humor, found that his own sense of humor was strained because he used it to cover a blow to his confidence caused by his son's drug problems.

- Project the consequences of your impatience into the future. This works wonders when you have been struggling with impatient behavior over a long period of time, a week or even a month. Set aside at least a half-hour. Become meditative. When you are relaxed, define the source of your impatient behavior, then ask yourself what it has caused you to do. Once you have defined the source and the effect on your behavior, project your actions as far into the future as you can by visualizing the consequences of continued impatience for your organization, your people, your vision, your other skills, and your family. Record the scenario on paper, highlighting all potentially damaging effects. An advertising executive did this recently and reported to us a terrible projected outcome that scared her into changing immediately. "I could have lost my job, and my husband, I was acting so crazy."

- Listen to calming music. Music can "soothe a savage breast." Select music that usually stirs you. Believe it or not, some people claim that a heavy metal rock band calms them more than a Beethoven symphony. Invest in a good car stereo system, portable radio, or tape recorder with earphones so that you can privately enjoy music's soothing effects in many different settings. Your favorite music can create a peaceful, relaxed state in which you can more clearly see the folly of your impatience. A publishing executive in Manhattan finds that listening to old Woodie Guthrie tapes for fifteen minutes after lunch puts a lot of patience into the remainder of his hectic day.

- Use your versatility to put you in a relaxed state where you can more dispassionately observe your impatience. Your exercise program should afford the best opportunity. Some runners experience a "high" or second wind during which they solve pesky problems that have eluded them. Solutions often spring into minds that change their pace. One executive uses racquetball to relax. "To me the most beautiful and graceful moment in the game is when I let the ball sink nearly to the floor before I return it," he says. "Those extra split seconds help me place the ball perfectly and control the game. At that moment I always remind myself to time my business decisions in just the same way. It's amazing how many problems I've solved with this finesse shot!"

• Conduct "impatience exploration" discussions. Find someone you can confide in, preferably someone not associated with your business, and let out everything that prompts your impatience. Ask your confidant to help you figure out why you exhibit such behavior. A spouse, a friend, a golf partner, or anyone who knows and likes you on a personal level will do. Don't stop until you have some answers or until you feel some confidence returning. Some executives who have confidence-keeping secretaries talk things out with them.

• Replay your vision. During one meditation marathon, review the broad vision of your organization's future. This will have one of two effects: a) it will ease your mind and reduce your impatience if you conclude that you are doing everything possible to carry out a viable vision, or b) it will uncover a flaw in the vision or the actions you're taking to carry out the vision. Either way, you'll reduce your impatience. One executive has put her vision of her department's future on paper so she can review it once a week. During a particularly hectic week, when her vision came under attack from several sides, she reviewed it twenty-two times. Her vision held up and so did her patience, which caused her to take more time to develop adhocracy with her people. The resulting exceptional performance of her department won her a promotion to executive vice-president.

• Completely shift gears. Bail out of the situation. Think about something entirely different. Take a weekend vacation or take a trip to Europe. Do whatever it takes to distance yourself from the circumstances causing your impatience. Sometimes you may be able to get out easily, other times it may take tremendous effort. Such a tactic requires versatility, changing your perspective so you can look at your impatience from afar. In this way, you can more objectively determine the threat your impatience poses to your organization. One group of executives has built a physical fitness facility at company headquarters complete with swimming pool, Jacuzzi, steam room, racquetball courts, and running track. They call it "The Refuge" because it never fails to help them squelch their impatience.

Any of these nine methods can provide temporary relief from the symptoms of impatience, but you must do even more to strike at the root cause of it, thereby building the long-term patience you need to create excellence.

Step Three: Living in the Long Term

Lasting patience comes from living in the long term, which means constructing an environment in which everything you and your people do is linked to the future. Again, that doesn't mean that you neglect the short term, but it does mean that you must fully consider the future impact of your actions. Such an orientation must become an underlying state of mind to the people within your organization. We recommend five ways to accomplish this goal.

Five Ways to Live in the Long Term

- Design a forward-looking compensation plan. You can do what Emhart Corp. did, tying executive bonuses to the company's long-term stock price. Consequently, when Emhart executives considered whether to modernize and expand a plant, they quickly decided to go ahead because such a move could enhance the company's stock price within five years. Under Emhart's old compensation system, the answer would have been "no" because next year's profits, upon which bonuses used to be based, would have suffered as a result of modernization and expansion. Sears & Roebuck also ties incentives to long-term performance and shareholder value, a change that has caused divestitures of retail operations overseas and the turnaround of the merchandising group in general; and Borden, Inc., is phasing in a return-on-equity plan for its top four hundred executives, thus placing more emphasis on long-term performance.

• Keep good people over the long term. In the words of John Young, CEO of Hewlett-Packard, "The challenge is to create the kind of environment where those [good people] see their futures here, as opposed to spending all their time looking around [for jobs elsewhere]." When good people stay for the long term, they begin to see the far horizons. As you recall, H-P accomplishes this by giving managers lots of autonomy and encouraging them to act like entrepreneurs.

• Keep your vision alive. Once you have mastered the vision skill, don't just sit back and let it take over your future. Exercise it daily. Otherwise, change may surprise you, perhaps putting you in the shoes of the remarkably successful founder of a West Coast chain of supermarkets, whom we'll call Harry. His stores were just like his competitors' stores except for one important difference: merchandising. Harry was a brilliant merchandiser, always able to keep his customers coming back. Sales and profits soared for Harry's chain until he met a Wall Street investment banker on an airplane one night. By the end of the flight Harry was convinced his company should go public, so he quit being a merchandiser and became a financier, taking his company public, then buying and selling chains of stores in food and nonfood retailing. He became so involved in numerous other activities, including gubernatorial and presidential commissions, that he forgot his long-term vision and soon merchandising in his stores became just like that of his competitors. Uniqueness vanished and his empire eventually crumbled. Though Harry had long-term vision in the beginning, he failed to keep it clear and alive.

- Measure your long-term success. If you only measure short-term success and progress, never tieing it to the long-term, your overall vision will quickly slip out of the minds of everyone in the organization. To live in the long term you need yardsticks that indicate progress over the long haul. These are especially important in a climate where quarterly earnings statements, stock analysts' reports, and hungry money managers who often control 50 percent or more of the stock of large corporations put pressure on short-term performance. According to *BusinessWeek*, C. J. Waidelich, past CEO of Cities Services prior to its takeover by Occidental Petroleum, felt a new pressure: "There is a very difficult situation evolving now. A company can have a few average years while putting a lot of money into long-term investments, and suddenly you're vulnerable to anyone offering 10 bucks a share more for your stock. I'm not sure that's healthy." To see what happens when a company measures performance in the long term, consider American Home Products, recently called the most profitable company in the last decade by *Fortune*. Better known by the names of such well-known products as Anacin, Chef Boy-Ar-Dee, Brach's candy, and Gulden's mustard, American Home Products' return on equity averaged 29.5 percent over the decade from 1974 to 1983. And for the past thirty years return on equity has not fallen below 20 percent (the median return for the Fortune 500 over the last decade was 13.2 percent). American Home Products uses the same measures of success that any other large corporation uses— with one dramatic difference: it applies the measures over the long term, not the short term. One year of phenomenal return on equity doesn't matter as much as thirty years of outstanding return above 20 percent.

- Talk about the long term—all the time. You will recall from the vision chapter that visionary executives articulate their visions into easy to grasp philosophies. Dow Jones, publisher of *The Wall Street Journal,* is one of the most respected companies in America, in 1983 earning $114 million on sales of $866 million and chalking up a whopping 27.4 percent return on equity. What do they talk about at Dow Jones? Long-term reputation. Speaking on this topic with a *Fortune* editor, Dow Jones CEO Warren Phillips said, "I think reputations are built very slowly over many years, on consistency of service to the consumer, high ethical standards, and in the case of journalism, accuracy, reliability, and trustworthiness. And those are not built overnight. Once the public judges well, that's great. But if you trip and do a number of things that are unreliable, untrustworthy, what you've built can collapse overnight. The companies on your [*Fortune*'s] list have probably gotten there due to a long period of pursuing quality and observing strict ethical standards. I'll bet none are there because of the good job they've done in the past year or two, there must be a long period of good performance. But a bad reputation you can get overnight."

Put yourself in the following predicament. You have just been hired as the new CEO of a $300-million plastics company that makes everything from furniture to automobile parts. The company has been reasonably profitable over the past ten years, but it has suffered the consequences of a decade of short-term decisions. You can't make sense out of the hodgepodge of product lines, your plants need renovation, your market share positions have declined, and your managers don't talk about anything but surviving the next six months. As the new CEO, you have been charged by the board to bring some long-term vision to this company. What would you do? Which of the above ways of living in the long term would you employ? Which would you implement first? Second? Meditate on the problem and devise a scenario before you read about what an executive in a similar predicament actually did.

Now imagine Frank Burke, CEO of a plastics firm, in such a situation. Although he recognized the importance of getting the organization to live in the long term, he also realized he couldn't change overnight the way people think, get paid, and measure their performance. He first had to help them fundamentally embrace change. After six months of familiarizing himself with the company and after endless hours of meditation, meetings, and interviews, Burke took his first step toward helping his organization live in the long term by implementing a company-wide communications program that stressed the importance of embarking upon a new era with a new long-term perspective. The campaign included "Breakfast with Burke" discussion sessions, a company newsletter focusing on long-term performance, and posters plastered on company walls saying "Think Tomorrow."

After a minor reorganization, Burke took his second step, individually calling into his office seven key executives—those who would be most critical to the company's turnaround. In each case, he increased their monthly salary by at least 25 percent—his analysis had confirmed that salaries in the company were slightly below the industry average. He then gave each a choice between staying on the current bonus system, which was based on annual profits, or moving to a new bonus system based on the long-term net worth of the company. All seven executives were shocked by the salary increase (one executive's raise was 50 percent) and all chose the new bonus system, under which executives would receive stock based on their own and the company's yearly stock performance. Bonuses were issued based on annual performance, and at the end of each five-year period the company would repurchase, if desired, accumulated stock at a value determined by current net worth. The new system thus helped executives focus on the long-term well-being and profitability of the company as well as annual performance.

In the ensuing twelve months, Burke formulated a vision for the company's future, at the same time devising measures that would monitor the company's progress toward it. The vision included 1) achieving a number one or two position in every market in which the company competed, or getting out of the market, and 2) emphasizing those markets that value product innovation. To measure progress toward achieving these two goals, he introduced a quarterly market share report, to be prepared by an outside, independent survey firm, and a monthly new product innovations report tracking the performance of every new product developed by the company in the previous eighteen months. Other elements of his vision related to the company's culture. Foremost among these was a goal that every employee come to feel that the company was the best place in the state to work. To measure progress toward this goal, Burke instituted an annual interviewing process in which he would individually meet with one hundred employees, selected through a random sampling method, to determine their level of satisfaction with the company.

In the five years since Burke assumed leadership, the company has dropped over thirty product lines, introduced over a hundred new products, grown from $300 million to $760 million, increased profit margins from 4 percent to 11 percent, and placed 75 percent of the company's new products in number one or two market positions. Ninety percent of the company's employees consider it the best place to work in the state.

The Strength of Patience: A Summary

Patience enables you to integrate and orchestrate the use of the other five New Age skills. Since it helps you employ the other skills at the right time and in the right combination and proportion, it allows for exquisite timing, a key ingredient in lasting excellence.

Impatience invariably leads to poor decisions, compromised competence, and a focus on short-range results at the expense of long-range ones. Patient executives, knowing that excellence never comes overnight, have the sort of staying power that invents the future.

In the words of Roswell Dwight Hitchcock, "The secret of all success is to know how to deny yourself. Prove that you can control yourself, and you are an educated man; and without this, all other education is good for nothing." By patiently committing yourself to the New Age skills, denying yourself the shortcuts, quick fixes, and shallow thinking that have hurt American productivity, you will finally be able to create excellence.

As we said at the outset, organizations and their problems are complex, and all organizations evolve through certain predictable stages. Since a given situation will demand all New Age skills but in different combinations and amounts, we have designed four problem-solving cases to which you can apply all you have learned from this book. Chances are you'll find one or more paralleling your own experience. If not, you many well encounter such problems in the future. These cases give you the opportunity to make hypothetical but realistic decisions related to four typical stages of an organization's life: start-up, growth, crisis, and evolution.

PART III

CREATING
EXCELLENCE

CHAPTER 11

Start-up: Originating Strategy and Culture

Silicon Valley is like an individual running around in front of a steamroller. You can outrun the steamroller on any given day. But if you ever sit down you get squashed.
—BOB BOSCHERT

Starting with a Strong Foundation

A company's culture starts forming the instant the founders begin conceiving their enterprise. From the very moment of conception, the company's culture begins to feed on various characters, events, products, strategies, and competitive environments. But some founders are so involved in breathing life into their ideas and strategies that they forget to nurture the infant culture. Sooner or later, they end up paying for the mistake.

Since so many new companies grow up in the fast lane, where change is always accelerating at a dizzying pace, it's easy for their executives to forget that the emerging strategy-culture foundation requires constant attention. Anyone managing a new enterprise must begin constructing the foundation of excellence right from the onset. During the emerging phase of any business, an executive faces a tough challenge in holding everything together because strategies often change from month to month, sending a steady stream of mixed signals to the organization's people. Although a leader can stress flexibility and

249

even weave it into the fabric of the developing culture, constant flux cannot be the culture's mainstay. Strong cultures depend on *long-term* commitment, competence, and consistency. When leaders of emerging companies let their strategies wander opportunistically, without taking their organization's developing culture into account, they end up with weak, fragmented cultures that are incapable of sustaining the next stage of growth. Consider two strikingly different examples, one in Atlanta, the other in Miami Beach.

Jim Shaw built Atlanta's Professional Travel Inc. (PTI) with his vision of a vertically integrated travel company that could control the customer's vacation experience from start to finish—it would plan the trip, sell the tickets, use a company-owned airplane, and book rooms in company-operated hotels. The vision, lauded by many observers as brilliant, would put the travel agent, the airline, and the hotel all under one management. Shaw embarked on his strategy in 1977 and over the next five years PTI grew to over $16 million. When, by 1982, the company was running four retail operations specializing in commercial and vacation travel, the vision seemed on the threshold of reality. Its tour-planning business had signed contracts with companies offering American and international ski packages, and PTI's three Boeing 727-100's gave it control over in-flight service to customers. So the industry was shocked when, on July 13, 1983, PTI filed for bankruptcy protection. That very day, Shaw, still promoting PTI's great advantages, was on a "get acquainted" trip to the Virgin Islands with a group of new travel agents. What had gone wrong? How had such a visionary executive gotten so out of touch with reality? One reason was that Shaw seemed, from the beginning, to take PTI's infant culture for granted, assuming his stunning strategy would take care of everything else. It didn't and it never does. Shaw's people never fully understood any of PTI's individual operations (retail travel, tour packaging, and the airline operation), let alone all three of them combined. The company's accounting system suffered basic problems no one ever resolved, and frequent squabbles between departments and businesses erupted, causing many managers to openly criticize the company's direction. In short, the neglected culture had become negative, disorganized, and confused. By 1982, failure was inevitable. Neither Shaw nor his people had ever worried about making sure their tour operators were solvent. When one tour operator under contract to PTI went bankrupt, PTI had to cover the booked vacations with its own money. In the spring of 1983 another tour company went bankrupt, again leaving PTI holding the bag. The company defaulted on its payments to Eastern Airlines for the three 727's, and when it couldn't meet its other obligations, a brilliant vision fled into Chapter Eleven.

CEO Al Burger of Miami-based "Bugs" Burger Bug Killers, Inc., also had a vision and a strategy, but unlike Shaw, he nurtured a culture to support them. Burger started his extermination business several years ago with the vision of eliminating, not just controlling, pests for his clients in the hotel and restaurant businesses. In six short years, this strategy, based on an unconditional guarantee to eliminate the breeding and nesting of rodents and roaches before requiring payment from the customer, added $20 million to company sales. The visionary Burger didn't just sit back and wait for the orders to come pouring in; he went out on jobs with his extermination crews, personally insuring that customers got the quality service his company promised. In this way he instilled in his four-hundred exterminators a deep commitment to superior service. To bolster his strategy, Burger paid for guest meals or rooms if a customer of one of his clients' restaurants or hotels spotted a pest and then sent individual letters of apology offering another free meal or room. His clients love the attention and happily pay four to six times more than the going rate to get his company's service.

If one of his exterminators loses a major account, Burger makes up for the lost compensation with a combination of salary and commission (exterminators can make $32,000 or more a year) until a new account is found. To avoid shortcutting any job, the company also subsidizes the employee's income when a job takes longer than expected. It also provides a cushion for employees whose customers neglect to prearrange for monthly visits, a common occurrence which can undo efficiency. With 12,000 restaurant and hotel accounts in 43 states, the $25-million business has won the admiration of customers and competitors alike. *Inc.* magazine reported that one employee, Alan Rosenberg, left BBBK, but then returned, saying, "I left 'Bugs' Burger for another company. It was a step backward. They had no standards. So I came back. This is the only company I ever saw where the owner and the people on the job all think the same way." A common commitment to superior service, high standards, and a dedication to stamping out roaches and rodents have combined to create the "Mercedes-Benz" of pest extermination.

Now that we've seen examples of the right and the wrong ways to lead an emerging enterprise, let's look at the future of a hypothetical high-tech company in the Silicon Valley.

A Case of Silicon Valley Fever

Brilliant engineer Bob Welch had worked for a prominent microcomputer firm for five years, during which he contributed significantly to his employer's technological leadership. He was especially proud of his accomplishments with voice-activated computing, which made input devices such as the keyboard, mouse, or optical reader obsolete. But his employer didn't share his enthusiasm for voice-activated computing and refused to budget sufficient money to develop a marketable product. Welch left the company in 1984, despite efforts of company officials, including the CEO, to keep him. Turning down offers of a 50 percent salary increase and more free time to pursue research in voice-activation, Welch decided to start his own firm. By December 1984, he had raised enough money from venture capitalist David Benson to launch Welcasco, Inc. Welch had to temporarily subdue his fascination with voice-activation in favor of launching the venture's first product, a sophisticated executive computer operated on the "mouse" principle, but using, in place of the mouse device, a hand-held stylus to point directly at data on the screen. The entire computer with a horizontally or vertically positioned screen, would fit into a medium-sized briefcase. Welcasco planned to sell to executives through a direct-marketing organization patterned after Tupperware's and Amway's approaches, but carefully modified to attract corporate executives. To design this marketing program, Welch hired JoAnn Casey, a savvy direct-sales marketer for a large cosmetic and housewares company. Casey had built similar organizations for two other companies and was excited by the prospect of taking her expertise into America's executive suites. Together Welch and Casey would own 51 percent of the company, while David Benson's venture capital firm would own 49 percent.

In the spring of 1985, Welch and Casey began pulling their organization together, with Welch supervising a group of seven handpicked engineers and Casey working with ten highly skilled direct marketers. By the fall of 1985, when the first Welcasco "Dax" computer went into production, the company had pre-sold five-hundred units at $10,000 each. The Dax package included a computer with a screen, two disc drives, a standard software package, and twenty-four hours of training and consulting per customer.

By the end of 1986 Welcasco hit paydirt with $12 million in sales and an avalanche of new orders. The system's technological innovations, combined with the company's unique selling approach, had made Dax an overnight success. By the end of 1987, sales jumped to $76 million, and Casey's direct-sales approach had turned the industry upside down. Seeing no limit to its continued success, the company contracted with two software houses to develop special programs for Dax. It also introduced a portable printer to give the marketing organization another product to sell. Since Casey desired to run the show, she became Welcasco's CEO at the beginning of 1987, with Welch moving into his own dream position as head of research and development.

Then came the spring of 1989, when the company faced a

critical decision. After two years of intense research and development, Welch had finally built a marketable voice-activated computer, making even the innovative Dax stylus obsolete. For her part, Casey had continued to strengthen the company's unbeatable direct-marketing organization and to further exploit its marketing strengths, Welcasco had taken over as marketing arm for several other high-tech companies that produced telecommunications devices, sophisticated audiovisual equipment, electronic presentation systems, a range of office gadgetry, and, of course, microcomputers. Most of Welcasco's growth had come from these other manufacturers' products. In fact, of the company's $200 million in sales at the end of 1988, only 25 percent came from Dax and related products. Now Welcasco had to make a choice. Should it continue to expand its marketing empire or should it return to its technological innovation roots and introduce the Voice-Activated Computer (VAC-1)?

Since Casey, Welch, and Benson were still the major stockholders, they met to review the company's situation and quickly identified three options:

A. Continue the direct-marketing approach but place priority emphasis on VAC. Introduce a competitively priced VAC-1 personal computer as quickly as possible through all viable channels of distribution, including the company's direct-marketing organization, to maximize market penetration. At the same time, expand plant facilities to mass produce the new machine and capitalize on the VAC research with intensified research and development.

B. Concentrate on building the company's marketing organization by increasing the number of direct-sales people and adding even more high-tech suppliers to broaden the line of products. Slowly introduce a premium-priced and sophisticated VAC-1 executive computer sold exclusively through the company's direct-marketing organization.

C. Implement both options simultaneously.

If you were in charge, which path would you choose? Why? To gain the maximum benefit from this exercise, spend some time building and testing your own scenario.

Now that you've thoroughly considered your case for one of the three options, watch how a New Age executive, armed with the six skills, would approach the decision.

The New Age executive would shun the first option because mass-producing and mass-marketing a revolutionary new computer within the existing Welcasco organization could invite disaster. Selection of this option indicates an obvious lack of insight in ignoring the strategic advantage of the direct-marketing organization, a lack of sensitivity in disregarding the impact on the Welcasco culture, and a lack of vision in not fully utilizing the company's strategic and cultural strengths. The company's marketing and sales culture has become highly competent by selling an ever expanding array of products to an elite group of customers. An all-out effort on the new VAC-1 would require the sort of mass merchandising to which Welcasco's existing culture is not geared. Nor is the company geared to mass production—only 25 percent of its sales has come from its own products. Technological innovation certainly served the company well at the outset, but such innovation comes from Bob Welch and his isolated staff of engineers, not from Welcasco's dominant culture. While the innovative products and sales methods received equal billing in the beginning, Welcasco has evolved in five years to stress the latter. Pursuing option A would grossly mismatch strategy and culture, preventing the company from achieving long-term success with either the new machine or its marketing empire. Casey has superbly rallied the troops around the common philosophy of providing executives with quick and useful access to high-tech products, and she has consistently recruited sales people, now numbering over two hundred, capable of carrying on the Welcasco tradition. Pursuing a strategy that does not take maximum advantage of these people would squander a valuable resource and mark the beginning of a strong culture's demise.

Although the New Age executive would find option B attractive, it does present one major drawback. On the positive side, it exploits the strengths of the direct-marketing organization by expanding into additional product lines while introducing the VAC in a limited way. That nicely matches strategy and culture. Casey invested five years in Welcasco's culture, and it wouldn't make sense to throw those years away. However, on the negative side, Bob Welch has invested five years developing a marketable computer that nontechnical business people can talk to—a potentially huge breakthrough, but option B will only capture a fraction of that potential. Would a company run by a New Age executive sit back and let someone else capitalize on its research and development? Not if vision and patience can find a way to catapult that R and D into a profitable future. It would be a grave mistake to ignore the breakthrough potential of the VAC-1 by introducing it slowly in limited numbers, thereby giving competitors time to duplicate and mass-market similar models. There must be a better alternative.

There is: option C. It allows Welcasco to take full advantage of its two major strengths: direct marketing of high-tech gear to executives, and technological innovation with microcomputers. The New Age executive must find a way to capitalize on all strengths. While the direct-marketing culture dominates at Welcasco, don't forget that Welch's technological innovation culture, while less pervasive, also contains the seeds of vast future potential. In this situation the best plan would be to draw upon all our six skills, but particularly insight, sensitivity, and vision to create a foundation of excellence in both the direct-marketing and technological innovation organizations. To do so, the company would need to be divided into two independent parts, one focused on implementing option A, the other focused on implementing option B. The two new business units could function as autonomous divisions within Welcasco, or they could operate as two separate companies. Either approach could work, but incorporating two separate companies would be the most streamlined and simple one. Although splitting the company in two, no matter how it's done, would require new capital, the company's past success, coupled with the breakthrough potential of the VAC-1, should make it easily possible to secure the necessary financing.

The two new units would offer some interesting advantages. Because the split would move the direct-marketing organization into one company and the production and R and D organization into another, Welcasco would enjoy a clean separation of two very different businesses, but it would, at the same time, maintain a complementary relationship. The marketing organization could still sell the R and D organization's products, but the production and R and D organization would be free to pursue other methods of distribution without squelching its corporate culture in the process. In fact, Welch and Casey had *informally* separated the company in 1987 when Casey became CEO and Welch immersed himself in research and development. All that is needed is to formalize that structure. Since splitting the company into two separate units and pursuing both options A and B could become burdensome, the company's leaders should devise a fallback position that gains as much advantage from both options as possible. The alternatives might include: a joint venture with another major personal computer company to introduce the VAC-1, a licensing of the VAC-1 technology to other manufacturers, or a sale of the direct-marketing organization to another, larger direct-marketing company that is eager to get into the high-tech arena. Whatever the fallback position, it should reflect the personal desires of the three major stockholders, as well as a sensitivity to the wants and needs of their employees.

What did Welch, Casey, and Benson actually do? Deciding to establish two divisions within the same company, they chose option C. By the end of 1990 both divisions had won excellence. The direct-marketing division reached $400 million in sales with further market penetration of existing and new product lines. Profits for the marketing division stood at a staggering $96 million, 24 percent of sales.

VAC-1 was introduced in the fall of 1989 and became an immediate success with over 1,000 units installed by Christmas. In 1990, that number soared to 7,000 with sales of $80 million and profits of $7 million by the end of the year. In January 1991, the VAC division had already begun shipping enhancements for the revolutionary machine. Of course Welcasco's success did not come without some serious problems. Over the years, tensions and disagreements between Welch, the innovator, and Casey, the marketer, constantly grew. Because their two divisions shared certain administrative functions, such as accounting, planning, corporate communications and public relations, personnel, and some staff marketing functions, a confrontation between executives with radically different points of view became inevitable. Welch passionately argued his positions, Casey equally defended her own, and Benson tried to play mediator; but the warring parties could not muster sufficient sensitivity to each other's viewpoint or enough versatility to adopt a differing perspective to avoid a major rift. By 1992, Welch, Casey, and Benson resolved the rift by finally and completely separating the businesses. The New Age executive would have used greater insight, sensitivity, and vision to have recognized from the beginning the need for two *totally* distinct organizations, incorporated as separate businesses with separate administrative functions.

Start-ups in the New Age

Executives of emerging businesses invariably rely on the two foundation skills, insight and sensitivity, and the integrative skill, vision. When these skills work together from the moment of a company's conception, they forge a strategy-culture alloy that will carry the company successfully through the predictable stages of development: growth, crisis, and evolution.

The start-up phase, more than any other, lends itself to culture neglect and the willy-nilly shifting of strategy, two dangers that account for the high mortality rate among new enterprises. Fortunately, conscientious use of New Age skills can prevent this, especially if enterprises muster them *before* they launch their ventures. Six months after incorporation may be too late.

• CHAPTER 12 •

Growth: Holding Strategy and Culture Together

> Think of the sequence. You create something. You grow it. You look for a competitive advantage. Then you really tie it down tight, making it as efficient as possible. Those are very different jobs.
>
> —ALAN ZAKON

Determining Appropriate Strategies

Even the most venerable and best-run organizations need new strategies from time to time, but new strategies can often conflict with the organization's existing culture. Executives in this position face one of the most difficult decisions of their careers: do they pursue an innovative strategy, changing the culture to match it, or do they keep looking for a strategy that more closely matches the existing culture? Choosing between these two courses of action requires a great deal of vision and patience, especially for a new CEO who has come aboard to harness, exploit, or direct the growth of an enterprise. Before you test your skills in a typical case involving a new strategy and culture, consider these two strikingly different situations.

Frank Sands, a Harvard Business School graduate, class of '63, took over his family's business, Sands, Taylor & Wood (ST & W), a Boston-based company that produces a natural wheat flour, King Arthur, that the company began selling in 1790. When young Sands came aboard, ST & W's annual sales were $3 million, derived exclusively from the unique product that had won the company admiration over the years. Armed

261

with his Harvard MBA and an eagerness to see the family firm grow, Frank took over as CEO in 1968. In his first year he began implementing a bold new strategy to help ST & W gain a larger and broader share of the bakery market through internal expansion and external acquisition. To launch this strategy, Sands acquired Allied Bakers Supply Company, a supplier of bakery ingredients whose profits were only marginal. Frank reasoned that in a declining flour market, Allied would provide instant relationships with new customers, thereby automatically winning ST & W a larger share of the overall bakery market. The move seemed to pay off when ST & W's sales doubled to $6 million by the end of the year. In 1973 Frank made his second acquisition. Convinced he could save money by manufacturing certain products his company had merely distributed in the past, he bought Joseph Middleby Jr. Co., a producer of pastry fillings and toppings. Again, sales doubled, this time to $12 million. In 1975 Sands acquired H. A. Johnson Company, also a manufacturer of bakery supplies, and ST & W's sales quickly shot to $25 million, with after-tax profits of $400,000. In the aftermath of such remarkable success, Frank hired a new general manager to run the company's day-to-day operations and bought a farm in Vermont, where he could take time to enjoy the dividends of his brilliant strategy. That turned out to be a mistake.

In 1977 ST & W contracted to provide bakery supplies to two-hundred Dunkin' Donuts stores, and although the margins were razor-thin, Frank believed the increased volume ($18 million a year) would do nothing but benefit ST & W. In 1978 he acquired Goodhue Products Inc., a producer of frozen bread dough. Sales soared to $45 million, but it didn't take long for excellence to fade under the pressure of a lagging economy and skyrocketing interest and gasoline prices, unforeseen costs that made the Dunkin' Donuts contract unprofitable and the rest of ST & W's operations only marginally profitable. Bankruptcy loomed on the horizon. How did such a stunningly successful strategy turn sour so quickly? Back in 1963, the company had been producing a unique, high-quality product that enjoyed an excellent reputation, and the small organization that had made that happen displayed a rich history of quality, performance, and dedication. When Frank Sands introduced his new strategy to enlarge ST & W's share of the bakery market through mergers, the apparent success of his moves blinded him to the fact that he was adding commodity products that lacked the high quality, reputation, and healthy margins his company's culture had instilled in King Arthur's Flour. Worse, the cultures Frank acquired cared little about the long tradition of excellence established by ST & W. In his headlong pursuit of growth, Sands had torn apart the company's strong strategy-culture alloy, but he did learn a hard lesson.

Barely avoiding bankruptcy in the late 1970s and early 1980s, ST & W has since divested itself of all its acquisitions, and today, with a sales volume of $3.5 million, the company has gone back to basics. Stressing its unique flour, the company is expanding its distribution of that product through an independent broker organization, and it has introduced a new product, stone-ground wheat flour, that has gotten off to a handsome start. By doing so, ST & W has once again harnessed its rich organizational culture. Although Frank Sands still desires growth, he has learned not to try to grow with strategies that require wrenching changes in his company's culture. His new vision, fortified with a healthy amount of patience, should help him create excellence in the future.

Unlike ST & W, Esquire, Inc., identified the bedrock of its strategic and cultural strengths before it began implementing an innovative growth strategy. In 1977 Bernard Krauss, CEO of Esquire, Inc., recognized that the company had lost its competitive advantages in mass market situations while it had retained its edge in the small market niches it dominated with unique products. Consequently, a new strategy emerged: divesting Esquire of some companies and expanding others through internal growth and acquisitions. After selling the company's loss-ridden *Esquire* magazine in 1977, Krauss moved Esquire completely out of the magazine business by 1979, at the same time expanding its educational publishing and specialty lighting businesses, both of which represented small niches with unique products. Now Krauss is buying businesses that fit the criteria he has formulated for excellence: unique specialty products that dominate small niches and produce high margins. According to Krauss's formula, the best markets are unique and noncompetitive. To augment the company's successful Wide-Lite operation, he has acquired four new businesses in the lighting area. He also purchased Cambridge Book, a textbook publisher, and Centron Corp., a maker of industrial training films. Remember the plight of Allyn and Bacon described in Chapter 3? A and B has begun to prosper under Esquire's management, finally getting out of the red and well into the black. Krauss has also taken Esquire into music publishing and television stations. Such diverse entities relate to a common strategy and culture because each dominates a small market niche with a unique product or service that allows it to position itself effectively against larger competitors. The Esquire culture thrives on decentralization, market dominance, and sustaining uniqueness. The bottom line? In the early 1980s earnings jumped over 500 percent to $8 million on sales of $110 million. Since then, the company has been acquired by Gulf & Western's Simon & Schuster division, which will reap great benefits if it has the patience to let Krauss's unique strategy and culture remain intact.

Whenever a firm embarks upon a new course to achieve greater growth, its culture will ultimately determine the success or failure of the changes. While AT & T's culture excelled in a monopolistic, regulated environment, where R and D, manufacturing, and marketing functioned noncompetitively both from within and without, the firm has recently found itself in the opposite situation: competition both from within and without. Whether AT & T's culture can successfully adapt has sparked tremendous debate, and many observers argue that it will take up to ten years to bring about the requisite changes. Obviously, vision and patience will determine the outcome.

While AT & T had no choice but to change, most other firms can choose their strategy after carefully weighing the consequences for the strategy-culture alloy. Any management unwilling to commit the time (it could take years) and money (it could take millions) to develop a new culture or adapt an old one should reconsider its goals. Remember, it took Frank Sands fifteen years to learn this lesson the hard way. To help you avoid learning the hard way, you can now test your vision and patience in a situation where growth had made it difficult to hold strategy and culture together.

A Case of Identity Crisis

Let's look at the future of another hypothetical firm. In 1955, Bob Jacobs and Dick Ross founded the Jacobs & Ross Advertising Agency in Dallas. In 1975 Bob died, leaving Dick, at age sixty-seven, chairman of the board but relatively uninvolved in day-to-day operations. President John Gibbs, forty-five, really runs the show these days, overseeing offices in Dallas, Houston, and San Antonio, with a few New Orleans accounts handled out of the Houston office. Agency revenues hit $50 million last year, profits a solid $2 million. The agency employs 103 people, 35 in Dallas, 42 in Houston, and 26 in San Antonio.

In the agency's early days it built an enviable reputation as the most creative advertising agency in Dallas. For twenty years, it delivered superb performance and won scores of advertising awards until clients and competitors alike knew that if a product was suffering from stale, worn-out approaches, Jacobs & Ross could solve the problem with creative advertising—for a price. J & R got the sort of results that made it possible to charge more than other local agencies. Behind his desk, John Gibbs had hung a chart depicting clients' sales before and after each of twenty J & R campaigns. The differences told the whole story.

Through the late 1970s, the agency was still benefiting from its strong beginnings and its traditions of creativity, but John Gibbs felt under increasing pressure to expand to allow good people ample opportunities to grow, develop, and advance. Consequently, in 1978, he opened the Houston office, followed by the San Antonio office in 1980. Then he brought in a few big New Orleans accounts in 1982, planning eventually to open an office there. He had even set his sights on Oklahoma City, Memphis, and Birmingham, not to mention smaller cities that also provided growth opportunities. Gibbs's focus on growth prompted two important events: 1) the client base shifted from industrial and consumer product and service companies to retail chains, and 2) quick, efficient ad production had supplanted creativity as the agency's most utilized skill. In shifting to retail clients, who generally budgeted heavily for advertising and could thus help J & R grow faster, the agency had to master the fast, efficient production of daily newspaper, radio, and TV ads. Retail clients didn't value creativity as much as timing. If an agency couldn't place timely ads, it soon lost the account, a fact of business that explains why most retailing companies across the country frequently switch agencies or establish in-house ones.

J & R's shift to retail was risky, but Gibbs felt it was a good gamble, given the potential growth benefits. Fortunately, as J & R's shift to retail clients evolved over seven years, the agency managed to retain its strong reputation for creativity. Approximately 30 percent of its clients, the old Dallas-based consumer and industrial products manufacturers or service companies, hired J & R because of that reputation. While these clients had come to represent only about 33 percent of the agency's total revenues, they accounted for 50 percent of the profits. Unfortunately, serving retail clients had become so demanding, and the opening of new offices so draining on management's time and attention, that the agency's ability to launch boldly creative campaigns no longer matched its reputation. Unless J & R took immediate action to close the gap between its reputation and its competence, it might lose its most profitable clients. Although you can regain a lost competence, a lost reputation can be impossible to recapture.

To remedy the situation, Dick Ross, John Gibbs, Mickey Christopherson, and Jerry Jackson flew to Nassau in the Bahamas for a three-day management retreat in October 1985.

Mickey was the senior vice-president responsible for the agency's consumer and industrial clients; Jerry Jackson was the senior vice-president responsible for the retail clients. The four knew they faced some tough decisions regarding the agency's future. Should they endorse Jerry Jackson's proposal for turning the company into a retailing specialist throughout the southern United States? Such a strategy would make J & R the first specialty agency of its kind in the United States, a move worth cautious and careful consideration. But the four executives felt pressure to decide quickly because one of the company's major clients, Sims Supers, a Texas-based grocery store chain, had just informed J & R that it was acquiring Delway Foods, an Atlanta-based grocery store chain with operations throughout the southeast. Could J & R service the combined group of three-hundred stores? To do so, J & R would have to open at least five new regional offices. If J & R couldn't agree to accept the assignment within two weeks, Sims would reluctantly switch agencies.

Struggling with the issues involved, the four executives spent their first two days in Nassau engaged in marathon discussions that led them to identify three basic options:

A. Open the five new offices to service Sims Supers and begin implementing Jackson's proposed retail advertising specialization strategy. Phase out nonretailing clients and open offices in all major cities in the South within the next five years, positioning the agency as the most efficient, responsive, and competent retail advertising organization in the region.

B. Respond to Sims Supers by opening five new offices but at the same time revitalize the agency's sagging creative capabilities. Maintain the current mix of retail and non-retail clients.

C. Tell Sims Supers that J & R cannot service them outside Dallas, Houston, and New Orleans. Refocus on the agency's longstanding strategic and cultural strength: creativity. Reduce the number of retailing clients and slow down growth to allow for revitalization of the agency's competence in creative campaigns.

Put yourself in the shoes of J & R's executives. Which option would you recommend? Why? Take some time to reflect on J & R's situation, carefully considering each of the three options, then discover what a New Age executive would do.

Option A deserves careful consideration, but it poses some fundamental problems that would eliminate it from the running. Given the fickleness of retail clients, the historical strength and current reputation of the J & R agency, and the risk associated with the new retail-oriented strategy, the New Age executive would move to the second and third options. Retail clients would always demand standard, uncreative ads rather than creative ones, and, regardless of an agency's competence in supplying their demands, clients could capriciously switch to another agency or develop their own in-house departments at any time. Margins are low and, in light of inevitably high account turnover, achieving a level of efficiency that would maintain reasonable profitability would be a constant headache. Hungry agencies just entering the market, recognizing retailers as an easy mark, could slice their fees to get the business. No New Age executive would select option A because pursuing an obviously short-term strategy would show a lack of vision and patience. A little organizational introspection would quickly reveal the great loss the agency would suffer if it discarded its reputation and continued to let its competence wane.

Quick growth could also be quite fleeting. New Age executives may take calculated risks, but they never mortgage their futures for the fast buck. The agency's track record came from a proven success formula. To throw that away in pursuit of an untried, risky strategy with fleeting rewards could ruin J & R. For all these reasons, option A would only make sense for an agency without J & R's strong culture and reputation for creativity.

The New Age executive would also find option B unacceptable. Unlike the case in the last chapter, this situation does not lend itself to splitting the company into two parts because the two alternatives do not offer equal opportunities. While separation could work for an agency with nothing to lose, J & R could not maintain the current mix of retail and nonretail business without eventually destroying its reputation and completely draining its creative competence. Since the past five years have proven that accepting too much retail business and opening new offices too rapidly takes its toll on the agency's distinctive competence and reputation, pursuing option B would simply continue an unwholesome trend. It also would display insensitivity by failing to recognize the nature and worth of the agency's culture, and a lack of focus by attempting to implement a strategy that requires a new culture while at the same time maintaining an old one.

Therefore, the New Age executive would select option C. While it doesn't take advantage of the immediate opportunity to expand with Sims Supers, that opportunity is in fact a threat to J & R's patiently developed culture and reputation. Rapid growth would certainly occur, but the agency's past pursuit of growth has brought negative results by eroding the agency's competence to deliver creative advertising approaches, a competence J & R can redevelop only by rededicating itself to its original vision. The agency's growth through retailing clients and new offices looks good on paper, but it's not the kind of growth to be relied on over time. Can a professional service firm rely on anything but its sterling reputation? Can it build an enviable reputation with traits other than creativity? Although a reputation based on production efficiency, quickness, and customer relations may also be desirable, it cannot replace a reputation for creative results. When a client suffers from sagging sales and profits, efficiency and speed and friendliness won't solve its problems. What about using growth to keep key people? Since J & R can't keep them all, it should pick the best ones and stop worrying about losing the others. What if they join competitors? If J & R rededicates itself to its former strategy and culture, it will keep far ahead of its competitors. This is where the skills of vision and patience really do their work. The New Age executive needs vision to hold strategy and culture together and to create a future based on long-standing strengths. Patience must temper the temptation to pursue rapid growth, particularly when it's offered on a silver platter. No fast-growth opportunity should be allowed to jeopardize J & R's magic strategy-culture alloy.

Unfortunately, in the beginning, Ross, Gibbs, Christopherson, and Jackson pursued option B, attempting to grow with Sims Supers while simultaneously revitalizing their reputation for creative advertising solutions. In the years after 1985, their competence in the area of creativity continued to decline despite frantic attempts to bolster it. Although the five new offices did bring fast growth and numerous retail clients, the Dallas office sank to being the worst performer in the agency. By the end of 1988, J & R reached revenues of $120 million, but profits lay stagnant at only $750,000, and the margins on retail business, which now accounted for 85 percent of total business, continued to be squeezed. Predictably, in the spring of 1989, Sims Supers' new CEO decided to establish an in-house advertising agency, immediately robbing J & R of 30 percent of its revenues. If two other major retailing chains also build in-house agencies, J & R could lose another 25 percent of its revenues. Did the growth keep good people? Several left to start Sims Supers' advertising department and several other key managers, complaining about the lack of creativity at J & R, are looking for jobs elsewhere. As John Gibbs put it, "We may have grown like a weed, but we're withering."

In the two years after 1989 J & R closed five offices and dropped twelve retail clients. Then began the long process of retrenching back to the agency's roots: creativity. Finally recognizing that the path will be difficult, the company nevertheless sees no alternative that promises long-term excellence. Vision and patience have finally come back to Ross, Gibbs, and Christopherson (Jackson left the agency when the firm decided to get out of the retail business). It took them longer than it should have, but they have finally gained some footing on the right path.

Growth in the New Age

What do you do when growth plans require a new strategy and a new culture, or when growth simply threatens to tear strategy and culture apart? Before embarking on any new strategy or succumbing to uncontrolled growth, you must bring your vision and patience to bear. While the former helps you keep an eye on both strategy and culture, the latter provides the long-term orientation you need to avoid opportunistic decisions that may destroy your strategy-culture alloy.

If growth requires a brilliant new strategy that poses a threat to the organization's culture, the brilliant strategy should be left on the drawing board. But if vision and patience uncover a weak strategy-culture marriage, a brilliant new strategy may provide the best means of appropriately modifying the culture. If so, vision and patience will help insure the durability of the new marriage.

CHAPTER 13

Crisis: Radically Altering Strategy and Culture

> Most ailing organizations have developed a functional blindness to their own defects. They are not suffering because they cannot resolve their problems but because they cannot see their problems.
>
> —JOHN GARDNER

Deciding What to Change

When the strategy and culture of an organization must radically change to enable management to rescue it from bankruptcy and failure, decisive action provides the surest turnaround. However, most executives who have been part of the management team that allowed the crisis to occur in the first place naturally resist recognizing and responding to the problems. Many even cling to the illusion that success lies just around the next corner. Such illusions prevent these executives from performing the radical surgery that so often determines the salvation of an enterprise. Although patience sometimes dictates that holding fast to a vision may help turn the corner from failure to success, many organizations pass beyond the point where it makes sense to continue patiently nurturing a vision, when the signals of decline (sagging sales and profits, personnel turnover, declining quality in products and services) persist year in and year out. When management does decide to perform radical surgery, it must ask the next tough question: what to change and how much?

Companies that have failed to promptly answer this question

will never achieve lasting excellence. We have cited numerous examples of failing and failed companies, companies like Braniff, which changed too much, too soon, and fell into bankruptcy; companies like International Harvester, which didn't change enough, soon enough, to avoid financial collapse; Woolco, which could never figure out what needed changing before all its stores had to be closed; Bausch & Lomb's instruments group, which mistakenly tried to imitate the style that had worked so well for IBM. Before exploring the New Age response to crisis, let's look at two troubled organizations which survived crisis in two dramatically different ways.

Brunswick Corp., best known for its bowling equipment, experienced crisis in 1982. The firm had just sold Sherwood Medical Company, the company's most promising and profitable business, to American Home Products, to avoid an unfriendly takeover by Whittaker Corp., which also wanted to get its hands on Sherwood. That left Brunswick with a group of lackluster recreation, defense, and technical businesses. According to a recent article in *BusinessWeek*, Wall Street investment bankers were calling for a "major redevelopment of assets" to guarantee Brunswick's survival. They sent a clear message: "Get out of the recreation business for good, then emphasize defense and technical businesses." But Brunswick CEO Jack Reichert said "No!" Armed with New Age skills, Reichert, the head of a $1-billion company in serious trouble (Brunswick lost $20 million in 1982), knew some things had to change, but he also saw the wisdom of keeping others the same. In Reichert's view, Wall Street demanded too much change, so he kept the company's bowling, billiard, and outboard motor businesses, but did embark on other changes.

First, Reichert altered the company's business strategies to put its products in market leadership positions. This meant eliminating overly cautious strategies that shortsightedly sought to prevent failure and replacing them with a stronger emphasis on aggressive new products. Obviously, such a major shift in emphasis would require shifts in culture, shifts Reichert knew should initiate his change program.

The severity of the situation, with Wall Street coaching and second-guessing on the sidelines, demanded quick, decisive action, but action calculated not to overwhelm Brunswick's culture. Convinced that his company's bureaucratic approach to decision-making would have to go before Brunswick could successfully implement winning market strategies, Reichert began his program by eliminating five senior management positions—the chief operating officer and four group executive positions—and reassigning the executives to streamline decision-making and reduce red tape. He reduced eleven divisions to eight, cut corporate staff from 560 to 230, eliminated lengthy reports and analyses, and increased incentive compensation. This crisis called for rather shocking measures, as crises usually do, but management had no reason to protect the culture at the expense of the organization's very life. Despite the gravity of the staff cuts, the decision eventually helped bolster face-to-face communications and provided more motivation for accomplishing goals. Reichert also instituted venture capital groups in each division to shelter new products with corporate, rather than division, funding, thus avoiding any need for his division managers to reduce profits and bonuses.

In the last two years, Brunswick has become more aggressive in its markets, more responsive to opportunities, and more profitable. 1983 produced profits of $66 million on sales of $1.2 billion, and the company's stock shot from $9 to $28 a share. 1984 looks even better.

As Brunswick's culture changed, the company grew more confident and aggressive about the new business strategies it could handle. New strategies and ventures include acquisition of a software company, creation of injection-molded parts made of powdered metal, a consolidation of the four outboard motor product lines, and numerous other projects that give the company's new culture a chance to flourish.

Across the Pacific, one Japanese company, which you would expect to value culture, met the challenge of crisis with strategy instead. Mazda Motor Corp. was suffering serious financial difficulty in 1974. The oil crisis had hit Mazda harder than other companies because its unique rotary engine really gobbled up the gas. Although Sumitomo Bank came to the rescue with the necessary financing to turn the company around, Mazda still needed a new CEO. It picked Yoshiki Yamasaki, who since the late 1930s had worked his way up through the ranks at Mazda.

Strategically, the company had bet its future on a rotary engine that could satisfy small car owners with the power of a large engine, but the oil crisis made further pursuit of that strategy ill-advised. Accepting this fact, Yamasaki quickly launched a new direction for the company: producing fast-selling cars that appealed to specific market segments by virtue of special designs or features.

In the years that followed, Mazda introduced the GLC sub-compact, targeted at customers interested in very small cars; the 626 sedan, emphasizing style and features, but still targeted at price-conscious buyers; and the RX-7 sports car, aimed at would-be Porsche drivers who wanted a sports car but couldn't afford one. It worked. In 1984 Mazda racked up its eighth consecutive increase in earnings and now enjoys a position as the world's ninth-largest car manufacturer.

Whether strategy, culture, or both must change to insure survival, executives must carefully identify exactly what must change and by how much before moving decisively.

A Case of Blindness

Let's look at how another hypothetical company dealt with change.

William McCovey was the president and CEO of Injection Molding Corporation of America (IMCA). McCovey had started the company in 1960 and built it up to $50 million in sales before Star Industries, an industrial products conglomerate, acquired it in 1974. McCovey, forty-eight at the time of the acquisition, agreed to stay on as president until he reached retirement age. Although the sale of his company had made him a multimillionaire, he loved the company and looked forward to playing a key role in a billion-dollar operation.

In true Horatio Alger style, McCovey had started IMCA on a shoestring to produce plastic pen barrels for a fledgling ballpoint pen manufacturer. As the ballpoint pen swept the country, it also swept IMCA into excellence. Eventually the pen company developed its own remarkably efficient injection-molding equipment and McCovey had mapped out a strategy for making IMCA the plastics division (with a full R and D staff and facilities) of major manufacturing companies. The company's slogan became "Flexible solutions for all plastics problems." Before long, IMCA's competence in R and D and its production flexibility allowed the company to move quickly from one injection-molded product to another, making ballpoint pen barrels one day, tracheotomy tubes the next. McCovey had an uncanny ability to predict a "hot" new application and then milk it as a supplier until the client acquired its own injection-molding equipment to reduce costs. By then, he'd be onto another trend. Recently, he had been making child-resistant closures, which was one of the main reasons IMCA was purchased by Star, whose pharmaceutical divisions demanded millions of the caps. Then, in the early 1980s, the "hot" products seemed to screech to a halt. When the situation reached the point that no one product accounted for more than 2 percent of IMCA's total sales volume, McCovey blamed it on the recession and sat back waiting for consumer buying to pick up steam. "Washington will fix that," he claimed.

He seemed oblivious to the fact that more and more IMCA customers consisted of smaller businesses, whose size and high percentage of bankruptcies caused IMCA colossal accounts-receivable problems. Competition had also increased over the years, until an injection-molding house seemed situated on every corner of the Los Angeles industrial area, where IMCA operated its own plant. Nevertheless, no competitor could match IMCA's R and D capability, so McCovey folded his hands behind his head and gazed comfortably at the smoggy skyline. "We're still the best," he insisted.

In 1982, despite signs of economic recovery on the horizon, IMCA's situation did not improve, and by mid-1983 the company's financial situation threatened Star's profitability. Before long, Star management assigned Bob Dresser, group vice-president of the pharmaceutical group, the responsibility of turning IMCA around. Dresser and McCovey spent hours analyzing the injection-molding industry and IMCA's position in it. Over the years, injection-molding had progressed from a specialty industry to a widespread process. Most large companies needed so many injection-molded plastic parts for their products that they had incorporated their own in-house injection-molding capabilities by the early 1980s. Those that lacked their own capability could get dozens of independent injection-molders bidding for the business. To gain a foothold with clients, some newer firms even settled for a few percentage points over cost. These developments explained IMCA's shift from larger to smaller customers.

As far as IMCA's R and D competence went, it had become less and less attractive to new but in many cases financially unstable customers who wanted low costs, not R and D. Dresser pointed out that rival upstarts were now facing long lines of creditors in bankruptcy courts across the nation. "That's how we've found ourselves in the credit business," he told McCovey. "Receivables have risen from forty-five days to sixty and even a hundred. Do you realize we're writing off 25 percent of our receivables?" Changing times had translated into hard times for IMCA's once brilliant strategy of serving as its customers' plastics divisions. As far as Dresser could determine, McCovey hadn't seen it coming. The founder just sat there shaking his head. "We'll make a comeback in 1984."

Dresser soon began scrutinizing the company's culture. Was it still strong, as McCovey so vehemently insisted? "We've got the best plastics engineers and technicians in the country at IMCA. And they believe in me. After all, I built this company out of thin air." Dresser had to agree that at least until now, the culture had maintained a consistent commitment to its competence, but how would they feel if they lost their jobs? Recently, the only thing between IMCA and collapse had been Star's financial shelter. Pull that away and 227 loyal plastics people would be pounding the pavement looking for jobs.

Dresser faced a difficult decision. On the one hand, IMCA's predicament demanded drastic action. On the other hand, he had only been with Star since the previous winter, when he had come aboard to replace the executive who had let IMCA drift into deepening trouble. He liked and admired McCovey and didn't want to be seen as a ruthless hatchet man for the front office. Unfortunately, the whole pharmaceutical group had drifted, and IMCA was just one of many headaches he had to cure. But his boss had ordered Dresser to fix IMCA, so he boiled his options down to three:

A. Position IMCA as the low-cost producer in the custom injection-molding industry. Reduce the company's R and D capabilities to the bare minimum, redirect all the company's resources toward increased productivity and efficiency. This would mean major cuts in overhead and personnel. With a healthy sales volume of $74 million, making it the largest custom injection-molder in Los Angeles, IMCA could profitably dominate the market if it became the lowest-cost producer.

B. Position IMCA as a high-tech plastics company capable of solving highly technical and sophisticated plastics problems. Reaffirm the company's old strategy and culture, but take it beyond its current sophistication and technological know-how to the edge of plastics technology that competitors and customers have not yet entered. The company's R and D function would have to be greatly expanded, but eventually margins would rise, and customers would be blue-chip.

C. Sell or liquidate the company, whichever makes the best financial sense.

Put yourself in Dresser's shoes. What would you do? Play out each scenario to its logical conclusions before you observe the actions of a New Age executive.

Option A would not appeal to the New Age executive. Insight into the nature of IMCA's industry exposes a marginal business opportunity at best. Even if IMCA became the low-cost producer in the Los Angeles area, the margins would be paper-thin, and competitors could squeeze them even thinner just to keep their facilities running. Versatility would allow the New Age executive to anticipate the inevitable reduction in the number of custom injection-molders as a reaction to the current glut.

Although option B merits some consideration, the New Age executive would quickly abandon it. The concept of becoming a premier, high-tech plastics research and development laboratory with production facilities would attract the entrepreneurial spirit and IMCA's culture could probably handle the change, but even a successful change might not insure the strategy's success. Insight would let the New Age executive see that large chemical and plastics companies like Du Pont and Monsanto would be more likely to make high-tech plastics breakthroughs. Customers looking for outside assistance in solving sophisticated plastics problems would be reluctant to go to a Los Angeles injection-molder turned high-tech researcher if they could go to established and reputable chemical companies. If Star Industries operated any other chemical or plastics units, a combination with IMCA might make sense, but Star has no similar units. Versatility would lead the New Age executive to examine the experience of other companies that have tried to effect similar changes, and he would quickly encounter a great many horror stories. It takes years for such a strategy to pay off and, frankly, IMCA doesn't enjoy that luxury. Even with an intense focus on the changes required by option B, the payoff would lie far in the future. During that time, IMCA would have to continue the low-margin injection-molding business which caused its crisis in the first place.

The New Age executive would select option C because insight, versatility, and focus would make it the only logical choice. Insight identifies the injection-molding business as forever marginally profitable, and it detects the high risk involved in turning it into a high-tech operation. The versatile executive would anticipate further industry decline and intense competition from major chemical companies, and the focused executive would turn his attention to other problems the pharmaceutical group must still resolve. The decision should focus on the changes that will most effectively benefit the whole pharmaceutical group strategically and culturally, otherwise an ailing IMCA could put even more than the IMCA workers out of their jobs. To the New Age executive, IMCA threatens the entire group, a price not worth paying. Selling or liquidating IMCA will create the most good for the greatest number of people.

What happened to IMCA? Despite McCovey's valiant efforts to persuade Dresser to pursue option B and make IMCA a high-tech plastics research, development, and production firm, Dresser stuck to his guns because option C made the most sense from Star Industries' point of view. But, displaying sensitivity to McCovey and his people, he helped McCovey position IMCA as an injection-molder evolving into a high-tech researcher before he put the company on the market.

In the spring of 1985, Calco Chemical Company bought IMCA for $20 million. Calco had already made some dramatic breakthroughs in injection-molded plastics research and desperately wanted to expand in the very areas McCovey had been attacking. It became a perfect marriage. Calco combined its plastics R and D efforts with IMCA's and committed itself to heavily invest in the area over the next five to seven years. The short-term profit pressure was taken off IMCA and McCovey, who could now take the necessary time to create excellence over the next decade.

By 1990, IMCA, whose name had been changed to Sci-tech Plastics, established itself as one of the foremost plastics research and development firms in the world. Large customers, even major chemical companies, sought Sci-tech's assistance in developing highly sophisticated injection-molded, blow-molded, and extruded plastics products. McCovey rose from being Sci-tech's CEO to a position as one of the directors of Calco. "We really are the best," he loves to say. "Dresser really did me a favor by not letting me rest on my laurels."

As for Bob Dresser, he went on to turn the Star Industries

pharmaceutical group around by focusing on its number one problem: product distribution. Over the next decade, the pharmaceutical group became the conglomerate's flagship ($1.4 billion in sales and before-tax profits of $180 million), ultimately winning Dresser the titles of president and CEO of Star Industries.

Crisis in the New Age

Executives in crisis situations must rely upon all six of the New Age skills, but particularly upon insight, versatility, and focus. Insight allows you to see the opportunities and threats involved in a business crisis, versatility helps you anticipate further changes that will face the company as the turnaround begins, and focus helps you determine exactly what and how much to change. By harnessing these three skills during times of crisis, you can chart a successful course. Once the turnaround has been achieved, sensitivity, vision, and patience will play more important roles. As Peter Drucker says in his book, *Managing in Turbulent Times*, "In turbulent times, the fundamentals have to be managed well." The fundamentals are strategy and culture, which often require radical alteration in times of crisis.

CHAPTER 14

Evolution: Fine-tuning Strategy and Culture

First we shape our structures, and afterwards
they shape us.
                          —WINSTON CHURCHILL

Carefully Evolving Strategy-Culture Alloys

As we discussed earlier, a strong culture displays commitment, competence, and consistency. These traits help organizations implement successful strategies that satisfy customers, gain competitive advantage, and capitalize on strengths. While excellence depends on strong strategy-culture alloys, what happens when a company with a strong corporate culture and successful business strategy, finds itself in a situation where it must adapt to new challenges, new environments? When circumstances dictate shifts in strategy, cultures must evolve to match them, or the cultures run the risk of extinction.

The Saturday Evening Post, once highly successful, ceased publication in 1969. The magazine industry contains a rich assortment of interesting organizations, from vast empires like Hearst, Time Inc., Times Mirror, and McGraw-Hill to thousands of idiosyncratic individual outfits that offer targeted products like *Boston* Magazine, *Savvy, Inc.*, and *Rolling Stone*. While the key to excellence may seem fairly obvious (target a market, build readership, then rake in the advertising profits), it's not quite that simple, because success inevitably depends, too, on the ability to move with the trends shaping our society. As mirrors

283

of public taste, successful periodicals reflect restless shifts in taste, shifts that strong publishing companies try to spot and report. Unfortunately, the culture of the Curtis Publishing Company, which put out *The Saturday Evening Post*, didn't possess such flexibility. Over the years Curtis Publishing had developed a strong corporate culture that established the *Post* as an American institution. Curtis's people followed a compelling vision of a magazine that contained something for everyone. Such an editorial policy worked until the world underwent dramatic changes in the late 1940s and early 1950s, when consumer preferences grew more and more fragmented. Curtis Publishing executives ignored this trend, despite the fact that it would have a major impact on advertising. The company's strong culture clung so steadfastly to the policies that had created excellence that it inadvertently caused the magazine's demise.

In contrast, Time Inc., which also displays a strong publishing culture, has been able to respond successfully to shifting tastes with strategies that harmonize with its strong culture. Over the years, Time's risk-oriented and entrepreneurial executives built a $2.7-billion publishing and communications empire by always launching their own ventures (*Money, People, Sports Illustrated, Fortune, Time,* and Home Box Office), and their confidence and patience led Time executives to nurture *Sports Illustrated* and HBO for years before they turned profitable. In 1978, they revived *Life*, which had ceased publication in 1972, by focusing on the ways in which consumers' and advertisers' tastes had changed and by making it a monthly rather than a weekly publication. Not surprisingly, Time's strong strategy-culture alloy won Time, Inc. the number six position on *Fortune*'s list of the most admired corporations in America in 1984. "Aggressive, innovative, risk-taking, entrepreneurial, blockbusting, arrogant" aptly summed up Time Inc.'s cultural traits, but could such traits survive a radically changing environment?

Changes began to accelerate in the communications industry as specialty magazines became the rage, cable TV competition intensified despite slowing customer growth, and circulation of traditionally popular magazines such as *Fortune* plateaued. In this whirlwind, Time Inc. suffered four major flops that have cost the company over $200 million. Its *TV-Cable Week*, a weekly program guide for cable TV, the *Washington Star* newspaper, subscription TV, and Teletext all failed.

How can Time's culture overcome these defeats? *BusinessWeek* quoted Time CEO Richard Munro's answer to this question: "We have been *laissez-faire* to the extreme. Now we have to pay more attention. We are not going to try to hit home runs. You could say we will try to hit singles." What challenges does his answer pose for Time's strategy-culture alloy? For one thing, the company will now look for acquisitions more than it has in the past because, by doing so, it will avoid giant risks on magazine concepts invented inside the organization. To better orchestrate the company's growth and direction, management should pay more attention to strategic thinking and should retrench to what it knows best. Toward these ends, Time recently divested itself of its forest products division, and it plans to shy away from markets that take it too far afield from magazines, books, and video. In the midst of these changes, Time should be careful not to destroy its strong culture or introduce strategies out of step with that culture. Although it can retain many of the culture's traits, such as confidence, patience, and aggressiveness, it needs to modify risk-taking and direct that energy toward sure-fire singles rather than risky home runs. It can still encourage and reward entrepreneurship, provided it refines that trait to be less wild-eyed and more sophisticated. Desired growth can come through acquisitions, and internal developments can be more steady, less explosive. At this point, Time seems to be reaping the benefit of its recent learning experiences by carefully evolving its strategy-culture alloy.

Strong cultures must adapt to changing environments. If they don't adapt, they may wither. If they overadapt, changing too many fundamental aspects at once, they may die. Companies will always need new strategies to reposition and redirect them in changing environments, but if new strategies require the culture to change too quickly or too much, they will fail. Fine-tuning strategy and culture provides the key to successful evolution, and successful evolution offers the key to maintaining excellence once you've created it.

A Case of Overadaptation

Let's look at how a hypothetical corporation deals with its evolution.

Phillip Gardner is the CEO of Segal Corp., a $2-billion consumer products manufacturer that makes and sells everything from soft drinks to detergent. For over four decades Segal has consistently introduced products that tower above competitors. Given the company's magnificent marketing prowess, many of its products have dominated their respective markets for years, leading observers to rank it as one of the premier consumer marketing firms in the country.

Not surprisingly, Segal's strategy-culture alloy has been a model of strength for over twenty years. Built upon a commitment to give customers the best products on the market, the company has made "marketing thoroughness" its distinctive competence and competitive advantage. It has so consistently developed and strengthened this competence and advantage that executive search firms, the business press, and industry analysts proclaim Segal the country's best training ground for marketing executives. Product managers at Segal learn so much about marketing soft drinks, snack foods, frozen pizza, salad dressing, deodorant, and dishwasher soap that if and when they leave Segal, they command the best positions and salaries. But although some do get lured away, Segal keeps its best people, thereby reinforcing its strong culture.

In 1984 Segal earned $325 million on sales of $2.2 billion, with a handsome 15 percent return on sales and a 22 percent return on equity. With such stellar bottom-line performance, it appeared that Segal could do no wrong, that nothing could ever threaten the company's excellence.

However, as so often happens, CEO Phillip Gardner learned during back-to-back difficult years in 1985 and 1986 that maintaining excellence takes even more effort than creating it in the first place. When Segal introduced thirty-two new or revised products in 1985, smaller competitors who could move faster than Segal beat twelve of them to the market by at least three months. But what most exasperated Gardner was the fact that in only two of the twelve cases did Segal gain its customary dominant position by the end of the year. To make matters worse, four of Segal's stand-by leaders, a salad oil, a deodorant soap, a cracker snack, and a window cleaner, lost their number one positions to new products introduced by competitors that same year. Although Segal's sales increased to $2.5 billion in 1985, profits stayed at $330 million.

When the alarming trend continued in 1986, Gardner and his management team realized that 1985 had not been a freak occurrence but a possible indication of vast environmental changes to which Segal would have to adapt. Of the twenty-five new or revised products Segal introduced in 1986, seventeen of them lost out to competitors who seemed to be smelling blood. Again, three more of the company's leading products took an uncomfortable backseat to new products. Sales rose to $3 billion, while profits sank to $225 million.

The once confident management team, led by Gardner, felt fear for the first time. Had they ignored an erosion of their company's strong marketing culture? Were Segal's strategies losing their edge? Had it mishandled its recruiting efforts over the last few years? These and other nagging questions filled Gardner's mind every night, and he found himself losing sleep as he desperately sought answers. At its annual meeting, the board of directors subtly made it clear that Gardner would have to halt the company's slide or he might be looking for a new job. When his most loyal senior vice-presidents began blaming each other for the crisis, Gardner felt overwhelming pressure to solve the company's problems. Time was running out.

Gardner had joined Segal Corp. twenty-six years earlier as a brand manager after graduating with honors from the University of Michigan. He assumed he would spend his entire career at Segal and had never worked for another company.

His hard work and loyalty propelled him through the product management ranks quickly until, at age forty-nine, he had become president and chief executive officer. By then he was clearly the company's primary strategist and cultural leader. "Our marketing thoroughness makes us invincible!" he would shout to large groups of company employees. "We're strong. We're committed. We're consistent. Nobody can beat us!" Gardner was truly the product of the organization he now headed, and he expressed great pride in the fact that his product managers learned the same system he had learned twenty-six years before. Sure, the system had become much more sophisticated in those twenty-six years, but the fundamental commitment to thoroughness had never changed. Unfortunately, Gardner's tenure with the same firm for so many years had not prepared him for the sweeping changes currently occurring in Segal's industry. Why wasn't the dependable Segal marketing system working its magic? Could Gardner do something he had never even contemplated before—tamper with Segal's marketing culture and the strategies it implemented? Gardner had no idea where to start, and lacking versatility, he couldn't even identify the specific environmental changes that had led to his company's recent difficulties. With his senior vice-presidents worrying about covering their own tracks, he found himself feeling increasingly cut off and alone. Whenever he tried to get them to confront the issues, he heard either cautious reactions or, worse, a deafening silence. So Gardner soon took matters into his own hands and went outside his management group for help, retaining the services of Warner & Company, a much-heralded management consulting firm.

Three months and $350,000 later, Warner & Company presented their findings to Phillip Gardner: 1) competition from smaller, more mobile companies was increasing; 2) competitors were becoming more sophisticated and proficient in marketing their products; 3) consumer product markets were growing more segmented and specialized. Based on these findings, Warner concluded that: 1) Segal must cut the time it takes to get a new product to market; 2) it must improve the sophistication and proficiency of its own marketing system to maintain its distinctiveness; 3) it must further segment markets to create new needs.

Because Warner's findings and conclusions clearly articulated the reasons for Segal's recent difficulties and the company's options for overcoming them, Gardner felt his confidence returning. Collecting its $350,000 fee, Warner left Gardner with the task of implementation. Though the consultants felt they had earned their fee, Gardner wished he'd gotten a more concrete game plan for his money. In the days and weeks after Warner's presentation, Gardner sketched three possible scenarios:

A. Make major changes within the next year in all three of the areas suggested by Warner's conclusions. This might prevent further slippage of the company's market positions.

B. Make minor changes in all three areas over a period of three years to minimize the upheaval in the company's strong culture.

C. Make major changes in one of the three areas over the next two years, moving to the other two areas after change in the first has proven successful.

If you were the CEO of a $2-billion consumer products firm faced with this decision, what would you do? Sketch and test your scenarios thoroughly. Put your decision and its anticipated consequences in writing, then compare your choice to that of the New Age executive.

Option A does not deserve a New Age executive's consideration because it represents a hasty, impatient response that could never result in lasting excellence. However, many executives, feeling tremendous pressure to make decisive changes, take this dangerous road, hoping they can implement change overnight with a barrage of memos and policies. Such hopes are bound to fail, particularly when you're dealing with a strong corporate culture, which an urgent plan can destroy. Gardner must keep Segal's strong culture intact. True, he must adapt it to changes in the environment, but he can't adapt it in one short year. This option disregards the skills of focus and patience, expecting too much change too soon. Adapting a strong strategy-culture alloy means evolving strategic and cultural traits critical to the organization's long-term well-being, carefully adding traits it can absorb naturally, and patiently nurturing the new traits until they become an organic part of the strategy-culture alloy.

Would a New Age executive pick option B? No. If option A tries to make too much happen too quickly, option B makes too little happen too slowly. The skills missing here are insight and vision, making this a watered-down, overly cautious option. Introducing minor changes on three different fronts simultaneously will not get results in a situation where a strong culture has become set in its ways. Trying to change Segal's culture with halfhearted efforts and strategies would be like trying to change the course of a charging army with a detour sign. Within three years, Segal will have lost the war (and its general) while wasting time waging small battles.

That leaves option C, the only viable path open to a New Age executive. Of course, the versatile executive would have anticipated earlier the changes that caught Segal by surprise in 1985. Segal's slowness to market had to be apparent in 1984. Had Gardner begun implementing one major change in that year, by 1986 he would already have made enough improvement in Segal's culture to pave the way for the other two changes. Option C will allow Gardner to focus resources on just one change in the company's strong strategy-culture alloy at a time, and its two-year schedule will allow sufficient time to ingrain the new element into the alloy. If the company focuses on just one of Warner's conclusions at a time, it will be able to successfully fine-tune its organization. Any strong culture or strategy can handle focused change, one step at a time. Rather than becoming disrupted or confused, the company can march in an orderly and concentrated fashion, adding one new trait, perhaps quickness to market, to its marketing thoroughness. Should the executive also consider deleting certain obsolete strategic or cultural traits at this time? Perhaps, but it's important to avoid deleting anything while in the process of adding something else. Otherwise, you risk confusion and, again, maybe forcing too much change at once. The New Age executive carefully focuses on one major change at a time, patiently awaiting its acceptance by the strategy-culture alloy before proceeding with any other major change.

What did Phillip Gardner do? Because Segal's approach had served him so well until recently, Gardner had never had to practice versatility. Not only couldn't he anticipate the changes occurring in Segal's environment, he did not appreciate focus, and he let pressure overrule his patience. He chose option A. Afraid of losing a job that had become his whole life, and anxious to get Segal back on track, he tried the impossible: implementing major changes in Segal's marketing culture in one year. "My people are great," he thought. "They can handle anything." Preaching fire-and-brimstone sermons about the need for change, he unveiled his three-point plan, which included a complete reorganization. But since no one had ever proposed anything this drastic before, confusion reigned throughout the organization as even the vice-presidents interpreted the plan as a panic move. While they went through the motions, none of them believed in the changes, and people further down in the organization felt overwhelmed by the push to introduce products faster, segment markets further, and improve the sophistication of the overall marketing system. Resentment replaced loyalty, fear replaced confidence, and failure seemed more likely than success. Instinctively, most employees went back to doing things the way they had always done them, because that was easier and more understandable. Seeing the strong resistance to change at all levels, Gardner grew so frustrated that he fired two senior vice-presidents and threatened to fire more if they didn't get behind the program. People who had reported to the fired vice-presidents began looking elsewhere for jobs until, by the end of 1987, Segal had not only lost many good people, it had lost more precious market share. The organization writhed in turmoil. Gardner was asked to resign.

To replace Gardner, the board picked Mario Ferraro, a feisty go-getter from New York City. By doing his homework, Ferraro observed Gardner's mistakes and extracted a commitment from the board to give him five years to reestablish the company's preeminence. Once hired, Ferraro selected option C and began implementing the first conclusion from Warner's report: cut the time it takes to get a product to market. He amended this change, adding "without compromising the company's marketing thoroughness."

Ferraro took time to ingrain this motto in Segal's culture. To insure its success, he slowly introduced a streamlined test-marketing process. Within months, instead of taking over a year for a new product to pass its tests, it only took six months. The key? A product introduction master plan. Plans had always been part of the test-market process, but in the past, R and D, new product development, product management, sales, and production each developed independent plans that were loosely tied together by the manager responsible for the new product. The new approach brought representatives from each of the different functions together to hammer out one plan together. This not only sped up test-marketing, it improved communications and strengthened the company's culture.

Segal worked with the new plan a full two years before it became an integral part of the marketing system. By the end of that period the test-marketing time had fallen to eight weeks. Along with other changes focused on cutting the time to market, Ferraro wrestled the company's profitability back to previous levels by recapturing 90 percent of its lost market leadership positions and maintaining an 80 percent success record of getting new products to market before or at the same time as competitors. Ferraro applied the six skills with adeptness, particularly versatility, focus, and patience—the skills that had eluded Gardner.

Evolution in the New Age

To successfully maintain a strong strategy-culture alloy in a changing environment, one must learn to adapt it carefully, applying versatility to anticipate changes, focus to make sure the adaptation takes hold, and patience to let the process run its natural course.

The life cycle of change can help one identify and evaluate changes, and the six steps for previewing change can help one exploit those changes to advantage.

Focus helps you zero in on critical changes, eliminating all unfocused activities that can distract you from successful adaptation. The five steps for implementing change insure successful, complete adaptation.

Patience reminds you to take the time to let versatility and focus do their jobs, to live in the long term. Most of all, it conquers the sort of fear that erodes confidence and guarantees failure and future fear, in a neverending destructive cycle.

As you begin to fine-tune your strong strategy-culture alloy, evolving it to adapt to a changing environment, remember the words of Thomas Watson, Jr., former chairman of IBM: "Thomas Watson, Sr., didn't move in and shake up the organization. Instead, he set out to buff and polish the people who were already there and to make a success of what he had."

Bibliography

Sources Referred to in the Text

Barnard, Chester. *The Functions of the Executive.* Cambridge, Mass.: Harvard University Press, 1938.

Bennis, Warren. *The Temporary Society.* New York: Harper & Row, Inc., 1968.

Benson, Dr. Herbert. *The Relaxation Response.* New York: William Morrow and Company, Inc., 1975; Avon Books, 1976.

Brown, Victor L. *Human Intimacy: Illusion and Reality.* Salt Lake City: Parliament Publishers, 1982.

Buckley, William F., Jr., *Overdrive.* Garden City, N.Y.: Doubleday, 1983.

Deal, Terrence E., and Kennedy, Allan A. *Corporate Cultures.* Reading, Mass.: Addison-Wesley Publishing Company, 1982.

Donaldson, Gordon, and Lorsch, Jay W. *Decision Making at the Top.* New York: Basic Books, Inc., 1983.

Drucker, Peter F. *Managing in Turbulent Times.* New York: Harper & Row, 1980.

Ferguson, Marilyn. *The Aquarian Conspiracy.* Los Angeles: J. P. Tarcher, Inc., 1980.

Gallwey, W. Timothy. *The Inner Game of Tennis.* New York: Random House, Inc., 1974.

Gluck, Frederick W., Kaufman, Stephen P., and Walleck, A. Steven. "Strategic Management for Competitive Advantage," *Harvard Business Review*, Vol. 58, No. 4, July–August 1980, pp. 154–161.

Grove, Andrew S. *High Output Management.* New York: Random House, Inc., 1983.

Hoff, Benjamin. *The Tao of Pooh.* New York: E. P. Dutton, Inc., 1982; Penguin Books, 1983.

Kanter, Rosabeth Moss. *The Change Masters.* New York: Simon and Schuster, 1983.

Kotter, John. *The General Managers*. New York: Macmillan Publishing Co., Inc. (The Free Press), 1982.

Levering, Robert, Moskowitz, Milton, and Katz, Michael. *The 100 Best Companies to Work for in America*. Reading, Mass.: Addison-Wesley Publishing Company, Inc., 1984.

Levinson, Harry. *The Exceptional Executive*. Cambridge, Mass.: Harvard University Press, 1968.; The New American Library, Inc., 1971.

Maccoby, Michael. *The Gamesman*. New York: Simon and Schuster, 1976.

————. *The Leader*. New York: Random House, Inc., 1981; Ballantine Books, 1983.

Miles, Robert H. *Coffin Nails and Corporate Strategies*. New Jersey: Prentice-Hall, Inc., 1982.

Milne, A. A. *Winnie the Pooh*. New York: Dutton, 1961 © 1954.

Naisbitt, John. *Megatrends*. New York: Warner Books, 1982, 1984.

Nierenberg, Gerard. *The Art of Creative Thinking*. New York: Simon & Schuster, 1982.

O'Toole, Patricia. *Corporate Messiah*. New York: William Morrow and Company, Inc., 1984.

Ohmae, Kenichi. *The Mind of the Strategist*. New York: McGraw-Hill Book Company, 1982.

Ouchi, William G. *Theory Z*. Reading, Mass.: Addison-Wesley Publishing Co., Inc., 1981; Avon Books, 1982.

Pascale, Richard Tanner, and Athos, Anthony G. *The Art of Japanese Management*. New York: Simon and Schuster, 1981.

Peters, Thomas J., and Waterman, Jr. Robert H. *In Search of Excellence*. New York: Harper & Row, Inc., 1982; Warner Books, Inc., 1982.

Raudsepp, Eugene. *How Creative Are You?* New York: G. P. Putnam's Sons, 1981.

Toffler, Alvin. *Future Shock*. New York: Random House, Inc., 1970.

Uttal, Bro. "The Corporate Culture Vultures," *Fortune* Magazine, Vol. 108, No. 8, October 17, 1983, pp. 66–72.

von Oech, Roger, Ph.D. *A Whack on the Side of the Head*. New York: Warner Books, Inc., 1983.

Zaleznik, Abraham. "Managers and Leaders: Are They Different?" *Harvard Business Review*, Vol. 55, No. 3, May–June 1977, pp. 67–78.

Other Books That Have Influenced Our Thinking and Writing

Albert, Kenneth J. *The Strategic Management Handbook.* New York: McGraw-Hill Book Company, 1983.

Bibeault, Donald B. *Corporate Turnaround.* New York: McGraw-Hill Book Company, 1982.

Bothwell, Lin. *The Art of Leadership.* New Jersey: Prentice-Hall, Inc., 1983.

Bradford, David L. and Allen R. Cohen. *Managing for Excellence.* New York: John Wiley & Sons, Inc., 1984.

Heller, Robert. *The Supermanagers.* New York: E. P. Dutton, Inc., (Truman Talley Books) 1984.

Henderson, Bruce D. *Henderson on Corporate Strategy.* Cambridge, Mass.: Abt Books, 1979.

Kiechel, Walter III. "Corporate Strategists Under Fire," *Fortune* Magazine, Vol. 106, No. 13, December 27, 1982, pp. 34–39.

Lawrence, Paul R., and Dyer, Davis. *Renewing American Industry.* New York: MacMillan, Inc. (The Free Press), 1983.

Levitt, Theodore. *The Marketing Imagination.* New York: MacMillan, Inc. (The Free Press), 1983.

Management Analysis Center, Inc., edited by Paul. J. Stonich. *Implementing Strategy.* Cambridge, Mass.: Ballinger Publishing Company, 1982.

Miller, Lawrence M. *American Spirit.* New York: William Morrow and Company, Inc., 1984.

Ouchi, William G. *The M-Form Society.* Reading, Mass.: Addison-Wesley Publishing Company, 1984.

Pirsig, Robert M. *Zen and the Art of Motorcycle Maintenance.* New York: William Morrow and Company, Inc., 1974; Bantam Books, 1982.

Porter, Michael E. *Competitive Strategy.* New York: MacMillan Publishing Co., Inc. (The Free Press), 1980.

Quinn, James Brian. *Strategies for Change.* Homewood, Ill.: Richard D. Irwin, Inc., 1980.

Rothschild, William E. *How to Gain (and Maintain) the Competitive Advantage in Business.* New York: McGraw-Hill Book Company, 1984.

Steiner, George A. *The New CEO.* New York: Macmillan Publishing Co., Inc., 1983.

Tregoe, Benjamin B., and Zimmerman, John W. *Top Management Strategy.* New York: Simon and Schuster, 1980.

Index